The Peace Keepers

Indian Police Service (IPS)

The Peace Keepers

Indian Police Service (IPS)

S R Arun, IPS

Director General Prosecution: Uttar Pradesh
Former Director General of Police: Uttar Pradesh

Manas Publications

New Delhi - 110 002 (India)

MANAS PUBLICATIONS
(Publishers, Distributors & Exporters)
4819/XI, Varun House, Mathur Lane,
24, Ansari Road, Daryaganj,
New Delhi-110002 (INDIA)
Ph. : 3260783, 3265523, 3984388
Fax : 011 - 3272766
E-Mail: manas.vkgarg@axcess.net.in

First Published *2000*

ISBN 81- 7049-107-X

Typeset at
Vrinda Graphics
Delhi-110 085

Printed in India at
New Gian Offsets Printers, Delhi
and Published by Mrs. Suman Lata for
Manas Publications, 4819/XI, Varun House,
Mathur Lane, 24, Ansari Road, Darya Ganj,
New Delhi - 110 002 (INDIA)

Preface

India celebrated the golden jubilee of Independence during 1997-98. The country has made great strides in various fields and become an important member of the international community. All this has been possible, because the internal peace was maintained and proper climate continued to exist for all round development. Although efforts had been made to disturb the security scenario by various forces, the State and Central security forces have done well to fight the terrorism and insurgency in maintaining communal and social harmony, conducting general elections which have strengthened the roots of democracy, and on various other fronts.

Immediately after India's freedom only two all India Services namely IAS and IPS were created. The first batch of the direct recruits of IPS joined at Mount Abu for training in 1948. Thus 1998 was also the golden jubilee year of the IPS. During the last 50 years, IPS officers have provided top leadership to police forces of the States and Centre. They have come out with flying colours in ensuring internal peace and security despite odds. Several IPS officers have made supreme sacrifices by laying down their lives at the altar of duty. The nation recognises their services with gratitude. Our salutations to these martyrs.

I have attempted to write the history of the IPS with a view to apprising the readers about this important "Service" engaged in the task of maintaining internal peace and security to ensure India's unity, integrity and prosperity. I hope the book will provide some insight into various aspects of the IP/IPS, the journey of which had started around 1861 when the Police Act was introduced.

The relevant information has been collected in about two months time, hence there may be many things which may be missing and if included would have made it still more useful. My apologies to those whose names are missing at relevant references, particularly in the chapter "Family Combinations in IPS".

Shri Subhash Joshi, Deputy Director, SVPNPA, Hyderabad, has been of great help to me who has taken immense pains in digging out information at the Academy and has supplied the same to me at short notice. My sincere gratitude to him, the staff of the Academy, Shri P S V Prasad, Joint Director, and Shri P V Rajgopal, Director.

My colleagues of UP cadre have done me a great favour not only by providing the relevant information and material but also by going through the manuscript. My special thanks to Shri S K Rizvi, IPS, Director, Prosecution, Shri Rizwan Ahmad, IPS, Aditional Director, Prosecution, UP, Shri S C Chaube, IPS, ADG, Technical, Services, UP and Sri K. D. Sharma, IPS (Retd.).

But for the active and ever willing cooperation of Shri R A S Tyagi, Suprintendent/Assistant Director, Computers, IP, and his staff it would not have been possible to produce this volume at a very short notice. I owe a great sense of gratitude to Shri Tyagi and his team of UP Police Computers Centre, Lucknow. I also appreciate the assistance rendered by Shri Piyush Misra, Head Constable, Computer Operator at UP PAC Headquarters, Lucknow. Shri Ambrish Misra, SI(M), Photographer PRO Wing of DGP Headquarters, UP and sh. Ratan Kumar, Naini Photo Service, Lucknow also deserve special mention and thanks for providing photographs of several IP/IPS Officers. I profusely thank Shri Moin-uddin,

Dy. Inspector (M)/Head Clerk of DGP Headquarters, Lucknow for providing material from old records. How can I forget to thank my P A, Shri A B Pant, and C A, Shri S K Shukla, who have been of immense help to me throughout.

I feel indebted to Sardar Vallabhbhai Patel National Police Academy, Hyderabad, and falicitate them on the memorable occasion of the golden jubilee of the Academy (1948-1998). As a humble product of Mount Abu (1964-passing out), I fail to express in words the positive role my Alma mater has played in moulding my personality as an IPS officer. My salutations to all those staff members of the Academy who during the last 50 years (half a century) have produced the excellent IPS material, engaged in the service of the Indian nation.

My sincere thanks to Manas Publications, especially to Shri V K Garg, for publishing this work at a very short notice and for doing it in an excellent manner.

Jai Hind

S. R. Arun

Contents

1

Evolution of Police Leadership

The concept of authority is as old as the civilisation itself. The early kings depended on the military for internal government as well as for war and conquest. However, military men because of their orientation to deal with an enemy were ill-suited to deal with problems of internal security. Thus the functionaries for maintenance of law and order had to be different from the military force and this force came to be known as police.

During early days the police in India was organised on the basis of land tenure and collective responsibility of village community. Zamindars were required to perform the police duties. Later on the Afghan and Mughal rulers introduced the Arabic-cum-feudalistic institutions of the Faujdar and Kotwal. Faujdar represented the executive authority of the government within the limits of a rural district. He was principally a military officer and also functioned as a chief police officer for the area of his command. In large towns, the police administration was under a Kotwal who had to maintain contingent of peons, horse patrols and spies. This system continued till the fall of Mughal empire.

In 1765, the East India Company acquired the Diwani in Bengal, Bihar and Orissa. In 1791, covenanted servants of the company were appointed to replace Faujdars. These servants of the Company acted both as judges and magistrates who had Darogas under them. The cities retained the office of Kotwal. In 1813, police functions were transferred to the Revenue Department and the control over police was transferred to the Collector from the District Judge. Later on, it was felt that police force in the district under Collector and District Magistrate failed to achieve the desired result without an authority to coordinate the collection of intelligence and operations against criminals and lawless elements. Therefore, in 1808, a Superintendent of Police (now Director General of Police of a State) was appointed for the divisions of Calcutta, Murshidabad and Decca (now in Bangladesh). This system proved satisfactory and thus it was extended to Patna, Banares (Varanasi) and Bareilly divisions in 1810. This system was abolished in 1829 when Divisional Commissioners of Revenue were appointed and the functions of Superintendent of Police were transferred to them to avoid duality of control over the magistrates.

The Civil Servants of East India Company, mainly of Bengal Civil Service and Madras Civil Service, were chosen in England based on patronage and nomination by the Directors of the Company. They used to be the kingpins of administration in their respective districts performing the functions of the revenue Collector, the Judge and the Police Officer, etc. all amalgamating in one. In 1833 a law was made that four young men nominated for each vacancy should appear in a competitive examination to decide which was the best. This system lasted for one year only. A decision was taken in 1853 by Government of India Act in favour of open competition based on interview in which pleasant manners, social background and intellectual standard were to be judged. This also ended in 1857.

In Bombay in 1853, the post of Superintendent of Police was created for each district who was in exclusive control of the police in the district. This system was adopted for Madras in 1855.

Court of Directors in 1856, desired that the police should be separated from the administration of land revenue and its management committed to an European officer with no other duties except police. In 1857, in a report it was mentioned that the combination of revenue, judicial and police functions in the Collector-Magistrate was objectionable as it placed them "above all law". A Chief Commissioner of Police was appointed in May 1858.

The Police Commission 1860

After the mutiny of 1857, a Police Commission consisting of six members with Mr. M. H. Court as President was appointed in 1860 to suggest reforms and improvements about police establishment. The commission in its report of September 1860 observed that "We have provided a complete Civil Organisation for the whole body, from the Inspector General to the common constable. We have been careful to provide a complete system of supervision by European officers. The want of this, has, we believe, been one of the greatest disadvantages of the Civil Police System here-to-before existing in India." The commission took particular care regarding the despatch from Her Majesty's Government which reads, "They (the Civil Police) should be under the control of the Magistrates of the Districts, subject to the supervision of the Commissioner of the Division, where such officer exists." The commission in their report mentioned, "We trust that our propositions will show the care we have taken to preserve the responsibility of the Magistrate for the general success of the Criminal Administration of the District, and to afford him prompt means of ensuring the obedience of the organised Constabulary to his lawful orders". They further said, "We have taken care to secure to the Police Officers that position which is necessary to the discharge of their responsibility for the efficiency of the police."

The Police Act 1861

Recommendations of the Police Commission 1860 led to the passing of the Police Act (Act V of 1861) which is still in operation. Under this Act, the entire police establishment under a provincial (now state) government was deemed to be one police force. The administration of the police was vested in an officer styled as the Inspector General of Police and such Deputy Inspectors General and Assistant Inspectors General as the provincial (state) government may deem fit. The administration of the police throughout local jurisdiction of the district vested in a District Superintendent and such other Assistant District Superintendents as considered necessary by the Provincial (State) Government (Sec. 4).

European Military Officers

ICS Act 1861

In 1861, the Indian Civil Service Act was passed by which several appointments were reserved under the control of the Secretary of State for India. Thus the institution of the I.C.S. popularly named 'Steel Frame' was established.

During the early years of the formation of the police forces, Inspector General of Police used to be generally an I.C.S. or a military officer. The Superintendent and Inspectors were taken form among regimental officers. The Commissioners of Divisions were appointed ex-officio Deputy Inspectors General as latter were too few in number and were not given sufficient responsibility. The higher ranks of the new police were filled entirely by Europeans drawn largely from the commissioned ranks of the native Army. To begin with in North West Provinces, 33 District

Superintendents were military officers drawn from the Military Police.

Superintendents and Assistant Superintendents of Police took charge of the police establishments (mainly in Bihar-then Bengal) from the District Magistrates on July 1, 1862.*

During the first two decades of the existence of the police constituted under Police Act of 1861, military men who were Britishers were directing the provincial forces; conditions were simple and work was light. Ambitious and able Britishers preferred to join either the Army or the I.C.S. in preference to the police. J.C. Curry, IP, in his book *The Indian Police* (1832) mentioned that the boy who joined the Indian Police was too lazy or too stupid to get into the Army, but prepared to go anywhere or do anything which did not involve drudgery.

In 1879, the appointment of military officers was discontinued. Police officers were to be recruited from the same classes as supplied the other branches of the uncovenanted service, such as Deputy Collectors and subordinate judges. Practically all appointments went to the 'nomination-wallahs' who were of the type mentioned by Curry.

The administrations of N.W. Province and Oudh (now U.P.) were merged in 1877 and as a result the police forces of the two provinces were also merged. The officer establishment of the amalgamated police officers consisted of one I.G.P. and two Inspector Generals, one Assistant I.G., and several Suprintendents and Assistant Suprintendents of Police in various pay grades. In 1879, the superior cadre was re-organised and their salaries were brought down, except for the officers drawn from the army.

---

* *Raj to Swaraj*, page 69 - SK Jha.

Demand for Indianisation

The Indian Civil Service Act 1861 had reserved the principal civil service offices to the I.C.S. the examination for which was held in England. Satyendra Nath Tagore (brother of Rabindra Nath Tagore - Nobel prize winner) was the first Indian to join the I.C.S. in 1864. It was difficult for Indians to go to England for appearing in the I.C.S. examination. The demand for Indianisation started gaining momentum. In 1867, the 'East India Association' founded by Dadabhai Naoroji, in a memorandum submitted to the Secretary of State asked for the recruitment of Indians to the I.C.S. Consequently in 1870 an Act was passed authorising the appointment of Indians to the higher offices without the necessity of undergoing an examination.

The Indian National Congress was born on December 28, 1885, on the recommendation of A.O. Hume, I.C.S., as he had seen the seeds of a national revolt, and the Congress was to act as a safety valve. The Congress demanded an enquiry into the working of the Indian administration. In 1886, a Public Service Commission was appointed to devise a scheme to do full justice to the claim of natives of India to higher and more extensive employment in the public services. A committee, appointed in 1890 under the chairmanship of W. Kaye, Member, Board of Revenue, Allahabad, which made various recommendations about U.P. Police, suggested that recruitment of gazetted officers to police department should be a proportion of military personnel who should be posted to it for good without the option of repatriation. Another suggestion was that recruitment be made from men who had just failed in the I.C.S. examination. Till then there was practice of certain Inspectors being placed in temporary charge of districts. Consequently, the 'Indian Police' was born.

Police Service of the Crown in India

I.P. meant the 'Indian Police', consisting of persons appointed to the Police Service of the Crown in India.

In 1892, it was decided that a certain proportion of officers for the 'Indian Police' should be recruited from the competition being held in England for the Indian Forest Service, as an experimental measure. The candidates were to be between the age of 19-20 years. The balance of the recruitment was to be made in India by recruitment from among Europeans as well as Indians. The first competitive examination was held in 1893 and 10 candidates were selected and thereafter, seven candidates were selected each year in 1894,1895, 1896 and 1897 . Out of these 28 officers selected from 1894 to 1897, six were allotted to N.W.P. and Oudh (now U.P.).

The appointments to the grade of Assistant Superintendent of Police were made by recruitment in England and India, and by promotion from the subordinate police service. Recruitment in England was carried out by competitive examination held annually in London by the Civil Service Commissioners, under regulations made by the Secretary of State for India. The candidates so selected were to enter the police force of the province to which they were allotted as probationers. For recruitment in India, a register of applicants for appointment as probationers to the grade of A.S.P. whose names had been approved by the Lt. Governor was maintained by the private secretary. The candidates were to be between the age of 19 and 24 years, pure natives of India, unmarried, British subjects and required to furnish satisfactory evidence of education and good conduct and ability to ride and with gentlemanly bearing and physical fitness. These qualifications were essential. The number of names admitted to the register were not to be more than five for each expected vacancy. A competitive examination was held once a year, to which only candidates whose names were entered in the register of approved applicants and who had received special permission to appear, were admitted. This examination was held by the Director of Public Instruction at Allahabad in United Provinces in the month of February. Promotions from the grade of Inspector to that of Assistant Superintendent of Police were occasionally made as a reward for exceptional merit and ability. An officer so promoted was not required to appear in any examination prescribed either for direct recruits or for departmental promotions, and he was not required to undergo any training.

Training

Probationers recruited in England and India were required to undergo training in two courses: the probationer course and further course for Assistant Superintendent. On joining their appointments they were posted to districts under the charge of experienced Superintendents of Police, who were responsible for grounding them in their duties and for supervising their studies. A probationer used to receive a salary of Rs. 250 a month. Police, judicial, vernacular and elementary drill and riding were main course of instruction. The duration of training was normally six months. A probationer on passing the probationary examination was appointed as an A.S.P. in the grade of Rs.300 a month and was placed under a selected District Superintendent of Police, who was to be his incharge of further training and studies which consisted practical training in drill and riding, office work of District Superintendent of Police, duties of Reserve Inspector, investigations, departmental enquiries, prosecution in courts and inspection work. One was not allowed to exercise executive powers as a police officer unless one had passed the examination for probationers.

The Police Commission 1902

The Police Commission 1902, which had been set up for analysing the causes of abuses of the powers by policemen along with many other points, averred that "the charges made against them (the Superintendents) are that they are often not well educated or intelligent men, that their training is defective, that their knowledge of the vernacular is not such as to enable them to have free intercourse with the people and to become acquainted with their feelings and circumstances." The commission was of the opinion that there was a great deal of truth in these complaints. It said, "The class of Superintendents found in all provinces is not what it should be, sufficient care has certainly not always been taken in appointing men to this service. These officers also are too often inclined to support their subordinates in an unreasonable manner and to receive complaints or strictures on public work in a hostile spirit". The commission condemned the old system of nominating candidates in India, which coexisted with the competition conducted in England, and appointments by the promotion of Inspectors. They approved the existing system of recruitment by competition in England but proposed reduction in age limit from 19-21 to 18-20 years, and also suggested certain improvements in their training in England and in provincial training schools in India. New entrants were to be promoted as Suprintendents of Police after seven years of their training.

The pay of an ASP ran from Rs. 250 to 400 and a SP from Rs. 500 to 1,000. The commission proposed considerable improvement in their scales — Rs. 300 to 500 for an ASP, Rs. 700 to 1200 for SP in five classes. The grade proposed for a native SP was Rs. 600 to 900.

Most of the recommendations of the Police Commission were accepted . European officers were to be recruited exclusively in England, but the Governor General retained the power to appoint Europeans in India in exceptional cases, and training was to be imparted for 18 months at a training school in India. Deputy Inspectors General were to be appointed by the selection from amongst Superintendents. These appointments were to be regarded as the highest posts absolutely reserved for the police Department. Full discretion was left to the local government to appoint the Inspector General of Police either from the I.C.S. or from the police. The I.G. was not to be Secretary to Government, but it was desired that he should have free access to the head of the local government. The pay of the gazetted officers was to be as recommended by the commission subject to the modification by the Secretary of State in the case of Deputy Inspectors General. However, only officers considered fit for the most important districts were to get more than Rs. 900.

The total strength of the police officers in British India in 1902 consisted of 10 IGs, 16 DIGs and Commissioners of City Police , 284 SPs , 233 ASPs and 1159 Inspectors. The Police Commission recommended substantial increase (14 DIGs, 39 SPs, 47 ASPs, 279 DSPs and 463 Inspectors) in these ranks.

Deputy Superintendents of Police - A New Cadre for Indians

A new rank of Deputy Superintendent of Police for Indians was proposed by the Commission. The pay proposed was Rs.250 to 500 and the incumbents were to be equal in status to an A.S.P. They were to be eligible for promotion to the post of Superintendent, but no fixed proportion was prescribed for this purpose. They formed a Provincial Service which was constituted largely by promotees from the rank of Inspector and occasionally by nomination .

The N.W.P. and Oudh were renamed as the United Provinces of Agra and Oudh by the Act VII of 1902. A reorganisation of the gazetted staff was carried out in 1906. One extra DIG was appointed, the number of SPs and ASPs was increased and posts of Dy. Supdts. were created. Half of Dy. Supdts. of Police were to be appointed from candidates who had qualified for or were serving in the revenue, judicial or police departments and the other half by promotion from Inspectors. Their pay was to be between Rs. 250 to 500 in four classes . In 1910, the strength of officers in U.P. was 1 IGP, 4 DIGs, 52 SPs, 48 ASPs and 28 DSPs of whom 1 SP and 26 DSPs were Indians.

Province	1912	1913	1914	1915	Total
Madras	3	3	2	1	9
Bombay	3	3	2	1	9
Bengal	5	5	4	2	16
United Provinces	4	3	5	2	14
Punjab	3	4	4	3	14
Bihar & Orissa	1	3	1	-	5
Central Provinces	2	2	2	-	6
Assam	2	1	1	-	4
Total	23	24	21	9	77

The recruitment for the service was stopped during the First World War.

In 1911, the total strength of police officers in India was 51 IGPs and DIGs, 331 SPs, 268 ASPs 234 DSPs and 1751 Inspectors. This increase was in the light of the recommendations of the Police Commission. The number of officers appointed in England for various provinces during 1912 to 1915 is given in Table 2.1.

The Royal Commission

The Royal Commission with Lord Islington as Chairman of the Public Services in India was appointed in August 1912. An 'Imperial Police Service Association' which was formed in 1911 submitted memorandum to the commission complaining their grievances. One of their demands was that the post of the I.G.P. which was hitherto filled by an I.C.S officer almost in every province, be filled from amongst the I.P. officers. On behalf of Government it was explained that there was full discretion with local governments to fill the post of I.G.P either from the I.C.S. or from the Police. The commission's report submitted in August 1915 could not be taken up for consideration till 1917 because of the World War I and the internal troubles. I.P. officers were appointed as Inspectors General of Police of provinces from 1919.

IP as I.P.S.

The I.P. in due course (the exact year is not known but is between 1912 to 1914) came to be known as I.P.S.

The Royal Commission recommended that there were grounds of policy for importing the bulk of officers for this service from Europe. They approved the system of recruitment through a competitive examination in England, and recommended that Europeans of mixed descent and Indians of unmixed Asiatic descent, educated in the United Kingdom for a period of five years, should be allowed to appear at the London Examination. The Governor General's power to make direct appointments in India, in exceptional cases, hitherto limited to domiciled Europeans, should be extended to include Indians also and used more frequently than had been done in the past, and not less than 10 per cent of the Superintendentship should be filled by promotion from the provincial service. This should gradually be extended to 20 per cent. Provincial Service Officers, permanently promoted to the I.P.S., should become full members thereof and be able to rise through all its grades. The heads of the various police schools and Inspectors General should see for themselves what was going on in provinces other than their own. Provision should be made for periodical conferences for police officers. The pay scale of the DIGs should be Rs. 1,500-100-2,000. There should be one selection grade for Superintendents with Rs.1,200 and the rest should be given salary in the scale of Rs. 700-60-1,000 without the existing efficiency bar at Rs. 900. An Assistant Superintendent should be paid Rs. 300-400-50-600. Indians, whether directly recruited or promoted, should be paid the same salary in large districts. Additional Superintendents should not be appointed until it was found possible to divide the districts. The formula for fixing the strength of the police cadre should be revised and based on up to date police experience. Blocks in promotion should be relieved by interprovincial transfers, premature retirement and personal allowances. Local Governments should fill the appointments of Inspectors General of Police from the best material available with due regard to the claims of senior police officers and to the advantages of local experience. Increased facilities should be provided in the matter of charges, and Indian officers should be placed under the Indian Service Leave Rules. The general pension rules should apply to all officers, and the Inspector General and Dy. Inspectors General should get a special additional pension.

With regard to the Provincial Police Service, they recommended that officers should no longer be appointed to this service from other departments; half the vacancies should be filled by direct recruitment by a committee of three officials and two nonofficials, including two Indians where possible all direct recruits should have taken a University degree; a direct recruit should serve for two years on an average before confirmation, and a grade of probationers should be created accordingly; there should be two selection grades of Rs. 700 and 600; for the res, the scale should be Rs. 250-4-/3-450-5-/3-500, probationers should get Rs. 150; there should be no hesitation in adding to the cadre to meet administrative requirements; the service should be styled after the provinces such as 'Bihar & Orissa Police services'; Indian DSP should be allowed to wear European uniform, and DSP should enjoy the same privileges as the members of the Provincial Civil Service in matters of attendance and leave, in the operation of the Arms Act and the like and get a fair share of executive work like ASP.

While the Government of India were still considering these recommendations, the U.P. branch of the IPA represented that pay of IPS officers was unjust and inequitable. On the other hand, Pandit Madan Mohan Malviya moved a resolution in 1918 in the Imperial Legislative Council, recommending that salaries of IPS officers should not be enhanced, the rule requiring that candidates for the IPS examination shall be of pure European descent should be abrogated, and that the recruitment examination should be held simultaneously in India and in England, or, if this is not accepted, then not less than one half of the total number of posts in the IPS should be recruited by an open competition in India. This resolution was opposed and rejected.

The Montague Chelmsford Report on Indian Constitutional Reforms was presented in British Parliament in April 1918. They were of the view that recruitment of a largely increased proportion of Indians should begin at once.

The Congress dubbed these proposals as unsatisfactory. Sir C. Shankaran Nair opposed the distinction between the Imperial and the Provincial branches of the Police Service, because there was no difference between the duties performed by the officers of the two branches, the recruitment examination held in London was of a low standard and by no means difficult to pass, whereas the directly appointed DSPs were graduates of universities and their work had been generally superior to that of their European colleagues, the London examination was closed to Indians, with the result that all the members of the superior service were Europeans, which amounted to racial discrimination against Indians. He suggested that the Imperial and the Provincial branches be amalgamated. He also said that it was universal belief among Indians that nomination was nothing more and nothing better than a system of patronage which was extremely demoralising and did not yield satisfactory results, and had proved a failure.

The Government orders were issued in installments in 1919. The existing division of Imperial and Provincial branches was retained, the London examination was not to be opened to Indians, Indians were to be recruited in India as recommended, the proportion of such vacancies was raised to 33 per cent (22 per cent by competition and 11 per cent by the promotion of DSPs), overseas allowance was introduced for the European members of the IPS, the pay scales of the IPS applicable to Indians and Europeans were made alike, which were - junior scale Rs. 325-325-350—150-375-400-400-450- -EB-500-500 -550-600-600-650, and senior scale Rs. 500 (4th year) 525-525-550-550-600-600-650-700-750-750-800-50-950-EB-1000-1000-1050-1100-1100-1150 to be introduced from January 1920, in supersession of the earlier orders, grants were to be made instead of advances for the purchase of uniform and horses, and the appointments to be made in India would be opted to "persons domiciled and born in British India of parents habitually resident in India and not established there for temporary purposes only." Fifteen Indians were appointed to the I.P.S. under the new arrangements in 1920.

The Government of India Act was passed in December 1919, which introduced "dyarchy" and the Governors were vested special powers with regard to internal law and order. The Civil Disobedience and Khilafat Movements, which started in 1920, gathered momentum giving way for Hindu-Muslim fraternisation. Subhas Chandra Bose resigned from the ICS. Mahatma Gandhi and 50 others issued a manifesto denouncing service -- civil or military — as being contrary to national dignity, under a Government which used the soldiery and the police for repressing national aspiration and called upon Indians to sever connections with the Government and find some other means of livelihood.

In this background it was decided that recruitment of Indians would be done in India. Examination was to be held in November/December by the Central Advisory Board of Educations. The Provincial Selection Committee consisted of a Minister, IGP and an experienced Commissioner and one member of Educational Service, three nonofficial and a member of Public Service Commission. Nominations of candidates having prescribed qualifications were made by the District Officers. The relative seniority of probationers recruited in India and in England was regulated by the number of marks obtained at the competitive examination. Representation of various communities was to be ensured while making nominations at the provincial level. This had already been accepted for the ICS. Out of the 25 candidates selected, 14 were Hindus, seven Muslims, three Anglo-Indians and one Indian Christian; three Hindus and two Muslims were nominated.

The relations between political classes and European officers kept on worsening giving adverse feeling of anxiety and discontent in European officers. In 1921, these European officers, who were dissatisfied with the conditions of service in the new situation, were given the option of retiring on proportional service, with the result that 69 ICS and 97 IPS and 121 other officers applied for retirement. Surplus officers of the British Army were also to be appointed.

Royal Commission (Lee Commission)

A Royal Commission with Viscount Lee as Chairman was appointed in 1923 to enquire into the organisation and general conditions of service, financial or otherwise of the Superior Civil Services in India, the possibility of transferring any of their present duties to provincial services and the recruitment of Indians and Europeans. The commission submitted their report in 1924, and on the basis of its recommendation a Public Service Commission was appointed in 1925. The commission also observed that the best type of Indian was not being obtained for the IPS partly due to inadequacy of emoluments offered and partly due to the hardships of a career in the police as compared to other services. The commission said that in the best interests of the state young men of good families and of the requisite physical and mental qualifications should be induced to enter the service. They also recommended following formula for giving greater representation to Indians in various Imperial Services.

Service	Indians (%)	Europeans (%)	By Promotion (%)
1. I.C.S.	40	40	20
2. I.P.	30	50	20
3. Indian Service of Engineers in Irrigation Branch	40	40	20

(Contd. . .)

(Contd. . .)

Service	Indians (%)	Europeans (%)	By Promotion (%)
4. Indian Service of Engineers Madras	45	33	22
5. Indian Forest Service	75	25	-

These recommendations were accepted by the Government of India. These arrangements continued till the outbreak of World War II.

Struggle for India's Freedom

The struggle for freedom continued. Revolutionary activities were revived in 1929. Attempts to kill IP and other senior European officers were made. Lowman, IGP Bengal, Saunders, ASP Lahore, and Col. Simpson, IG Prisons, Calcutta, were killed and several others were injured. The civil disobedience movement continued. The London examination for entry into the IPS was closed to Indians with 5 years' residence in England in 1929. The Simon Commission in their report mentioned that the reorganisation of the services as recommended by the Lee Commission was still incomplete. The IPS Association in a memorandum suggested the appointment of a Police Commission to consider reasonable conditions of employment and remuneration to all the members of Police force, but this was ignored by the Government

There were 665 IPS officers in January 1933, of whom 505 were Europeans, 152 Indians and 8 others.

'IPS' Renamed as 'IP'

The IPS Association had been pressing for changing the designation of the service from the 'Indian Police Service' to the 'Indian Police'. This request was turned down in 1930 but approved in 1933 because of service sentiments.

There was wide spread anxiety in the minds of European Police officers in regard to the impending constitutional changes. The Viceroy addressed a special conference of the Inspectors General of Police and other I.P. officers on November 26, 1934, and praised the role of officers and men for all that they had done during those years particularly since April 1931, which were stormy times.

With the Government of India Act coming into effect in 1935, greater autonomy was given to the provinces and that gave rise to several apprehensions and further misgivings in the minds of European officers. The strength and the composition of the I.P. in January 1936 was as follows:

TABLE 2.2

Provinces	Europeans	Hindus	Muslims	Others	Total
Madras	48	16	4	4	72
Bombay	63	6	3	2	74
Bengal	71	18	13	-	102
U.P.	75	49	11	2	137
Punjab	82	4	14	9	109
Bihar & Orissa	40	13	4	-	57
C.P.	39	9	3	4	55
Assam	19	5	2	-	26
Total	437	120	54	21	632

The orders passed on the recommendations of the Lee Commission had fixed the proportions of Europeans and Indians for direct recruitment at 40:40 for Madras and

Bengal; 50:30 for Bombay, U.P., C.P. , Bihar and Orissa; 65:17 for Punjab; and 60:20 for Assam. It was pointed out in 1938 that this was delaying the attainment of the target for Indianisation contemplated by the commission. The Secretary of State, thereupon, decided that in all provinces where the proportion fixed was 30:30 it would be changed to 40:40 from the examination to be held in 1939. This resulted in five more Indians being appointed on the basis of that examination.

The Second World War Effect on 'IP'

The Second World War broke out on September 3, 1939. Recruitment to I.P. was stopped and all the IP officers including those availing leave in Europe were recalled. The IGPs' conference held in March 1940 besides other points also discussed the method of recruitment of Indians in India for the IP and the block in promotion of Assistant Suprintendents, as a result of the recall from leave of a number of senior officers. As the right kind of European candidates were not forthcoming for the competitive examination for the IP one-third of the vacancies in England were filled by nomination in 1939. The last examination for Europeans was held in London in March 1940. There was no recruitment of Europeans from 1943 and of Indians from 1944. The number of Europeans and Indians in the IP changed as follows during the period from 1939 to 1944.

Date	Europeans	Indians	Total
1.1.1939	428	181	609
1.1.1940	429	187	616
1.1.1944	361	216	577
1.1.1945	344	215	559

Anxiety of European Officers

The Indian Police Association had developed the anxiety about the future of the service with reopening under the scheme of the Act of 1935. In the January 1940 bulletin of the Association, the anxiety of the service members was expressed as "what will dominion status for India have in store for the members of the All India Services? That a Constitutional change of this magnitude will affect our conditions of service materially, goes without saying. Already Public Service Commissions have been set up in most provinces and the Federal Public Service Commission (set up in 1935) has been functioning for some time. Will the control of the All India Services ultimately pass to this body or will all the services be completely provincialised and the Imperial Services abolished? Time alone will provide the answer. . . . ." Regarding the future recruitment to the services, *The Statesman* in its issue dated 17th January, 1940, wrote, "yet another important question to which in the light of experience a fresh approach is needed is that of recruitment in Great Britain for the services. It should by this time be clear that India cannot go on indefinitely overloading her services and mortgaging the future because she is compelled to take in every year a fresh consignment of young Englishmen from the universities. There is no longer any urge from the universities or from the young men to come. A good many who do come discover that the situation has been seriously misrepresented to them by some retired Governors and others with the laudable intention of keeping the services going. Coming out with enthusiasm, carefully educated about the new regime and fully in sympathy with the march to self government, they find themselves regarded as obstacles to Indianisation and as overpaid importations who prevent a general scaling down of salaries to a normal level. Now that Britain is likely to have urgent other uses for such young men it would seem to be a good moment to reconsider the whole question."

The European officers were worried about the future of the Indian Police in view of the constitutional reforms. The I.P. Association in their bulletin of February 1940 mentioned in the editorial that "the conditions of service would be bound to change. . . . . . As there was a possibility that we should have to retreat from this position we should be ready with our cases for compensation for loss of career in addition to the payment of pensions which had been earned."

Transition from IP to IPS

The partition of the country into India and Pakistan (West and East - now Bangladesh since 1971) was announced on June 3,1947. At that time there were 10 All-India Services and 22 Central Services . The Government of India gave certain guarantees in matters of pay, pension and disciplinary matters and were allowed the same pay which they were drawing prior to independence. Those unwilling to serve could retire on proportionate pension. Before actual transfer of power, wishes of indiviudual officers were ascertained. Most of the European officers decided to leave because they felt that their anti-national activities would be revenged upon by the leaders, they were afraid of the curtailment of their bureaucratic independence and their colour prejudice. While some Muslim officers decided to migrate to Pakistan, the Hindu officers stayed on.

The Depletion

Immediately before Independence, the IP consisted of 516 officers including 323 Europeans, 63 Muslims and 130 Hindus and others. The majority of the European officers opted for retirement and compensation for loss of career. Practically all the Muslim officers opted for Pakistan. The

Hindu officers and men in the N.W.F.P. and the Sind Police were allowed to migrate to India. Similar situation was allowed about migration of Dy. Suprintendents of Police from India to Pakistan and vice-versa. This resulted in a serious depletion of the strength of police officers and men in the northern provinces of India. From U.P., one IGP, seven DIGs (all Europeans) and one Muslim DIG (Mr. Kazim Raza) opted out. Thirty out of 56 Superintendents of Police and 42 Assistant Suprintenents either sought voluntary retirement or migrated to Pakistan. Mr. J.D.A. Pollock, IP, decided to continue in U.P., and retired in 1966.

After India's Independence

Indian Independence Act 1947 had given guarantee to members of the Secretary of State services which were incorporated in Draft Article 283A (Subsequently Article 314 of the Indian Constitution). During debate about retention or otherwise of ICS and IP, Sardar Vallabhbhai Patel in his powerful speech in the Constituent Assembly pleading for these services said:*

> "The leaders of the nation were called for, the Cabinet was there,the Congress President was there . Your President (Dr. Rajendra Prasad) was there and your leader to-day (Pandit Jawaharlal Nehru) was there. Mahatma Gandhi was also present... Every section (of the proposed Indian Independence Act) was scrutinized and the draft approved. After that it was passed (in the British Parliament). Now, these guarantees were circulated before that to the provinces. All provinces agreed. It was also agreed to incorporate these into the Constituent Assembly's new Constitution. That is one part of the guarantee. Have you read that history? Or you do not care for recent history after you began to make history? If you do that, then I tell you we have a dark future. Learn to stand upon your

* *Constitutional Law of India*, by H.M. Seervai.

> pledged word, and, also, as a man of experience, I tell you, do not quarrel with the instruments with which you want to work." While paying tributes to the patriotism, loyality and sincerity of the members of the Civil Services he remarked:
>
> "Their shoulders held the sky suspended;
> They stood, and earth's foundations stay."

Sardar Patel further said "...we have difficult times ahead. We are talking here under security kept in very difficult circumstances. These people are the instruments, remove them and I see nothing but a picture of chaos all over the country."

Ultimately it was decided to retain only two All-India Services namely the ICS/IAS and the IP/IPS.

Special Recruitments

After the Independence only two All India Services namely IAS and IPS were retained. Names of ICS and IP were allowed to be used. Due to wholesale exodus of European and Muslim officers, the shortfall in the higher ranks became acute. In police, certain confirmed Inspectors had to be put as Superintendents of Police in-charge of districts. State Police Service officers with very little experience and having put in few years and even months service were also posted against the senior posts, held so far by the IP officers. The officers of the All India Services were also needed for the newly merged states.

On the basis of the competitive examination held in 1947, 38 IPS officers were selected who reported at the Central Police Training College, Mount Abu on September 15,1948, and they got the honour of being the first batch of regular recruits of the service, as prior to that IP officers were never trained centrally as they used to be trained in training colleges of the provinces and thereafter remained posted locally. This number was not sufficient to meet the acute shortage of experienced senior officers. With a view to reducing the shortage, special recruitment was made in 1948 by Special Recruitment Board. This Board prepared lists of officers who were considered fit for immediate appointments. There was no written test and selection was made on the basis of service records and the interview. The Special Recruitment Board was also authorised to fill the remaining vacancies from the open market candidates for which higher age limits were prescribed and only interview was held . Any candidate having put in five years service in gazetted rank or an advocate having five years practice, etc., were eligible to compete. On Board's recommendation 40 Provincial Police Service officers and 39 open market candidates were appointed to I.P.S. initially.

At this stage following categories of officers formed part of the Indian Police Service:

1. IP	Indian Police
2. IPS (RR)	Officers appointed from regular recruitment on the basis of competitive examination.
3. IPS (WS)	Officers appointed to IPS on the basis of war service (Regular Commissioned Officers) released from the Defence Forces.
4. IPS (EROM)	Officers appointed through emergency recruitment scheme of 1949 from the open market.
5. IPS-EC/SSC	Officers appointed to the IPS through the released Emergency Commissioned Officers/Short Service Commissioned Officers of the Defence Forces.

6. IPS-PPS-ER	Officers selected from the Provincial Police Service through emergency recruitment.
7. IPS-PPS	Officers promoted to IPS from the Provincial Police Service against promotion quota.

Constitutional and Legal Provisions

Articles 312,313 and 314 of the Constitution of India (commencement date - 26-1-1950) provided for the All India Services. Article 312(1) says that if it is necessary or expedient in the national interest so to do, Parliament may by law provide for the creation of one or more All-India Services common to the Union and the States, and regulate the recruitment and the conditions of the persons appointed, to any such service. Article 312(2) reads, "The Services known at the commencement of this Constitution as the Indian Administrative Service and the Indian Police Service shall be deemed to be services created by Parliament under this Article."

Article 313 of the Constitution made provisions for transition which were "Until other provision is made in this behalf under this Constitution, all the laws in force immediately before the commencement of this Constitution and applicable to any public service or any post which continues to exist after commencement of this Constitution, as an All India Service or as service or post under the Union or a State shall continue in force so far as consistent with the provisions of this Constitution."

Article 314 made provision for the protection of the then existing officers recruited by the Secretary of State, and provided as "Except as otherwise expressly provided by this Constitution, every person who having been appointed by the Secretary of State or Secretary of State in Council to a civil service of the Crown in India continues on and after the commencement of this Constitution to serve under the Government of India or of a State shall be entitled to receive from the Government of India and the Government of the State, which he is from time to time serving, the same conditions of service as respect to remuneration, leave and pension, and the same rights as respect to disciplinary matters or rights as similar thereto as changed circumstances may permit as that person was entitled to immediately before such commencement."

This Article was subsequently repealed by the Constitution (Twenty Eighth Amendment) Act 1972 which came into force on 29-8-1972. By the same Act, a new Article 312-A was added which empowered Parliament to vary or revoke conditions of service of certain services (ICS and IP).

Former Secretary of State Service Officers (Conditions of Service) Act 1972

The preamble of this Act reads, "An Act to provide for variation or revocation of the conditions of service of former Secretary of State Service Officers in respect of certain matters and for matters connected therewith or incidental thereto." Section 2(b) defined "former Secretary of State service," while section -2 (c) defined " ICS members of the Indian Administrative Service" and Section 2 (d) gave the definition of the "IP" as "IP members of the Indian Police Service means a person who was appointed to the Police Service of the Crown in India known as the Indian Police and who on the appointed day is a member of the Indian Police Service."

As per section 4 of this Act conditions of service of IP members of the IPS were to be the same as were for the members of the IPS, under the provisions of the All India Services Act 1951).

The All India Services Act 1951

An Act to regulate the recruitment, and the conditions of service of persons appointed, to the All India Services common to the Union and the States" was passed which came into force on October 29,1951. According to Section-2, "The expression" an "All India Service" means the service known as the Indian Administrative Service or the service known as the Indian Police Service, or any other service specified in Sec. 2-A."

Section-3 provided for the regulation of recruitment and conditions of service, according to which "the Central Government, may, after consultation with the Governments of the States concerned make rules for the regulation of recruitment and the conditions of service of persons appointed to the All-India Service." According to Section 4, "All Rules in force immediately before the commencement of this Act and applicable to an All -India Service shall continue to be in force and shall be deemed to be rules made under this Act."

The All -India Services Rules

The Government of India in consultation with the State Governments made the following rules from time to time which were applicable to the members of the All India Services:

1. The All India Services (Medical Attendance) Rules 1954

2. The All India Services (Compensatory Allowance) Rules 1954
3. The All India Services (Travelling Allowance)Rules 1954
4. Miscellaneous Executive Instructions concerning All India Services 1954.
5. The All India Services (Leave) Rules 1955.
6. The All India Services (Provident Fund) Rules 1955.
7. The All India Services (Special Disability Leave) Regulations 1957.
8. The All India Services (Overseas Pay, Passage and Leave Salary) Rules 1957.
9. The All India Services (Death -cum-Retirement Benefits) Rules 1958.
10. The All India Services (Remittance into and Payments from Provident and Family Pension Funds) Rules 1958.
11. The All India Services (Commutation of Pension) Regulations 1959.
12. The All India Services (Study Leave) Regulations 1960.
13. The All India Services (Conditions of Service-Residuary Matters) Rules 1960.
14. The All India Services (Conduct) Rules 1968.
15. All India Services (Discipline And Appeal) Rules 1969.
16. All India Services (Confidential Rolls) Rules 1970.
17. The All India Services (Joint Cadre) Rules 1972.
18. All India Services (Dearness Allowance) Rules 1972.

19. The All India Services (Leave Travel Concession) Rules 1975.

20 The All India Services (House Rent Allowance) Rules 1977.

21. The All India Services (House Building Allowance) Rules 1978.

22. All India Services (Group Insurance) Rules-1981.

The Indian Police Service Rules

Following rules applicable to the members of the IPS were made from time to time:

1. The Indian Police Service (Cadre) Rules 1954.
2. The Indian Police Service (Recruitment) Rules 1954.
3. The Indian Police Service (Probation) Rules 1954.
4. The Indian Police Service (Pay) Rules 1954.
5. The Indian Police Service (Uniform) Rules 1954.
6. The Indian Police Service (Fixation of Cadre Strength) Regulations 1955.
7. The Indian Police Service (Appointment by Competitive Examination) Regulations 1955.
8. The Indian Police Service (Appointment by Promotion) Regulations 1955.
9. Indian Police Service (Special Allowance) Rules 1977.
10. Indian Police Service (Probationer's Final Examination) Regulations 1987.
11. Indian Police Service (Regulation of Seniority) Rules 1988.

Cadre Strength

The Government of India, by virtue of powers conferred under All-India Services Act 1951, in consultation with the State Governments made "The Indian Police Service (Cadre) Rules 1954". In pursuance of these Rules "The Indian Police Service (Fixation of Cadre Strength) Regulations, 1955 were made.

Cadre Formation

The constitution of the cadre for each State or group of States is done under rules and they are referred to as "State Cadre" or "Joint Cadre". The strength of each cadre is determined by the Central Government in consultation with the concerned State Governments and there is provision for triennial review. Cadre officers are sent on deputation to Government of India for postings in Central Police Organisations, other departments and organisations against 'Central Deputation Reserve'. There is also provision for deputation from one State to another which is known as 'State to State deputation'. The cadre strength is determined on the basis of following components:

1. All the posts of Suprintendents of Police and above, under the State Government, are called Senior Duty posts.

2. Central Deputation Reserve @ 40% of item (1) above.
3. Training Reserve @ 3.5% of item (1) above.
4. State Deputation Reserve @ 25% of item (1) above.
5. Posts to be filled by promotion and selection under Rule 8 of the IPS (Recruitment) Rules, 1954 not exceeding 33.33% of items (1), (2), (3) and (4) above.
6. Leave Reserve and junior posts Reserve @ 16.5% of item (1) above.
7. Posts to be filled by direct recruitment (items 1+2+3+4+6-5).

Initially the officers selected for IPS were generally allotted to the home states. There was no ceiling for insiders or outsiders. The States Re-organision Commission recommended that at least 50% of the new entrants in any State cadre should be from outside. These recommendations were accepted and implemented from 1960. This was done keeping in view the national integration. Since 1960, some of the directly recruited IPS officers are being allotted to non-home states. Earlier the candidates were required to indicate the choice of States to be allotted in case one did not get the home state. Subsequently this was withdrawn and the candidates were required to indicate that, in case of selection for IAS or IPS, would they like to be allotted to home state. No option was asked for outside states as the allotment of cadre was done on a roaster system. The officers promoted from the State Police Services formed part of the home cadre and they are not allotted to the 'out side state cadre'.

The Cadre Strength

The position of the IPS cadre in the country, as reflected below will show that the number kept on increasing gradually, until a decision was taken, not to expand the cadres and reduce the strength after thorough review of the State cadres.

Year	Recruitment Posts	Promotional Posts	Total Authorised Strength
1967	1340	273	1613
1970	1492	299	1791
1971	1483	307	1790
1975	1716	375	2091
1976	1804	390	2194
1980	1838	566	2404
1982	1982	608	2590
1987	2273	705	2978
1989	2380	756	3136
1992	2588	832	3420
1993	2590	832	3472
1994	2605	838	3443
1995	2668	851	3519
1997	2493	851	3344

State Cadres

Cadre strength of various States, including the new cadres formed from time to time, is indicated in the following table:

Year and Strength

Cadre	Year								
	1967	1970	1975	1980	1987	1989	1993	1995	1997
1. Andhra Pradesh	91	91	123	150	129	194	194	194	183
2. Arunachal Pradesh Goa-Mizoram-Union Territories (AGMUT-Notified on 20-6-1990)	-	-	-	-	-	-	170	171	162
3. Assam & Meghalaya (Joint cadre from 1992)	67	67	79	98	121	142	144	144	136
4. Bihar	117	117	150	176	219	215	253	263	250
5. Gujarat	74	85	91	102	135	132	141	141	133
6. Haryana	39	39	58	70	93	92	116	116	109
7. Himachal Pradesh (+ Delhi)	90	-	46	54	58	77	77	77	72
8. Jammu & Kashmir	27	56	49	49	80	84	99	99	94

9. Karnataka	85	87	89	101	130	138	138	147	147
10. Kerala	51	53	70	78	111	117	126	126	121
11. Madhya Pradesh	170	189	209	219	303	297	293	293	278
12. Maharashtra	143	154	156	178	207	203	216	216	205
13. Manipur & Tripura	-	-	51	58	84	99	111	111	105
14. Nagaland	-	-	-	-	-	-	45	52	49
15. Orissa	88	99	99	104	123	122	131	160	151
16. Punjab	70	70	84	94	119	116	142	142	144
17. Rajasthan	88	91	95	107	136	147	155	155	146
18. Sikkim	-	-	-	14	22	24	27	27	21
19. Tamil Nadu	77	81	108	130	160	156	180	200	189
20. Uttar Pradesh	193	233	274	333	350	396	396	417	395
21. West Bengal	143	176	190	204	233	258	268	268	254
22. Union Territories	-	103	70	85	115	127	-	-	-
TOTAL	1613	1791	2091	2404	2978	3136	3422	3519	3344

The National Police Commission

The National Police Commission in their 6th report of March 1981 indicated following facts about the cadre strength:

1. There are 664 directly recruited Deputy Superintendents of Police and their total number including both directly recruited and promoted is 2800. They have put in varying number of years of service as DSP The total number of promotion posts is 552. It is, therefore, inevitable that some able and competent Deputy Superintendents of Police are not promoted to the IPS even on acquiring eligibility for promotion due to the structure of the service and the percentage reserved for promotion.

2. The Central Police Organisations have a total number of 1416 posts of Class I officers out of which 269 i.e. 19% are occupied by IPS officers and the bulk of these are in the ranks of DIGs, IGs and above. There are only 2 non-IPS IGs and 31 non-IPS DIGs and they belong to the respective CPOs. There are now 114 officers in the Senior Time Scale belonging to these organisations who aspire for the higher posts in the Central Police Organisations.

This commission also made following observations about cadre structure:

1. There is a wide variation in the promotion prospects to the level of DIG and IG from cadre to cadre. There is need for uniformity of prospects irrespective of cadres.

2. The alliances that develop between some IPS officers and the local interests of caste, creed etc., in their home states are a matter of concern as these alliances come in the way of honest and clean administration. Therefore, every direct recruit he posted outside one's home state.

3. Every officer should do a spell of duty in a CPO cadre the period of which should not exceed five years.

4. Each and every IPS officer promoted from the state police service should work in the Central Government.

5. IPS officers should be exposed to a variety of jobs in and outside the police organisation in order to broaden their outlook.

6. The management of the IPS cadre should be by Police officers at the Centre, through the Central Police Establishment and in the States by similar Boards set up under the State Security Commissions.

6

Recruitment and Promotions

RECRUITMENT

The first ever competitive examination for IP was held in England in 1893. The minimum educational qualification was 'Senior Cambridge Examination' and age was to be between 19-20 years. This age limit was to be between 19 to 24 years for Indian natives when Indians were allowed to compete. In 1939, the minimum educational qualification was prescribed to be graduation.

The minimum qualification for appointment to the post of Deputy Superintendent of Police was graduation. Deputy Suprintendents of Police were later on promoted as IP.

After Independence

We have seen in chapter 3, various categories of IPS officers and the special recruitment made to fill up a large number of vacancies caused due to migration or premature retirement. The minimum qualification was graduation and other eligibility conditions varied for each source of recruitment and minimum physical standards like height were not prescribed. The examination was conducted by the Federal Public Service Commission of India, now U.P.S.C.

In exercise of the powers conferred by the All-India Services Act 1951, the Central Government in consultation with the State Governments made 'The Indian Police Service (Recruitment) Rules 1954'. According to rule 3, the service consisted of (1) members IP, (2) members recruited to the service before the commencement of these rules; and (3) persons recruited to the service in accordance with the provisions of these rules. The methods of recruitment, as prescribed by rule 4, were (a) by a competitive examination, (a) by selection of persons from among the Emergency Commissioned Officers and Short Service Commissioned Officers of the Armed Forces of the Union, who were commissioned on or after Ist November 1962, but before 10th January, 1968, or who had joined any pre-commission training at later date, but who were commissioned on or after that date, and who were released in the manner specified; and (b) by promotion of Substantive members of a State Police Service.

The Indian Police Service

The Indian Police Service (Appointment by Competitive Examinations) regulations 1955 were made by the Central Government in consultation with the State Governments and the Union Public Service Commission. These regulations provided for holding of competitive examination by the Union Public Service Commission, conditions of eligibility of candidates, disqualifications for admission, reservations for certain classes, disqualification on grounds of plural marriage, penalty for impersonation etc., disqualification for appointment on medical grounds, etc.

The Central Government in consultation with the State Governments and the UPSC made The Indian Police Service (Appointment by Promotions) Regulations 1955 which, besides defining certain things, provided for constitution of the committee to make selection, preparation of a list of suitable officers, consultation with the UPSC, appointment to cadre posts from the select list, appointment to the service from the select list etc. The promotion quota remained 25% which was increased to 33.33% in 1977.

The Civil Services Examination

The UPSC holds competitive examination for Civil Services every year. Civil Services mainly include, the Indian Foreign Service, IAS, IPS and other Central Services Class I and Class II.

Written Examination

Besides three compulsory papers of (1) English Essay (2) General English and (3) General Knowledge, in which all the candidates were required to appear, for IPS, only two optional subjects were prescribed out of three prescribed for the IFS/IAS and Central Services. Candidates appearing for IFS/IAS were required to write two more advanced subjects and answer books of these were not evaluated unless one passed in the three optional subjects. It was subsequently provided that candidates who successfully competed for IPS would not be offered appointment for any other central service except IAS and IFS.

Subsequently the system of written examination was revised from time to time . The preliminary examination was started from 1979 to weed out the substandard candidates because of the ever-increasing number. All the candidates were to appear in the prescribed minimum subjects and selection was made on the basis of marks obtained.

The Interview

Immediately after Independence, the recruitment to IPS except for the direct recruits, was made on the basis of interview only. Subsequently it was provided that a basic minimum percentage of marks were compulsorily to be obtained failing which the candidate would not be eligible for selection even if one had done well in the written examination. This system was subsequently revised and the selection was to be made on the merit of the total marks obtained in written examination and the interview . In Sixties the maximum marks for interview for IFS/IAS were 400 and for IPS 200. Subsequently this was revised and maximum marks for interview for all the services were to be the same.

Age Limit

The lower age limit was prescribed for IPS with a view to encouraging the candidates to join the IPS. It was 20 to 24 years for IPS and 21 to 24 years for IFS/IAS and other Central Services. Subsequently the lower age limit distinction was given up and whereas the lower age limit remained 21 years, the upper age limit was revised from time to time to 24 to 26 and 28 years. The upper age limits were relaxed from time to time for displaced persons from Pakistan, scheduled castes, scheduled tribes and other backward castes.

Physical Standards

Initially no separate physical standards were prescribed for the IPS. Subsequently minimum height (5 feet 5 inches for candidates from plains), chest measurements and eyesight etc., were prescribed. Certain deformities like flat foot, knock knees, colour blindness etc., were made disqualifications.

The medical tests of successful candidates after the declaration of the final result by the UPSC, used to be conducted by the Medical Boards of respective states. This system used to cause delay in respect of some candidates and it affected their joining the training. This system was subsequently modified and all those candidates who appeared in interview were subjected to Medical Examination on the following day of the interview at an indicated medical centre.

Quality of Candidates

According to a study made by a committee set up in 1968, by the Government of India, Ministry of Home Affairs , of Directors General /Inspectors General of Police, there has been a fall in the quality of candidates during the years 1948 to 1966. This is reflected in the Sixth Report of the National Police Commission the gist of which is given below indicating the degrees held by the candidates prior to entering the service.

Year	IPS			IAS		
	I Class	II Class	III Class	I Class	II Class	III Class
1948	34.1%	63.3%	2.6 %	57.6%	33.3%	9.1%
1959	50.9%	45.3%	3.8%	-	-	-
1960	50.7%	45.2%	4.1%	-	-	-
1965	24.6%	65.84%	9.6%	34.9%	58.1%	-
1966	16.1%	61.4%	22.5%	52.9%	39.9%	7.2%

Educational Disciplines

The data of three decades relating to 1963 to 1993 regular recruits compiled from the Civil Lists of IPS officers of the country shows that earlier the candidates from 'Arts' followed by 'Pure Science' streams used to dominate. In 1966 the percentage of 'Arts' stream was as high as 87 which came down to 27 in 1993. 'Pure Science' stream contributed 40% selected candidates which came down to 9% in 1992. Candidates from 'Technology' kept on gradually increasing which rose from 1% in 1967 to 36% in 1993. Candidates from 'Management' discipline did not show much variation over years but 'Medicine' which contributed 2% in 1983 rose to 11% in 1993. The overall percentage of 31 years comes to Arts - 55.60, Science - 27.13, Technology - 11.24, Management - 2.6, Medicine - 1.80 and others 1.55, the details of which are reflected in the chart given on the following page.

Attraction for I P S

The National Police Commission (Report of 1981) observed, "it is found that, of late, the IPS is generally given higher preference after IAS/IFS by candidates taking the combined competitive examinations. It is, however, seen that after being selected for and even after joining the IPS most candidates continue if they are eligible, to try for the IAS and IFS. . . ." Studies have shown that after 1973 the preference for the IPS has improved due to improvement in the scales of pay after the Third Pay Commission. Subsequently interaction with the IPS probationers revealed that there were candidates who had given IPS as their first choice as compared to IAS . In many cases the choice had been IAS, IPS and IFS or IPS, IAS and IFS.

PROMOTIONS

Directly recruited IP officers, who used to be Europeans only, were initially posted as Assistant Suprintendents of Police. Certain selected Inspectors, very few in numbers, were given promotion to IP as Assistant Superintendent of Police and they usually retired from that rank. On the recommendations of the Indian Police Commission 1902-03 a new designation of 'Deputy Superintendent of Police' was created on the analogy of the Provincial Civil Service. This rank was to be manned by Indians only, who were to be appointed either by direct recruitment or by promoting the Inspectors. This

Educational Disciplines of Candidates Appearing for Civil Services

Year	Arts Stream	%	Pure Science	%	Tech-nology	%	Manage-ment	%	Medi-cine	%	Others	%	Total
1963	29	66	14	32	-	0	1	2	-	0	-	0	44
1964	38	79	10	21	-	0	-	0	-	0	-	0	48
1965	40	77	9	17	3	6	-	0	-	0	-	0	52
1966	54	87	8	13	-	0	-	0	-	0	-	0	62
1967	45	66	20	29	1	1	2	3	-	0	-	0	68
1968	35	83	7	17	-	0	-	0	-	0	-	0	42
1969	26	74	7	20	2	6	-	0	-	0	-	0	35
1970	20	57	14	40	1	3	-	0	-	0	-	0	35
1971	17	61	9	32	1	4	1	4	-	0	-	0	28
1972	35	60	18	31	4	7	1	2	-	0	-	0	58
1973	41	69	14	24	4	7	-	0	-	0	-	0	59
1974	47	65	21	29	3	4	1	1	-	0	-	0	72
1975	32	58	20	36	3	5	-	0	-	0	-	0	55
1976	42	47	41	46	6	7	-	0	-	0	-	0	89
1977	54	52	48	46	1	1	-	0	1	1	-	0	104

1978	20	44	22	49	3	7	-	0	-	0	-	0	45
1979	25	56	16	36	1	2	2	4	1	2	-	0	45
1980	22	58	16	42	-	0	-	0	-	0	-	0	38
1981	32	64	13	26	3	6	2	4	-	0	-	0	50
1982	32	59	14	26	5	9	3	6	-	0	-	0	54
1983	31	58	16	30	2	4	2	4	1	2	-	1	53
1984	36	48	23	31	11	15	4	5	1	1	-	0	75
1985	48	48	25	25	20	20	5	5	3	3	-	0	101
1986	52	49	31	29	13	12	4	4	6	6	-	0	106
1987	57	56	16	16	20	20	4	4	3	3	2	2	102
1988	50	57	15	17	18	20	3	3	1	1	1	1	88
1989	29	37	17	22	22	28	4	5	3	4	3	4	78
1990	30	42	16	23	13	18	3	4	3	4	6	8	71
1991	19	37	13	25	10	20	3	6	3	6	3	6	51
1992	25	33	7	9	28	37	4	5	3	4	9	12	76
1993	15	27	6	11	20	36	3	5	6	11	5	9	55
Total	1078	55.60	526	27.13	218	11.24	52	2.68	35	1.80	30	1.55	1939

system continues even now for the officers of the State Police Services.

Superintendent of Police

Usually the European IP Officers were posted as District Suprintendents of Police. The Indian Police Commission 1902-03 after carefully considering the question whether natives be employed as Suprintendents, were of the opinion that, "in provinces where the ordinary circumstances prevail, it is both safe and expedient to throw open some superintendentships to natives ------------ at present, such officers do not exist to any extent in the police ---------. The employment of natives as Suprintendents, however, is more or less an experiment; and therefore, it ought to be tried within reasonable limits wherever circumstances permit" In pursuance of these recommendations, in due course, when Deputy Suprintendents, who were first appointed in 1906, gained sufficient seniority were promoted to IP and were posted as Suprintendents. Mr. Alakh Kumar Sinha of Bihar a directly recruited DSP and subsequently promoted to IP, was the first ever Indian to head the Police force of a province in 1938 when elected Congress Government came to power. Regarding directly recruited IP Officers the Commission mentioned that, "Seven years of work as an Assistant following on this training (with short terms of duty as officiating Superintendent) ought to be enough to fit him for the efficient performance of the duties of Superintendent." An ASP got his promotion as SP usually after 7 years and this continued till 1947. Consequent to large scale departure of IP Officers in 1947, the ASPs with few months service had to be promoted as SPs but once sufficient number of directly recruited IPS Officers were available, it generally took six to seven years to get promoted to the rank of Superintendent of Police. During 1960 the ASP got his promotion in the senior scale of the IPS as Superintendent of Police in three to four years of service which included training period also. On the recommendation of the Fourth Pay Commission it was provided that ASP will get promoted to senior scale of pay on completion of four years of service and this was given effect to from January 1986. The Fifth Pay Commission also maintained this.

Substantive members of the State Police Service are appointed to the IPS by promotion in accordance with the Indian Police Service (Recruitment) Rules 1954 and the Indian Police Service (Appointment by Promotion) Regulations 1955. The promotion quota was 25% of the senior duty posts of a particular cadre which was subsequently raised to 33.33%. State Police Service Officers on first appointment to IPS get posted in the Senior Scale of pay as Superintendent of Police.

DIG

The Indian Police Commission 1902-03 observed, "Passing now to the higher classes of inspecting officers, the Commission find that adequate advantage has not been taken of the provision of the law which permits the appointment of "such Deputy Inspectors General as to the Local Government shall deem fit." In all provinces these officers are too few in number. Some of their most important duties are entrusted to Commissioners and District Magistrates and many of them are entirely neglected. They are practically confined to work of a comparatively unimportant character; and their usefulness is consequently impaired. The Commission would, therefore, propose to increase their number and to place a Deputy Inspector General in full administrative charge of a range comprising as many districts as he can reasonably be expected to control. This arrangement will not only lead to the maintenance of a higher standard of work among Suprintendents, but also to their more cordial and intelligent cooperation with one another. One Deputy

Inspector General in each province should be placed in administrative charge of the railway police; and it will be both convenient and expedient to place him also in charge of the Provincial Criminal Investigation Department, the constitution and objects of which will be discussed later. Deputy Inspector General should be carefully selected from among the Suprintendents. Their pay should run from Rs. 1,500 to Rs. 2,000 in three classes. These appointments should be regarded as the highest prizes absolutely reserved for the police department." These recommendations were generally carried out.

As there used to be only one post of the IGP in a Province/State, very few could get to this highest rank and the remaining IP/IPS officers had to retire from the rank of DIG of Police. This statement continued till early nineteen eighties, when upgradation of Senior supervisory posts was ordered and Government of India issued guidelines for time bound promotions, as far as possible, in various ranks.

Additional IGP

Till 1960 this post did not exist. In order to accommodate certain officers of the same batch in the same rank and pay the posts of Additional Inspector General of Police were created in some States. In U.P. when Sri Shanti Prasad, IP was made the IGP, his batch-mate Sri S. C. Mitra IP was promoted as Additional IGP. Sri Misra later on went to Mount Abu as Commandant, Central Police Training College in the rank of IGP from where he retired as Director, National Police Academy. In 1982 the post of Additional IGP having pay scale of Rs. 2250-2500 was abolished and Government of India ordered two scales in the rank of DIG i.e., Rs. 2000-2250 for DIG Grade Second and Rs. 2250-2500 for Grade First. Fourth Pay Commission did not favour this rank of Additional IGP, hence it was abolished.

IGP

From 1861 to 1919 the IGP of a province used to be an ICS officer, who was the head of the police department. The Indian Police Commission 1902-03 in their report said, "The Commission thoroughly approve of the provision of Act V of 1861, that the administration of the Police throughout a province shall be vested in an Inspector General, who should be the departmental head of Police force. After consideration of all the evidence that the Commission have heard on the subject, and their experience of the duties and work of the Inspector General, they are of opinion that this office should for the present ordinarily be held by a selected District Magistrate. They do not think that the door should be absolutely closed against the officers of the police Department."

From 1919 onwards Police officers were posted as Inspector General of Police of a Province, the highest rank. From 1973 onwards this post used to be upgraded to that of Director General of Police-cum-Inspector General of Police, in some States, as and when the State Governments so desired. This practice continued till 1985.

Additional DGP

Rank of Additional Director General of Police in the pay scale of Rs. 7,300-100-7,600 was recognised by the Fourth Pay Commission for certain Central Police Organisations which took effect from January 1, 1986. Post of DGP of smaller States were also placed in this pay scale. Though the posts of Additional DGP were not mentioned for the States, some States did create these posts in order to promote the IPS officers who were stagnating in the rank of IGP. The Fifth Pay Commission has recognised this rank in the pay scale of Rs. 22,400-525-24,500 which has taken effect from 1st January 1996.

Director General of Police

This is the highest post for the IPS. Till 1985, it was for the States to create this post for the State Police Chief, as till then the recognised post was that of IGP. Fourth Pay Commission recognised this highest rank for the IPS in the pay scale of Rs. 7,600-8,000 for bigger States and some Central Police Organisations and Rs. 8,000 fixed for selected posts under the Government of India. From January 1, 1996 the DGP has been placed in the pay scale of Rs. 24,050-650-26,000.

7

Pay

Initially the pay scales of Army Officers drafted as Police Officers differed from province to province. By and large these pay scales as per old records available in 1888 were :

1.	I.G.P.	Rs. 2500.00
2.	D.I.G.	
	(i)	Rs. 1800.00
	(ii)	Rs. 1500.00
3.	A.I.G.	Rs. 700.00
4.	S.P.	
	(i) First Grade	Rs. 1000.00
	(ii) Second Grade	Rs. 800.00
	(iii) Third Grade	Rs. 700.00
	(iv) Fourth Grade	Rs. 600.00
	(v) Fifth Grade	Rs. 500.00
5.	A. S. P	
	(i) First Grade	Rs. 400.00
	(ii) Second Grade	Rs. 300.00

In 1879, the UP cadre was re-organised and the pay scales were brought down except for the officers drawn from the army.

The direct recruitment for the I.P. was started in 1893. The pay admissible to Asstt. Superintendents of Police (I.P.) was Rs. 250.00 as probationer and Rs. 300.00 in the second grade on completion of training and posting as regular A.S.P.

The pay scales of the A.S.P. were revised from Rs. 300.00 to 500.00 and of S.P. from Rs. 700.00 to Rs. 1200.00 in 5 classes for Europeans and Rs. 600.00 to 900.00 for the natives.

Orders for revision of pay of I.P. officers were issued in 1919 which were made applicable from 1.1.1920. Following scales were allowed:

Junior Scale

I Year	Rs. 325.00
II Year	Rs. 325.00
III Year	Rs. 350.00
IV Year	Rs. 350.00
V Year	Rs. 375.00
VI Year	Rs. 375.00
VI Year	Rs. 400.00
VI Year	Rs. 400.00
VII Year	Rs. 450.00
VIII Year	Rs. 500.00
IX Year	Rs. 500.00

X Year	Rs.	550.00
XI Year	Rs.	600.00
XII Year	Rs.	600.00
XIII Year	Rs.	650.00

Senior Scale

Rs. 500 (4th year) -525-525-550-550-600-600-650-700-750-750 -800-850-950-EB-1,000-1,000-1050-1100-1100-1150.

Time Scale to Indian Police Officers from 1st April, 1924

Following pay scales were allowed to IP officers in 1924 which remained applicable even after India's Independence:

	Basic Pay		Overseas Pay	
Year of Service	Junior	Senior	If drawn in Sterling	If drawn in Rupees
Ist	350	650	-	100
2nd	375	650	-	100
3rd	400	650	-	100
4th	425	650	-	125
5th	450	650	15	150
6th	475	650	15	150
7th	500	675	15	150
8th	525	700	15	150
9th	550	725	15	250
		Efficiency Bar		
10th	575	750	25	250
11th	600	800	25	250
12th	625	825	25	250
13th	650	850	25	250
14th	675	900	25	250
15th	700	925	30	300

(Contd. . .)

(Contd. . .)

Year of Service	Basic Pay: Junior	Basic Pay: Senior	Overseas Pay: If drawn in Sterling	Overseas Pay: If drawn in Rupees
16th	950		30	300
17th	1,000		30	300
	Efficiency Bar			
18th	1,050		30	300
19th	1,050		30	300
20th	1,100		30	300
21st	1,100		30	300
22nd	1,150		30	300
23rd	1,200		30	300
24th	1,250		30	300
25th	1,300		30	300
26th	1,350		30	300
	Selection Grade			
	1,450		30	300

1. Efficiency bars were to be in force after the ninth year of service in the junior and the seventeenth year in the senior scale. An officer, who was not considered fit for a superior appointment, was not allowed to rise above Rs. 550 in the junior scale. An officer who was not considered fit to hold charge of a first class district, was not allowed to rise above Rs. 1,000 in the senior scale.
2. Under Government of India letter no. F 728/22-Police dated the 27th August, 1923, appointments to the selection grade were made strictly by selection, all officers who had rendered exceptionally meritorious service as Superintendents of Police, being eligible. Fitness for promotion to administrative rank was regarded as enhancing an officer's claim to appointment but was not the sole criterion of selection.
3. Officers of non-Asiatic domicile only were to receive overseas pay.
4. Officers entitled to overseas pay were to draw it in sterling or in rupees accordingly as they came under rule 4 or rule 5 of the Statutory rules and orders of 1924 published under Resolution no. F-172-B-11-24, dated the 15th January, 1925, at pages 125 to 133 of the Police Gazette dated the 18th February, 1925.

From 1.4.1935, the pay-scale of D.I.G. Police (I.P. officers) was fixed as Rs. 1950-50-2150. Pay-scales of other ranks remained the same.

I.P.S. Pay-Scales from 1949

Pay-scales as applicable from 1.4.1949 were :

Year of Service	Basic Pay Junior Rs.	Senior Rs.
Ist	350	-
2nd	350	-
3rd	380	-
4th	380	-
5th	410	-
6th	440	600
7th	470	640
8th	500	680
9th	530	720
10th	560	760
11th	590	800
	Efficiency Bar	
12th	620	840
13th	650	880
14th	680	920
15th	710	960
	740	1,000
16th	770	1,000
17th	810	1,050
18th	850	1,050
19th		1,100
20th		1,100
21th		1,150
22nd		1,150

Posts Carrying Pay Above the Time Scale

1. DIG	(i)	Rs. 1950-50-2150 (for IP officers)
	(ii)	Rs. 1450-50-1650 (for IPS officers)
2. IG	(i)	Rs. 2500-125-3,000 (for IP officers)
	(ii)	Rs. 1850-100-2250 (for IPS officers)

Marriage Allowance

Marriage allowance of Rs. 30/- per month was admissible to married officers only and bachelors used to be the losers.

Indian Police Service (Pay) Rules-1954

Government of India, in consultation with the State Governments, as per provisions of All-India Services Act 1951, made " Indian Police Service (Pay) Rule 1954". These rules provide for:

1. The scales of pay admissible to a member of the service and the dates of effect.
2. Regulation of increment including stagnation increment.
3. Withholding of increment.
4. Grants of advance increments.
5. Pay fixation in various kinds of appointments including initial appointment to IPS on promotion from the State Police Service, etc.

Pay Scales in force from 1960

Revised pay scales of the I.P.S. officers as applicable from 1.4.1960 were:

Year of Service	Basic Pay Junior Rs.	Senior Rs.
Ist	400	740
2nd	400	740
3rd	450	740
4th	490	740
5th	510	740
6th	540	740
7th	570	780
8th	600	820
9th	635	860
10th	670	900
11th	705	940
12th	740	980
13th	775	1,020
14th	810	1,060
15th	845	1,100
	Efficiency Bar	
	890	1,100
16th	915	1,150
17th	950	1,150
18th		1,200
19th		1,200
20th		1,250
21th		1,300
22nd		1,400
Selection grade		1,400

Posts Carrying Pay Above the Time Scale

Rank	I.P.S. Rs.	I.P. Rs.
1. D.I.G. of Police	1600 - 100 - 1800	1950 -50- 2150
2. Addl. I.G. P.	2000 - 125 - 2250	2500 - 125 - 2750
3. I.G. P.	2250 - 125 - 2500	2500 - 125 - 2750

From 1982, two grades of pay were allowed in the rank of DIG which were:

1. DIG Grade-II	Rs. 2000-125-2250
2. DIG Grade-I	Rs. 2250-125-2500

Revised Pay from 1.1.1986

On recommendations of the Fourth Pay Commission the pay scales of Indian Police Service officers with effect from January 1, 1986, as fixed by Government of India, Ministry of Personnel & Training, Administrative Reforms and Public Grievances and Pensions, Department of Personnel & Training vide notification no. 11030/16/87- AIS.II dated 13th March, 1987, were as under :

1. Junior Scale	Rs. 2200-75-2000-EB-100-4000
2. Senior Scale	
(a) Time Scale	Rs. 3000 (fifth & sixth year) 100 - 3500 - 125 - 4500
(b) Junior Administrative Grade	Rs. 3700-125-4700-150-5000
3. Selection Grade	Rs. 4500 - 150 - 5700
4. Super Time Scale	
(a) D.I.G.	Rs.5100-150-5400 (10th year or later- 150 - 6150

(b) I.G.	Rs. 5900 - 200 - 6700
5. Above Super Time Scale	
(a) Addl. D.G.	Rs. 7300 - 100 -7600
(b) D.G. (1) Smaller States-	Rs. 7300-100-7600
(2) Bigger States	Rs. 7600-100-8000

On the recommendations of the Fifth Pay Commission of India, the following pay scales have been allowed to I.P.S. Ooficers from 1.1. 1996:

Grade	Pay Scale (Rs.)
1. Junior Time Scale	8,000 - 275 - 13,500
2. Senior Time Scale	10,000 - 325 - 15,200
3. Junior Administrative Grade	12,000 - 375 - 16,500
4. Selection Grade	14,300 - 400 - 18,300
5. Super Time Scale	
(1) D.I.G.	16,400 - 450 - 20,000
(2) I.G.	18,400 - 500 - 22,400
6. Above Super Time Scale	
1. Addl. D.G.P.	22,400 - 525 - 24,500
2. D.G.P.	24,050 - 650 - 26,000

Comparative Pay Scales

Keeping in view the rise in prices etc., the pay scales were also revised from time to time, as per details given earlier. The starting pay of various ranks of police officers, IP and IPS remained more or less remained the same for about one hundred years (1888-1985). From 1986, there has been phenomenal increase in price index which in turn led to increase in pay scales of various services including the IPS (see Table on the next page).

Starting Pay of Various Ranks

Year	ASP	SP	Selection Grade	DIG	IG	Addl. DGP	DGP	Remarks
1888	300	500	-	1500	2500	-	-	ICS/Army Officers
1893	250	500	-	1500	2500	-	-	IP and other Officers
1920	325	525	-	1500	2500	-	-	IP Officers
1924	350	650	1450	1500	2500	-	-	IP Officers
1935	350	650	1450	1950	2500	-	-	IP Officers
1949	350	600	-	1450	1850	-	-	For IPS Officers
								For IP Officers scales remained unchanged.
1960	400	740	1400	1600	2250	-	-	IPS Officers
1986	2200	3000	4500	5100	5900	7300	7600	IPS Officers
1996	8000	10000	14300	16400	18400	22400	24050	IPS Officers

Training of IPS Officers

As we know the Police in India took the shape of an organisation with the introduction of the Police Act (Act-V of 1861). Initially the Army officers, mostly upto the rank of Captain, were put as Superintendents of Police of the districts. They were trained as Army officers and were not given any training as Police officers. From 1893, onwards the I.P. officers were appointed on the basis of examination held in England. They were trained in India mostly in the provinces of their allotment. Police Training Colleges (then Schools) at Moradabad (U.P.), Phillaur (Punjab), Bhagalpur (Bihar) Saugor (M.P.), and Vellore (T.N.) are the oldest institutions where I.P. officers of one or a group of provinces used to be trained. I.P. officers were also trained in districts under selected Superintendents of Police, for want of any centralised training in the country. The I.P. officers, hardly got an all-India exposure and many of them even did not know each other for years.

Immediately after India's Independence, I.P.S. became the successor service of the I.P. The IPS officers of the new generation were drawn from all regions and social groups of the country. In 1948 (September 15) a Central Police Training College was established at Mount Abu (Rajasthan) with a view to fostering an all-India outlook and for achieving uniformity. The first batch of I.P.S.(RR) joined Abu in September 1948.

In 1956, a committee headed by Shri B.N. Mullick, the then D.I.B., examined the training programmes of the I.P.S. probationers, highlighted certain deficiencies and recommended inclusion of police principles and administration, investigation procedures, criminology, scientific, medical and technical aids. These recommendations were accepted.

In 1966, another committee was constituted under the chairmanship of the then Director, C.B.I. Shri D.P. Kohli, and Director, C.P.T.C as member, to assess the training programmes and suggest measures for improvement. Several measures were suggested which were later on implemented.

A committee (Gore Committee) constituted in 1972 about Police Training in India gave its recommendations in 1974 after making exhaustive study of the training needs. This committee suggested shifting of the Academy to a convenient central location in the country. The Academy was shifted to Hyderabad in February 1975. Gore Committee observed that in a changing social context the role of a Police Officer would be much more than maintaining law and order. They, therefore, needed to be trained in management concepts and techniques through modern concepts of criminology and penology. The training programmes were suitably revised.

The National Police Commission (1977-81) also examined the role of senior police leadership and recommended certain changes in the training schedule of IPS officers under chapter XLV-sixth report- March 1981 'Training and Career Development of Indian Police Service Officers'.

Till 1958, I.P.S. probationers used to report at CPTC at Mount Abu for one year's initial course. In 1960, the 'Foundational Course' was introduced for the probationers of all the Services i.e. Indian Foreign Service, Indian

Administrative Service, Indian Police Service and other class I Central Services. Candidates selected by the Union Public Service Commission were asked to report at National Academy of Administration, Mussoorie (UP), where they remained from middle of July to middle of December each year. From there officers used to report to training Institutions of the respective services. The philosophy behind this foundational course was to broaden the outlook of the newly recruited officers, give them exposure about various services, inculcate feeling of belonging to a particular batch and transform them from University students to responsible officers, so that they serve the country well. From Mussoorie, IPS officers were sent to Mount Abu for one year's training and after passing out from there they were sent to training colleges of the States of their allotment for being imparted training about local laws, procedures and drill, etc.

Till 1960, C.P.T.C. used to train IPS probationers only. Few officers from other countries and Dy. Supdt. of Police-probationers from some States also got trained with IPS probationers. An 'Advanced Course' for Superintendents of Police was introduced in 1960. In 1973, this programme was renamed as 'Senior Officers Course.'

Central Police Training College (C.P.T.C.) was established on 15.9.1948 at Mount Abu (Rajasthan), the summer capital of Rajasthan and Gujarat, firstly in the army barracks and then in the Rajputana Hotel Estate and the Abu Lawrence School. The Institution was renamed as National Police Academy in 1967 and was named after Sardar Vallabhbhai Patel in 1974.

I.P.S. officers of 27 batches 1948 to 1973 had the privilege of being trained and passing out from Mount Abu.

The Academy moved to Hyderabad in February 1975, and started functioning at the new campus from 10 February,

1975. This Academy has a sprawling campus, full of greenery where one can feel relaxed in a quiet atmosphere.

Academy's Mission

The primary purpose of the National Police Academy is to prepare leaders for the Indian Police, who will lead/ command the force with courage, uprightness, dedication and a strong sense of service to the people.

The Academy endeavours to inculcate in them, such values and norms as would help them serve the people better. In particular, it tries to inculcate integrity of the highest order, sensitivity to aspirations of people in a fast-changing social and economic milieu, respect for human rights, broad liberal perspective of law and justice, high standard of professionalism, physical fitness and mental alertness.

The Academy is a focal point for training of the trainers of police training institutions all over the country. It seeks to create an ideal training environment through dedicated, committed and skilled faculty.

The Academy is a centre for research studies on police subjects and expanding its resource base through tie-ups with similar institutions in and outside the country.

The Faculty

This institution has the selected members on its faculty who are experts of their field and are handpicked as best lot out of several aspirants from various parts of the country. Its alumni are proud of them.

Training Courses

The Academy conducts a basic course for I.P.S. probationers, three in-service management courses for I.P.S. officers of the junior, middle and senior levels, training of trainers course for the trainers of various Police Training Institutions of India, induction course for State Police Service officers promoted to I.P.S., short specialised courses, seminars/ workshops for various levels of Police officers and officers from other departments. Academy also runs Foundational Course for new entrants of certain services.

Calender of courses at SVP NPA, Hyderabad, includes following programmes for 1998, which gives an insight about the training being imparted there.

Course	Duration
1. IPS Probs-50 RR Phase I	44 weeks
2. IPS Probs-49 RR-Phase II	1 week
3. Level-I Management Course for 6-10 yrs. Service	3 weeks
4. Level-II Management Course for IPS officers	4 weeks
5. Level-III Management Course for DIG/IG on 11 yrs.	2 weeks
6. Basic Management Course for Probationers	4 weeks
7. Induction Training Course	6 weeks
8. Training of Trainers' Course	6 weeks
9. Training Administrators' Workshop	10 days
10. Management of Training	9 days
11. Coordinated Approach to Criminal Justice System	5 days
12. Traffic Management	5 days
13. Recent Trends in Economic Crimes	5 days
14. Human Resource Management in Police	5 days
15. Science & Technology and DNA	5 days
16. Reunion Seminar : IPS 1968 (on 30 years)	3 days
17. Reunion Seminar : IPS 1973 (on 25 years)	3 days
18. Vertical Interaction Course for IPS (of various levels)	1 week
19. Vertical Interaction Training Programme for I.A.S. Officers (of various levels)	5 days

Number of Probationers Trained

Sl. No.	Year	IPS	Dy. SP	Foreigners	Total
1.	1948-49	38(RR-1) 20(SRB-1)	-	-	58
2.	1949-50	14(RR-2) 19(SRB-II)	15(WB-1 Hyderabad-14)	-	48
3.	1950	35(SRB-III)	-	-	35
4.	1950-51	37(RR-3) 5(SRB-IV)	-	-	42
5.	1951	7(SRB-V)	-	-	7
6.	1951-52	33(RR-4)	-	-	33
7.	1951-52	(SRB-VI) 10(SRBVII)	-	-	31
8.	1952-53	39(RR-5)	-	-	39
9.	1953-54	37(RR-6)	3 (Tripura)	-	40

10.	1954-55	45(RR-7)	2(J & K)	2(Nepal)	49
11.	1955-56	32(RR-8)	4(J&K-3 Hyderabad-1	2(Nepal)	38
12.	1956-57	44(RR-9)	3(M.P.)	8(Nepal)	55
13.	1957-58	67(RR-10)	3(Kerala-1) (J&K-2)	-	70
14.	1958-59	33(RR-11)	-	-	35
15.	1959-60	42(RR-12)	-	-	42
16.	1960-61	48(RR-13)	8(M.P.)	-	56
17.	1961-62	63(RR-14)	12(CRP-6 MP-6)	-	75
18.	1962-63	69(RR-15)	15(MP-7 Goa-3 Delhi &HP-1 CRP-4	4 (Nepal)	88

19.	1963-64		29(CBI-10) Manipur-3 CRP-13 Tripura-3		29
20.	1964	63(RR-16)	12(Manipur-2) MP-10		75
21.	1964-65	61(RR-17)	7(Nagaland-3) Delhi &HP-4	2(Nepal)	70
22.	1965-66	65(RR-18)	10 (Manipur-2) Delhi &HP-8	2(Bhutan)	77
23.	1966-67	69(RR-19)	7(Delhi &HP-7)	2(Korea)	78
24.	1967-68	82(RR-20)	5(DHANI-2) CBI-3	2(Bhutan)	89
25.	1968-69	74(RR-21)	1(UT)	2(Nepal)	77
26.	1969-70	57(RR-22)	7(DHANI-1 Manipur-4 CBI-2		64

27.	1970-71	50(RR-23)	9(CBI-4) Nagaland-3 Tripura-2		59
28.	1971-72	49(RR-24)	4(Manipur-3) Tripura-1	3(Sikkim-1) Bhutan-2	56
29.	1972-73	64(RR-25)	6(Nagaland-4 CBI-2	2(Sikkim-1) Lesotha-1	72
30.	1973-74	87(RR-26)	2(Nagaland-1) CBI-1	2(Bhutan)	91
31.	1974-75	95(RR-27)	16(Nagaland-9 Mizoram-6 CBI-1		111
32.	1975-76	81(RR-28)	2(Nagaland-1) CBI-1	6(Bhutan-2) Afghan-4	89
33.	1976-77	106(RR-29)		7(Sikkim-5) Bhutan-2	113
34.	1977-78	112(RR-30)	8(Nagaland-3) Sikkim-5	2(Bhutan)	122

35.	1978-79	49(RR-31)	8(Nagaland-2) AP-1 Sikkim-2 CBI-3		57
36.	1979-80	50(RR-32)	3(Nagaland)	2(Bhutan)	55
37.	1980-81	41(RR-33)	2(Goa)	1(Bhutan)	41
38.	1981-82	59(RR-34)	-	-	59
39.	1982-83	57(RR-35)	-	-	57
40.	1983-84	57(RR-36)	-	2(Bhutan)	59
41.	1984-85	76(RR-37)	-	2(Bhutan)	78
42.	1985-86	84(RR-38)	-	2(Bhutan)	86
43.	1986-87	102(RR-39)	-	4(Bhutan)	106
44.	1987-88	108(RR-40)	-	1(Bhutan)	109
45.	1988-89	70(RR-41)	-	-	70
46.	1989-90	74(RR-42)	-	-	74

47.	1990-91	79(RR-43)	-	2(Bhutan)	81
48.	1991-92	81(RR-44)	-	-	81
49.	1992-93	70(RR-45)	-	5(Bhutan-2) Nepal-3	75
50.	1993-94	77(RR-46)	2(CBI)	-	79
51.	1994-95	84(RR-47)	-	-	84
52.	1995-96	81(RR-48)	-	-	81
53.	1996-97	91(RR-49)	-	-	91
54.	1997-98	114(RR-50)	12(RPFClass-I	5 Palestine	131
	Total	3262(RR) 117(SRB) 3379	Dy.SP 205 RPF 12	74	3670

1. Bhutan	32
2. Nepal	23
3. Sikkim	07
4. Afghanistan	04
5. Palestine	05
6. Korea	02
7. Lesotha	01
Total	74

Officers Trained

Fifty batches have been trained from 1948 to 1997-98 and the total number of officers trained workout to 3670 which includes 3262 I.P.S.-Regular Recruits, 117 SRB, 205 Dy. Superintendents of Police and 74 foreigners. The number of probationers trained in various batches is indicated on previous pages.

On both sides of the rear gate of the parade ground of the Academy some brass plates have been displayed on which names of the probationers trained in each batch since 1948, have been inscribed. This is a continuous exercise and probationers of successive batches get the chance of knowing about those who were trained prior to them. Those who find the names of their relatives feel happy and elated.

The Academy has been awarding various trophies, cups and medals in indoor and outdoor subjects, languages and over all performance of the probationers. This has been generating a lot of competition in various items of training, good conduct, discipline, punctuality and attendance. Here is a list of them.

INDOOR SUBJECTS

The President of India Cup

This cup is awarded to a probationer who stands first in the combined total of marks obtained in the final examination in Police Sciences viz. Police in Modern India; Investigation; Forensic Medicine; Forensic Science (Theory & Practical) and Maintenance of Public Peace and Order, together with marks obtained in snap tests (if any) held from time to time during the period of training in these subjects.

The Manipur Cup for Law

The cup is awarded to a probationer who stands first in the combined total of marks obtained in the final examination in Law subjects viz. Constitution of India and Indian Evidence Act; Indian Penal Code and Special Laws; and Criminal Procedure Code together with marks obtained in snap tests (if any) held from time to time during the period of training in these subjects.

Shri K.K. Shah Trophy

This trophy is awarded to a probationer who stands first in the combined total of marks obtained in the final examination in the subjects of Forensic Medicine and Forensic Science (Theory & Practical) together with marks obtained in snap tests (if any) held from time to time during the period of training in these subjects.

The Mehta Cup

This cup is awarded to a probationer who stands first in the combined total of marks obtained in the final examination in all the compulsory indoor subjects together with marks obtained in snap tests (if any) held from time to time during the period of training in these subjects.

Shri Teja Singh Memorial Trophy

This trophy is awarded to a probationer who secures the highest number of marks in the final examination in the subject of Criminology and in snap tests (if any) conducted.

The 1957 Batch of IPS Officers' Trophy

This trophy is awarded to a probationer who secures the highest number of marks in the final examination in the subject of 'Police Leadership and Management — Theory and Practice' and in the snap tests (if any) held during the period of training in the subject.

Arun Kumar Arora Memorial Trophy

The trophy is awarded to a probationer who secures the highest number of marks in the final examination in the subject of Personality Development & Ethical Behaviour and in the snap tests (if any) held during the period of training in the subject.

The 1964 Batch of IPS Officers' Trophy

This trophy is awarded to a probationer who secures the highest number of marks in the final examination in the subject of ' Police in Modern India' and in snap tests (if any) held during the period of training in the subject.

Shri Alakh Sinha Trophy

This trophy is awarded to the probationer who secures the highest number of marks in the final examination in Investigation and in the snap tests (if any) held during the period of training in the subject.

Shri Bijay Shanker Memorial Trophy

This trophy is awarded to a probationer who secures the highest number of marks in the final examination in the subject of 'Maintenance of Public Peace and Order' and in the snap tests (if any) held during the period of training in the subject.

OUTDOOR SUBJECTS

1. The Jaipur Cup for P.T.

2. The Tonk Cup for Equitation.
3. The S.R.B. Cup for Drill.
4. Shri R.D.Singh Cup for Swimming
5. The 51st batch of Senior Course Officers' Trophy for Unarmed Combat.
6. Gandhi Gyan Mandir Yoga Kendra Trophy for Yoga.
7. Smt. Vinodini Verma Memorial Cup for Musketry.
8. The Maharaj Singh Cup for Games & Sports.
9. The BSF Trophy for proficiency in Outdoor subjects.

The BSF Trophy is awarded to a probationer who stands first in the combined total of marks obtained in (1) the final examination in all the compulsory outdoor subjects and (2) periodical tests if any held during the period of training in these subjects.

10. The IPS Association's Sword of Honour for the Best Outdoor probationer.

The Sword of Honour is awarded to a probationer who stands first in the combined total of marks obtained in the final examination in all the compulsory outdoor subjects; games and sports and periodical tests, if any, held during the period of training in these subjects.

LANGUAGES

1. Banerji Cup for Hindi.
2. Assam Government Trophy for Assamese.
3. West Bengal Government Trophy for Bengali.
4. Kerala Government Trophy for Malayalam.

5. Gujarat Government Trophy for Gujarati.
6. N.P.A. Trophy for Kannada.
7. Maharashtra Government Trophy for Marathi.
8. Tamilnadu Government Trophy for Tamil.
9. Union Home Minister's Trophy for Telugu.
10. Orissa Government Trophy for Oriya.
11. Punjab Government Trophy for Punjabi.
12. Jammu & Kashmir Government Trophy for Urdu.
13. The 7th Top Management Course Trophy for Manipuri.
14. N.P.A. Trophy for Nepali.

GENERAL

1. The Vice President of India's Trophy for Exemplary Conduct.
2. L. Sewa Memorial Trophy for best probationer in co-curricular activities.
3. Vandana Malik Trophy for Dedication and Hardwork.
4. The 55th batch of Senior Course Officers' Trophy for Best Turn Out
5. Shri Surendranath Trophy for the Best Squad.
6. B.P. Singhal Trophy for Hindi Elocution.
7. Suprobha Deb Memorial Trophy for Best English Essay.
8. Ashesh Singhal Memorial Prize for English Debate.
9. Director's prize for Best Photo-album.

10. Compaq Trophy for Computer Studies.

OVERALL

1. The Prime Minister's Baton and Home Ministry's Revolver for the best all-round probationer.
2. Shri Bhubanananda Misra Memorial Trophy for the Second best all-round Probationer.

Best All-round Probationers

Following officers had the distinction and honour of being the best trainees of their respective batches, since 1948:

Sl. No.	Name	State	Batch
	Shri		
1.	C.V. Narasimhan, IPS	Madras	1948
2.	R.D. Singh, IPS	Bihar	1949
3.	Surendranath, IPS	Punjab	1950
4.	Baldev Singh, IPS	Madhya Pradesh	1951
5.	B.M. Mathur, IPS	Uttar Pradesh	1952
6.	A.K. Varma, IPS	Madhya Pradesh	1953
7.	M.K. Barooah, IPS	Assam	1954
8.	M.K. Narayanan, IPS	Madras	1955
9.	S.S. Lamba, IPS	Madhya Pradesh	1956
10.	K.V.H.Padmanabhan,IPS	Andhra Pradesh	1957
11.	P.S. Bhinder, IPS	Punjab	1958
12.	S.S. Brar, IPS	Punjab	1959
13.	B.K. Chaudhary, IPS	Uttar Pradesh	1960

14.	S.V.M. Tripathi, IPS	Uttar Pradesh	1961
15.	Devendra singh, IPS	Rajasthan	1962
16.	W.I. Devaram, IPS	Tamil Nadu	1963
17.	G.B.S. Sidhu, IPS	Uttar Pradesh	1964
18.	Sarabjit Singh, IPS	Punjab	1965
19.	Shanthanu Kumar, IPS	Rajasthan	1966
20.	Sunder Singh, IPS	West Bengal	1967
21.	R.D. Tyagi, IPS	Maharashtra	1968
22.	K.J. Joseph, IPS	Kerala	1969
23.	R.K. Pandit, IPS	Uttar Pradesh	1970
24.	Tilak Kak, IPS	Uttar Pradesh	1971
25.	Avtar Krishan, IPS	Madhya Pradesh	1972
26.	Ajit Singh, IPS	Punjab	1973
27.	Raj Kumar, IPS	Tamil Nadu	1974
28.	J. Punnoose, IPS	Kerala	1975
29.	K.V.S. Murthy, IPS	Tamil Nadu	1976
30.	Ajay Chadha, IPS	U.T.	1977
31.	K. Ramananujam, IPS	Tamil Nadu	1978
32.	B.S. Sidhu, IPS	Uttar Pradesh	1979
33.	Rajiv Jain, IPS	Bihar	1980
34.	Manoj Bhatt, IPS	Rajasthan	1981
35.	V.K. Gupta, IPS	Uttar Pradesh	1982
36.	S.P.S. Parihar, IPS	Madhya Pradesh	1983
37.	A.K. Arora, IPS	Rajasthan	1984
38.	A.K. Singh, IPS	Gujarat	1985

39.	V.S.K. Kaumudi, IPS	Andhra Pradesh	1986
40.	N.S. Saravade, IPS	West Bengal	1987
41.	Atul Karwal, IPS	Gujarat	1988
42.	Sanjay Kundu, IPS	Himanchal Pradesh	1989
43.	Ajay Bhatnagar, IPS	Bihar	1990
44.	Alok Sharma, IPS	Uttar Pradesh	1991
45.	Gaurav Yadav, IPS	Punjab	1992
46.	Sharad Chauhan, IPS	Punjab	1993
47.	V. Prabhakar Apte, IPS	Andhra Pradesh	1994
48.	Madhup Kumar, IPS	AGMUT	1995
49.	Vinay Hande, IPS	Bihar	1996.

President's Colours to the Academy- 1988

The Academy had the honour of receiving the President's colours on September 15, 1988, in recognition of its outstanding achievements and service to the nation.

Distinguished Alumni

Alumni of the institution have successfully provided senior leadership to police forces of the country including State and Central Police Forces. They have also successfully held high ranking positions out of the police. Several officers have been awarded Police Medals for long and Meritorious Services, President's Police Medal for Distinguished Services, Gallantry Medals, Param Vishishta Sewa Medals, Padma Shri, Padma Bhushan and Magsasey Award. Several IPS officers have had the distinction of becoming the Governors of various States, India's Ambassadors in other countries, Members/ Chairman of the Union Public Service Commission etc.

Several IPS officers in various parts of the country have laid down their lives at the altar of duty. We pay our homage to them who have made supreme sacrifices. I.P.S. and the country is proud of them.

Golden Jubilee

India celebrated the golden jubilee of the Independence of the country (1997-98). It was a happy coincidence that while I.P.S. was completing 50 years of its existence since 1948 in free India, the Sardar Vallabhbhai Patel National Police Academy celebrated its golden jubilee (15.9.1948 to 15.9.1998) and the golden jubilee batch of the I.P.S.(1997) received their training. What a proud and happy occasion for all of us.

Training at C.S.W.T. Indore

About two weeks training is imparted to I.P.S. probationers at B.S.F's 'Central School of Weapons and Tactics' at Indore. Here they have to undergo very rigorous training, both indoor and outdoor including field training. The officers are exposed to the latest weaponry, including night firing with tracer ammunition. They are also given intensive training in Field Craft, Camouflage and Field Tactics, vital for anti-terrorist and anti-insurgency operations.

Army Attachment

Probationers are sent for two weeks attachment with Army, deployed in difficult areas, either in western sector, particularly J&K , or in North East, where they are exposed to various facets of the Army, the difficulties that they face at the borders, the spirit behind the civil-military liaison, the attention which the families of the members of the Armed forces need in the districts where these I.P.S. officers will in due course be posted and many other good points about each other.

Bharat Darshan

I.P.S. probationers are taken out from the Academy for about two weeks to various parts of the country for a study tour about the police of the states visited and to give them chance to see certain parts of the country. Every batch is usually divided into four groups and probationers of each group are sent to states which are neither their home states nor states of cadre allotted. This exposure becomes very useful from various angles.

State Police Academies/Training Colleges

Before the introduction of the sandwitch pattern course, the I.P.S. probationers, after passing out from Mount Abu / Hyderabad, were sent to Police Academy or Police Training College of the State to which they were allotted, where they were kept for about three months and were given training about the laws and police rules, regulations and police drill etc., of the State. Later on this period was reduced to about four weeks and the probationers, on completion of the first phase of their training at Hyderabad, are now sent to the State Police Training Institutions.

Training in Districts

After training in the State Police Training Academy/College, the probationers are sent to districts for five to six months practical training. Normally one probationer is posted under a good Superintendent of Police and to a selected district in which one could get exposure to various police problems. The probationer is required to pick up the practical knowledge of the district police work. He/she, during attachment with the S.P., usually observes the functioning of the District Superintendent of police, public dealing, disposal of public complaints, personnel management, correspondence with other departments particularly the District Magistrate, within the district. They also learn about the functioning of the District Police Office, Local Intelligence Unit, District Crime Record Bureau, Police Lines, the Prosecution Branch, the functioning of courts dealing with criminal cases and the Executive Magistrates. Probationers also learn the work of the Sub-Divisional Police Officer, while being attached with one of them. They are attached to city police station for about two weeks. They also hold charge of a rural police station for about three months.

Attachment at State Headquarters

In Uttar Pradesh, on completion of the training in the district, the probationers are collected at the State Headquarters, where they are exposed to functioning of various State Police Units like DGP, Headquarters, C.I.D., State Intelligence Wing, State Crime Record Bureau, State Forensic Science Laboratory, P.A.C. Headquarters, etc. Probationers also call on the Senior Police Officers, DGP, State Chief Minister and the Governor.

Second Phase of Training

After completion of the training in the states, probationers are collected at Hyderabad for debriefing session of about a week. Earlier it used to be three months, after which the final 'Passing Out Parade' was held. From 47th R.R. batch, the practice of Passing Out Parade after the second phase was discontinued. In 1995, the Passing Out Parade of two batches namely 46(RR) and 47 (RR) was held together. Since 1995 i.e. 47th batch onwards the Passing Out Parade is held on completion of the first phase at the Academy.

Attachment with CPOs

Government of India decided that the IPS probationers also be exposed to the functioning and problems of the Central Police Organisations deployed in difficult areas particularly in J & K and the North East. For the first time 47th batch was sent to J & K /North Eastern States for three months attachment with the C.P.O. BNs, either of CRPF or BSF. This practice now continues but for a duration of about a month.

Attachment at Delhi

A new beginning is being made to send the I.P.S. probationers of the Golden Jubilee Batch (50RR) to Delhi for training. Here they will see the functioning of various Central Police Organisations, Delhi Police, the Parliament, and call on various dignitaries including Union Home Minister, Prime Minister and the President.

Completion of Training

The total period of training for I.P.S. probationers is about 26 months i.e. two years and two months which starts with the Foundational Course at the Lal Bahadur Shastri Academy of Administration, Mussoorie, and gets completed with the Second phase of the training at the Sardar Vallabhbhai Patel National Police Academy, Hyderabad. Thereafter they are posted to respective states of allotment where they get posted to districts to function as Asstt. Superintendents of Police incharge of a Police Circle/Sub-Division. Every officer eagerly awaits the completion of this initial rigorous training and looks forward to start career on first posting. What a happy moment it becomes when one joins at the first place of posting as a juniormost IPS officer. In Uttar Pradesh the A.S.P. in a district gets the treatment of a 'Prince'.

9

Uniform

The European Army officers posted in the police department, immediately after the commencement of Police Act-1861 used to put on the Army uniform with Captain's badges' of rank or the rank that they held in Army. Because of this the Superintendents of Police in some states, particularly in U.P., are known as "Kaptan Saheb" even now. The army pattern of uniforms like `full dress', `undress' and `mess dress' were also used. These uniforms used to be very expensive.

The 1902 Police Commission said that "there is no objection to the adoption of the same pattern of uniform in the case of European officers, but the only recommendations that the commission have to make on the subject are, that whatever general uniform is worn, it should be as inexpensive as possible, and that the distinguishing letters I.P. (Indian Police) be worn on the shoulder strap."

From 1907 onwards, on appointment of Deputy Supdts. of Police in provinces 'Indian Police' officers were directed to wear I.P. on shoulders which distinguished them from Dy. Superintendents of Police. The IP (Uniform) Rules were made from time to time, the last being the Indian Police (Uniform) Rules 1942. Rule 37 of the Indian Police Service (Uniform) Rules 1954 provided that IP officers may continue to use the letters "IP" instead of the letters "IPS" in the devices prescribed for the crest, badges and buttons.

Indian Police Service (Uniform) Rules 1954

The Central Government in consultation with Governments of the States made the 'Indian Police Service' (Uniform) Rules 1954 in exercise of the powers conferred by the All India Services Act 1951. According to these Rules, the uniform to be worn by a member of the Service (IPS) shall be the same as specified in the schedule of these rules . The State Police Service officers officiating in IPS cadre posts are allowed to wear all items of the uniform prescribed for IPS officers except the badge, crest and the buttons. The excepted items can be worn by an officer on actual appointment to the IPS. The IPS officers on deputation to Police Forces like CRPF, etc., are allowed to wear the uniform prescribed for the officers of those Forces under the rules and regulations applicable to them as per orders issued on 22.6.1962, by the Ministry of Home Affairs, Government of India.

Wearing of Uniform by Retired IPS Officers

The Ministry of Home Affairs, Government of India, vide its order dated 7.10.1958, said that there is no objection to permission being granted by State Government to IPS officers to wear, after retirement, uniform of the rank last held by them immediately before retirement on ceremonial occasions and police parades. According to another order of 1960, members of the service should not, after their retirement from service, wear the uniform prescribed in these rules while they are re-employed in non-police posts.

Grant for Uniform

Every member of the service, on appointment to IPS is entitled to receive from the Government an initial grant and renewal grant at the each interval of seven years. The grant could be withheld to the members who are due to retire within two years of the date when the grant is due.

The initial grant used to be Rs. 1000 which was raised to Rs.3000 by the Fourth Pay Commission, which became applicable from 1986. The renewal grant was Rs. 500 which was raised to Rs. 800 from 1986. By the Indian Police Service (Uniform) Amendment Rules, 1998, the initial grant has been raised to six thousand five hundred rupees and the renewal grant to three thousand rupees with effect from August 1, 1997.

Kit Maintenance Allowance

Every IPS officer is entitled to receive a kit maintenance allowance of eighty rupess per month, when one is holding a post, the duties of which require him to put on a uniform. Words "when he is holding a post, the duties of which required him to put on a uniform" have been omitted by the Indian Police Service (Uniform) Amendment Rules, 1998. Now kit maintenance allowance is admissible at the rate of one hundred fifty rupees per month from August 1, 1997.

Grant for Horse and Saddlery

Every member of the Service, shall, if the Government considers that he should maintain a horse / a hill pony while posted in a hill district, receive an initial grant of not exceeding Rs. 1200, towards the cost of the horse and the saddlery. In UP, IP and IPS officers were entitled to horse maintenance allowance at the rate of Rs. 60 per month.

Working Dress

According to Rule 6 the Central Government, after consultation with the State Government concerned, may from time to time, make such modification in the working dress which a member of the service may wear while engaged in work of an informal character as local circumstances may require. According to an order of 1969 the following working uniform has been prescribed but the type of working dress to be worn may be decided by the DGP/IGP of the state or the force, as the case may be. Following are the types of prescribed working dress:

Type-1	Type-2	Type-3	Type-4
1. Peak Cap	1. Peak Cap	1. Peak Cap	1. Peak Cap
2. (1) Jacket (2) Slacks of the same material as the jacket (gabardine or drill or khaki gabardine cotton)	2. (1) Bush Shirt (2) Jacket/ slacks of the same material	2. (1) Shirt with or without (2) Jersy (3) Slacks	2. (1) Shirt (angola or cellular) (2) with or without jersy (3) Slacks (gabardine or drill)
3. Whistle and lanyard	3. Whistle and lanyard	3. Whistle and lanyard	--
4. Shoes/Ankle boots	4. Shoes/Ankle boots	4. Shoes/Ankle boots	4. Shoes/ Ankle jungle boots
5. Khaki Socks	5. Khaki Socks	5. Khaki Socks	5. Socks
6. Khaki Shirt	--	--	--
7. Blue Tie	--	--	--
8. Cloth belt of the same material as the jacket or Sam brown belt	8. Cloth belt	8. Sam brown belt	8. Web belt
9. Ribbons	9. Ribbons	9. Ribbons	--

Review Order

The review order uniform shall be worn on all state ceremonies (e.g. public arrivals and departure of President, or the Governor, presentation of Guards of Honour or such occasions) at ceremonial parades or whenever full dress is ordered. The type of Review Order to be worn on any occasion may be prescribed by the DGP/IGP of the state or the force concerned. The Review Order consists of mounted and non-mounted duties the details of which are given below:

Mounted Duty

1. Peak Cap, (2) Jacket (3) Whistle and lanyards (4) Breaches, (5) Field boots (optional), (6) Spurs (optional) (7) Khaki shirts (8) Blue tie, (9) Khaki socks (10) Sam Browne belt, (11) Sword, and (12) Medals and decorations.

Review Order for Non Mounted Duty

Type (A) (for winters)	Type (B) (for summers)
1. Peak Cap	1. Peak Cap
2. Jacket (gabardine or drill)	2. Shirt (khaki cellular)
3. Whistle and lanyard	3. Whistle and lanyard
4. Slacks of the same material as jackets	4. Slacks , khaki drill or cotton terrene or khaki gabardine cotton.
5. Brown Ankle boots/shoes	5. Brown shoes
6. Khaki shirts	-
7. Blue tie	-
8. Khaki socks	8. Khaki socks
9. Sam Browne belt	9. Sam Browne belt

10. Sword	10. Sword
11. Medals and decorations	11. Ribbons, medals and decorations.

Mess Dress

Mess dress shall be worn at messes, at official public entertainment or when invited to meet the President or Governor at dinner or at an official function, formal or ceremonial occasions, unless Review Order is specially ordered. This dress shall consist of (a) black shirt buttoned up coat with black trousers or white trousers or white shirt buttoned up coat with white or black trousers; (b) miniature medals for mess functions, bottom edge of the bar to touch the top edge of the left breast pocket - for state functions full size medals will be worn and (c) Footwear - plain black leather oxford shoes with plain toe caps with five pairs of eye-lets.

The Mess dress for I.P. officers and even for IPS officers before 1960 was different. They used to wear badges of ranks on shoulders which were made of dark blue and white woollen material. IP officers also wore spurs with black shoes.

Other Dress Items

1. Head dress 1. Peak Cap - Khaki gabardine
   or
   Pagri of Khaki silk or muslin
   or
   Beret Cap of Navy Blue Colour

2. Jaket - Khaki Drill / gabardine
   Cotton terrene (during hot weather)
   or
   Khaki gabardine woollen
   or

Woollen terrene
(during cold weather)

3. Trousers (Slacks) - to match the jacket.
4. Breaches (Bedford or Jodhpur type)
5. Boots Ankle
6. Shoes - Plain brown leather
7. Boots, Field
8. Spurs (optional for mounted duty only)
9. Belts - Sam Browne of Army Regulation pattern
10. Sword - Infantry Pattern
11. Sword Knot - Brown leather with acorn
12. Scabbard - Brown leather - infantry pattern
13. Whistle
14. Revolver / automatic pistol (optional)
15. Helmet for informal working dress
16. Bush shirts - infantry pattern
17. Gorget patches - for selection grade and above
18. Jersey
19. Shorts - Khaki
20. Shirts - Khaki
21. PT. Vests - For under training probationers
22. Putties ankle - Khaki woollen

23. Hose Tops - Khaki woollen
24. Stockings - Khaki woollen
25. Overcoat (optional) - Khaki
26. Gloves - To be worn when necessary

Special Provisions for Women Officers

(a) **Working Dress** : This shall consist of same items as prescribed for male officers with the following alterations in the specifications in respect of slacks and footwear :

(i) *Slacks* : Plateless trousers of Khaki colour with two side pockets similar in pattern to those prescribed for the male officers with front flap closed and a zip flap on the right side at a position under the arm, the front flap being optional.

(ii) *Shoes* : Derby brown leather shoes or plain brown leather shoes with heels not more than 1" measured from the base of the rear stitching of the uppers.

(iii) *Ankle Boots and Field Boots* : Of the same specifications as those prescribed for male officers, with heels not more than 1 1/2" measured from the base of the rear stitching of the uppers.

(b) **Mess Dress** : This shall consist of :

(i) *Saree* : Cream-colour silk saree in winter and cotton or terrycot saree of the same colour in summer, normal length with red zari border of minimum width 3" and maximum width 5". The zari border may be either of gold plated silver thread or silk thread in a floral pattern.

(ii) *Blouse* : Colour matching with saree, air hostess sleeves. The saree being draped over the left shoulder and anchored by an Indian Police Service badge chromed on in silver metal. The blouse would be of waist length with minimum of four buttons and the length of the blouse ending where the saree begins, and without stand and fall collars, concealed hooks may be used instead of buttons in appropriate numbers, if desired.

(iii) *Footwear* : Cream colored sandal/shoes with straps and covered toes; heels not exceeding 2 1/2".

(iv) *Medals* : May be worn on the saree over the left breast.

(c) **P.T. Kit** : It shall consist of :

(i) Shorts / white track pants (white with police blue stripes)

(ii) High-collared white 'T' shirts with Indian Police Service colours with 3 buttons in the front

(iii) White socks with appropriate footwear as prescribed for male officers

(d) **Cosmetics** : No cosmetics shall be used by lady officers except a `bindi' on the forehead and 'sindhur' filling the head parting and special cream which does not leave a shade on the skin and which otherwise suited may be used according the requirement of the weather and both `bindi' and `sindhur' shall be as inconspicuous as possible.

(e) **Ornaments** : Women officers may wear 'Mangal sutra' wedding rings and ear-studs. But these shall be as inconspicuous as possible. No other ornaments should be worn by lady officers when in uniform.

Alternative Uniform for Lady Officers

Lady officers with about 16 weeks of pregnancy may switch-over to the following alternative working dress:

(a) *Khaki Saree :* Khaki silk saree in winter and khaki cotton or khaki terry-cot saree in summer; to be draped over the left shoulder passing under the shoulder straps with Indian Police Service badge.

(b) *Khaki blouse :* Khaki cotton blouse of waist length worn up to the elbow ; buttoned up all the way down in the front with front buttons or concealed hooks; stand and fall collar; shoulder straps to be sewn at the outer end and fixed by a single button at the inner end, two breast pockets ; and back plain without pleats.

(c) *Badges of ranks :* To be worn on the shoulder straps of the blouse.

(d) *Footwear :* Brown leather sandals/shoes with straps; toes not visible; heels not exceeding 2".

(e) Khaki socks.

(f) *Head-gear (optional) :* Same as worn in normal times.

BADGES OF RANKS

For I.P. officers, during early stages of appointment following badges of ranks were prescribed:

1. I.G.P.	Crown and 2 Stars.
2. D.I.G	Crown and 1 Star.
3- Supdt. of Police 3rd grade and above.	1 Crown
4. S.P. below 3rd Grade	3 Stars

5. A.S.P.	2 Stars
6. Probationer	1 Star

Immediately before India's Independence in 1947, the badges of ranks were revised as under, and the IG and the DIG were permitted to use 'Gorjette Patches'.

1. IGP	3 Stars with Crown
2. DIG	2 Stars with Crown
3. SP	Crown
4. ASP	1 to 3 Stars depending upon the service put in

IPS Officers from 1948 till 1969

ASP	IPS with 1 to 3 Stars depending upon service put-in/Incharge of Sub-Division
SP	IPS with State Emblem
SP with 15-20 years service	IPS with one Star and State Emblem
Selection Grade SP or with 20 years service	IPS - Two Stars with State Emblem
DIG	IPS with 3 Stars and State Emblem
IG	IPS with crossed sword and baton with one Star
Director, IB	Crossed Sword and baton with State Emblem

Badges of Ranks from 1969

1. Director I B	Crossed sword and baton, the State Emblem and one Star
2. Other DGs and Addl.DGs	Crossed sword and baton and State Emblem
3. IGP	Crossed sword and baton with one Star
4. DIG	The State Emblem and three Stars
5. Selection Grade SP or 15 years service	State Emblem and 2 Stars
6. Distt. SP/Comdt. of a Bn. or SP with 10 years service	State Emblem with 1 Star
7. All other IPS officers in Senior scale of pay with less than 10 years of service	State Emblem
8. ASP with 5 years service or in-charge of a Sub-Division	3 Stars
9. ASP with 2 to 5 years service	2 Stars
10. ASP with less than 2 years service	1 Star

10

Women in IPS

Our glowing tributes to late Ms. Vandana Malik, I.P.S. (1987 Manipur and Tripura cadre) who laid down her life while fighting insurgents in 1989.

In the pre-Independence days there was no scope for the women to join the Police Forces, more so for the I.P./I.P.S. During the post-Independence period also, there was no induction of any lady I.P.S. officer for the first 25 years i.e. a quarter of a century, of the country gaining freedom. The Indian Administrative Service (Recruitment) Rules and the Indian Police Service (Recruitment) Rules laid down that "No married woman shall be entitled as a matter of right to be appointed to the service and where a woman appointed to the service subsequently marries, the Central Government may, if the maintenance of service so requires, call upon her to resign". For Indian Foreign Service also married women were disqualified. This rule was subsequently amended as the Constitution of India provided for equal rights to women and no discrimination was to be made on the basis of sex. Despite the open All India Competition for Civil Services in India, held by the Union Public Service Commission, each year, the ladies getting selected opted for Indian Foreign Service, IAS and other central services and avoided joining I.P.S. as this service was considered to be the males' domain.

It was in the silver jubilee year of our Independence when Ms. Kiran Bedi (1972 batch) joined the I.P.S. and the service had the privilege of having its first woman officer. Since then, in next 25 years, i.e. between the silver jubilee and golden jubilee of India's Independence (1972 to 1997), 103 women officers joined the I.P.S. as regular recruits. Their number as compared to total probationers for various years is as under:

Sl. No.	Year	Total R.R. Officers	Women Officers	%
1.	1972	64	1	1.56
2.	1973	81	1	1.23
3.	1974	84	1	1.20
4.	1975	70	1	1.45
5.	1976	95	5	5.26
6.	1977	112	3	2.67
7.	1978	49	1	2:04
8.	1979	52	2	3.85
9.	1980	49	1	2.04
10.	1981	58	1	1.72
11.	1982	57	4	7.01
12.	1983	57	4	7.01
13.	1984	76	1	1.31
14.	1985	84	1	1.20
15.	1986	102	2	1.96
16.	1987	108	5	4.62
17.	1988	70	3	4.29
18.	1989	74	5	6.79
19.	1990	79	10	12.66
20.	1991	81	4	4.94
21.	1992	71	3	4.23
22.	1993	78	6	7.70
23.	1994	84	9	10.71
24.	1995	82	13	15.85
25.	1996	91	13	14.29
26.	1997	114	13	11.40
Total		2022	103	5.09

Names of Officers

Sardar Vallabhbhai Patel National Police Academy, Mount Abu/Hyderabad, had the distinction of training the following lady I.P.S. probatiners:

Sl.No.	Name of the Officer	Cadre	Year of Allotment
1.	Mrs. Kiran Bedi Pashawaria	U.T.	1972
2.	Ms. Kanchan C. Bhattacharya	U.P.	1973
3.	Mrs. Suraj Kaur Mehra	U.P.	1974
4.	Mrs. Jija S. Hari Singh	M.P.	1975
5.	Ms. Asha Gopal	M.P.	1976
6.	Mrs. Letika Saran	Tamil Nadu	1976
7.	Mrs. Manjari Jaruhar	Bihar	1976
8.	Ms. Renuka Mutto	U.P.	1976
9.	Mrs. G. Thilakavathi	Tamil Nadu	1976
10.	Mrs. Deepa Mehta	Haryana	1977
11.	Mrs. Kanwaljit Deol	U.T.	1977
12.	Mrs. Sridevi Goel	Maharashtra	1977
13.	Mrs. Vimla Mehra	U.T.	1978
14.	Mrs. Aruna M. Bahuguna	A.P.	1979
15.	Mrs. Kumud Choudhary	Bihar	1979
16.	Mrs. Archana Ramasunderam	Tamil Nadu	1980
17.	Mrs. Neeran Chadha Borwarkar	Maharashtra	1981
18.	Mrs. Asha Sinha	Bihar	1982

(Contd. . .)

(Contd. . .)

Sl. No.	Name of the Officer	Cadre	Year of Allotment
19.	Ms. Geeta Johari	Gujarat	1982
20.	Mrs. Mamatha Anurag Sharma	West Bengal	1982
21.	Ms.(Dr.) Prabha H.Rao	Karnataka	1982
22.	Mrs. Tejdeep Pratihast	A.P.	1983
23.	Ms. Nirmal Abhitabh Choudhary	Bihar	1983
24.	Ms. Neelamani N. Raju	Karnataka	1983
25.	Mrs. Rina Mitra	M.P.	1983
26.	Ms. Sutapa Sanyal	U.P.	1984
27.	Ms. Meera Ram Nivas	Gujarat	1985
28.	Ms. Dyuti Rani Doley Barman	J & K	1986
29.	Ms. Srilakshmi Prasad	Tamil Nadu	1986
30.	Ms. R.Sreelekha	Kerala	1987
31.	Mrs. Aruna Mohan Rao	M.P.	1987
32.	Ms. A.R. Anuradha	A.P.	1987
33.	Ms. Suman Bala	West Bengal	1987
34.	Ms. Vandana Malik	Manipur &Tripura	1987
35.	Ms.B. Sandhya	Kerala	1988
36.	Ms. Rashmi Shukla	Maharashtra	1988
37.	Mrs. Sivagami Sundari Nanda	U.T.	1988
38.	Mrs. Archana N. Sandawale	Karnataka	1989
39.	Mrs. Sushma Singh	M.P.	1989

(Contd. . .)

(Contd. . .)

Sl. No.	Name of the Officer	Cadre	Year of Allotment
40.	Mrs. Nina Singh	Manipur	1989
41.	Mrs. B. Radhika	Orissa	1989
42.	Dr.(Mrs.) Pradmya Saravede	West Bengal/ Maharashtra	1989
43.	Mrs. Anjana Sinha	A.P.	1990
44.	Ms. Tilotama Varma	U.P.	1990
45.	Mrs. Anju Gupta	U.P.	1990
46.	Mrs. Seema Agarwal	Tamil Nadu	1992
47.	Mrs. Savitha Dharmadhikari	Karnataka	1990
48.	Mrs. Anuradha Shanker	M.P.	1990
49.	Mrs. S. Renuka Sastry	U.P.	1990
50.	Ms. Tanuja Srivastava	U.P.	1990
51.	Ms. Shobha Ohatker	Bihar	1990
52.	Ms. Pragya Richa	M.P.	1991
53.	Ms. Marie Lou Fernandes	Maharashtra	1991
54.	Ma. Nuzhat Khan	U.T.	1991
55.	Ms. Anita Roy	U.T.	1990
56.	Ms Mongrang Indashisha	Assam/ Meghalaya	1992
57.	Ms. Preeta Varma	Bihar	1991
58.	Ms. Meera Rawat	Kerala	1992

(Contd. . .)

(Contd. . .)

Sl. No.	Name of the Officer	Cadre	Year of Allotment
59.	Ms. Sapna Tewari	Orissa	1992
60.	Ms. Malini Krishnamoorthy	Karnataka	1993
61.	Ms. Neeraja Gotru	Gujarat	1993
62.	Ms. Sonali Mishra	M.P.	1993
63.	Ms. Archana Tyagi	Maharashtra	1993
64.	Ms. Deo Gurpreet Kaur	Punjab	1993
65.	Ms. Jyoti S. Belur	U.P.	1993
66.	Ms. Anupama S. Nilekar	Bihar	1994
67.	Ms Tadasha Mishra (1) Sister	Bihar	1994
68.	Ms Soumya Mishra (2) Sister	AP	1994
69.	Ms. Anita Punj	Punjab	1994
70.	Ms. Anjana Singh	Nagaland	1994
71.	Ms. Kala Ramchandran	Tamil Nadu	1994
72.	Ms. Garima Bhatnagar	West Bengal	1994
73.	Ms. Abhilasha Bisht	West Bengal	1994
74.	Ms. Shashi Prabha Dwivedi	Punjab	1994
75.	Ms. Meena Sampat	Bihar	1995
76.	Ms. Ritu Thakur	Orissa	1995
77.	Ms. R. Malar Vizhi	Bihar	1995
78.	Ms. Swati Lakra	A.P.	1995
79.	Ms. Charu Bali	Haryana	1995

(Contd. . .)

(Contd. . .)

Sl. No.	Name of the Officer	Cadre	Year of Allotment
80.	Ms.(Dr.) Bala Santosh	Haryana	1995
81.	Ms. Shikha Goel	J & K.	1995
82.	Ms. Meenakshi Chawla	M.P.	1995
83.	Ms. Anupam Saxena	Bihar	1995
84.	Ms. Neerja Voruvuru	Punjab	1995
85.	Ms. Malini Srivastava	Rajasthan	1995
86.	Ms. Smita Khare	Rajasthan	1995
87.	Ms. B.Bala Naga Devi	Tamil Nadu	1995
88.	Ms. Charu Sinha	A.P.	1996
89.	Ms. Vineeta Sharma	Assam/Meghalaya	1996
90.	Ms. Mamta Singh	Haryana	1996
91.	Ms. Satwant Atwal	H.P.	1996
92.	Ms. Ritu Mishra	J & K	1996
93.	Ms. Sunita Kakran	Orissa	1996
94.	Ms. Vibhu Raj	Punjab	1996
95.	Ms. Vinita Yadav	Rajasthan	1996
96.	Ms. Prashakha Mathur	Rajasthan	1996
97.	Ms. Shalini Singh	Tamil Nadu	1996
98.	Ms. Bhavna Saxena	Tamil Nadu	1996
99.	Ms. Damayanti Sen	West Bengal	1996

(Contd. . .)

(Contd. . .)

Sl. No.	Name of the Officer	Cadre	Year of Allotment
100.	Ms. Rashmi Sinha	West Bengal	1996
101.	Ms. Suman Gupta	Bihar	1997
102.	Ms. Karuna Kesharwani	Nagaland	1997
103.	Ms. Rekha Khare	Orissa	1997

The cadre allotment between 1972 to 1997 of women I.P.S. officers remained as under:

	Cadre	No. of Lady I.P.S. Officers
1.	Andhra Pradesh	7
2.	Assam & Meghalaya	2
3.	Bihar	12
4.	Gujarat	3
5.	Haryana	4
6.	Himachal Pradesh	1
7.	J & K	3
8.	Karnataka	6
9.	Kerala	3
10.	Maharashtra	5
11.	Madhya Pradesh	8
12.	Manipur	2
13.	Nagaland	2
14.	Orissa	5
15.	Punjab	5
16.	Rajasthan	4
17.	Tamil Nadu	9
18.	Uttar Pradesh	9
19.	U.T.	6
20.	West Bengal	7
	Total	103

11

Family Combinations in IPS

In Indian society being an I.P.S. officer is considered to be a matter of great pride and satisfaction. If in any family there are more than one officers, it becomes a rare privilege. Here are some family combinations, which may be of some interest to readers. The details given below have been collected by personal contacts based on the personal knowledge of certain officers. If due to ignorance certain names are found missing, author would like to be excused, as no official record is available about these family-facts.

Fathers and Sons

Father	Son	Grand Son
1. Alakh Kumar Sinha IP, The first IGP of Bihar in 1939	M.K. Sinha, IP 1928 IGP of Bihar	Jyoti Niwas Kumar Sinha, IPS - Bihar, 1967
2. M. S. Mathur IP-UP, 1931 Former IGP-UP (Then Police Chief)	Vijai Shanker Mathur IPS-UP, RR-1962 Former DGP-UP and Spl. Secy.-MHA	
3. B.S. Chaturvedi SPS/IPS-UP		Ashok Chaturvedi IPS-MP-RR-1969

(Contd. . .)

(Contd. . .)

Father	Son	Grand Son
4. K.P. Srivastava SPS/IPS-UP-1951 Former IGP, Arunachal Pradesh	(1) Vikram Srivastava IPS-UP-RR-1973 (2) Raman Srivastava IPS-Kerala-RR-1973	
5. K.R. Bhatnagar IPS-UP-1948- E.R.O.M.	Rajiv Rai Bhatnagar IPS-UP-RR-1983	
6. Prakash Singh IPS-UP-RR-1959 Former DGP, UP and B.S.F.	Pankaj Kumar Singh IPS-Rajasthan-RR-1988	
7. Ram Asrey IPS-UP-RR-1960	Sunil Kumar IPS-Tamilnadu, RR-1988	
8. Ram Lal SPS/IPS-UP	(1) Rajiv M. Singh IPS-Assam-RR-1984 (2) Sujan Vir Singh IPS-UP-RR-1986	
9. S. R. Arun IPS-UP-RR-1963	Asim Kumar Arun IPS-UP-RR-1994	
10. A.K. Sharan IPS-UP-RR-1965	Sumit Sharan IPS-Tamilnadu-RR-1997 Golden Jubilee Batch	
11. A.K. Ghosh I.P, Bihar-1940	Anjan Ghosh IPS-J & K-RR-1970	
12. K.P. Medhekar IPS-Maharashtra RR-1949	R.K. Medhekar IPS-Maharashtra/Kerala RR-1975	
13. S.S. Jog IPS-Maharashtra RR-1953	D.S. Jog (Expired) IPS-Maharashtra RR-1986	

(Contd. . .)

(Contd. . .)

Father	Son	Grand Son
14. A.K. Chaudhary IPS-Bihar-RR-1956	Krishna Chaudhary IPS-Bihar-RR-1979	
15. Baljit Rai Sur IPS-UT-RR-1954	Rahul Rai Sur IPS-Maharastra-RR-1981	
16. Ram Chand Negi IPS-WB	S. D. Negi IPS-Sikkim-RR-1987	
17. Surender Kr. Seth IPS-Maharashtra- RR-1960	Rajnish Seth IPS-Maharashtra RR-1986	
18. Amar K. Chaudhary IPS-Bihar-RR-1956	Arun Kumar Chaudhary IPS-Bihar-RR-1977	
19. M.G. Narvane IPS-Maharashtra- RR-1967	Sidharth M. Marvane IPS-Orissa-RR-1989	
20. D.S. Mohi IPS-Punjab	Nalin Prabhat	
21. Kalyan Rudra IPS-Haryana- RR-1960 Former DGP-Haryana	Ritwik Rudra IPS-RR-1994 Bihar	
22. K.K. Zutshi IPS-Haryana- RR-1959 Former-DGP	Sidharth Zutshi IPS-RR-1994 Tamilnadu	
23. Mohd. Nizam IPS-WB	Jawed Shamim	
24. Ram Ratan IPS-MP-RR-1959	Deepak Ratan IPS-AP-RR-1997	
25. A. P. Mukherjee IPS-WB-RR-1956	Sanjai Mukherjee IPS-WB-RR-1989	

(Contd. . .)

(Contd. . .)

Father	Son	Grand Son
26. B.N. Patnaik SPS/IPS-Orissa SPS-1971	Diptesh Kumar Patnaik IPS-Orissa-RR-1997	
27. A.S. Aulakh IPS-MP-RR-1971	Naunihal Singh IPS-RR-1997-Punjab	
28. Ram Yash Singh IPS-Bihar	Amitabh Yash IPS	

Fathers and Daughters

Following are some of the distinguished daughters who have done pride to their fathers and families by joining the I.P.S.

Father	Daughter
1. Rati Ram Verma IPS-HP-RR-1961 Former DGP, HP	Tilottama Verma IPS-UP-RR-1990
2. Krishnamoorthy IPS(SPS)/AP	Malini Krishnamoorthy IPS-Karnataka-RR-1993
3. Puran Singh IPS-SPS-U.T.	Dr.(Ms.) Santosh Bala IPS-Haryana-RR-1993
4. Y.N. Saxena IPS-UP-RR-1959	Anupam Saxena IPS-Bihar-RR-1995
5. Bhagwat Narain Sharma IPS(PPS-1954)-UP-1968	Vineeta Sharma IPS-Assam & Meghalaya RR-1996
6. Uma Shanker (UPPS-1960) IPS-UP-1973	Karuna Kesherwani IPS-Nagaland-RR-1997

Sisters

1.	Tadasha Mishra IPS-Bihar-1994-RR-47	Soumya Mishra IPS- AP-1994-RR-47

Brothers

1.	D. Sen, IPS Former Director, CBI	N. S. Saksena, IP UP, 1941
2.	C.K. Mallick IPS-UP-RR-1963 DG, Vigilance, UP.	A.K. Mallick IPS-Assam (UP), RR-1979
3.	P. K. Bansal IPS-Gujarat-RR-1963 Former DGP, Gujarat	K. K. Bansal IPS-UP-RR-1967
4.	M. K. Shukla IPS-MP-RR-1965	R. M. Shukla IPS-UP-RR-1967
5.	J. N. Roy IPS-MP-1960	K. N. Roy SPS/IPS (UP)
6.	Vikram Srivastava IPS-UP-RR-1973	Raman Srivastava IPS-Kerala-RR-1973
7.	Neyaz Ahmad IPS-Bihar-RR-1974	Mumtaz Ahmad IPS-UP-RR-1977
8.	Rajiv Mohan Singh IPS-Assam-RR-1984	Sujan Vir Singh IPS-UP- RR-1986
9.	M.V. Bhaskar Rao IPS-AP-RR-1962	M.V. Krishna Rao IPS-AP-RR-1974

IPS COUPLES

	Husband	Wife
1.	Inder Singh Mehra (Expired) IPS-UP-RR-1974	Suraj Kaur Mehra (Expired) IPS-UP-RR-1974

(Contd. . .)

(Contd. . .)

Husband	Wife
2. Rakesh Jaruhar IPS-Bihar-RR-1976	Manjari Jaruhar IPS-Bihar-RR-1976
3. Nanchil Kumar IPS-Tamilnadu-RR-1976	Tilakavasthi IPS-Tamilnadu-RR-1976
4. M. Bahuguna (Expired) IPS-AP-RR-1979	Aruna M. Bahuguna IPS-AP-RR-1979
5. Anurag Sharma IPS-AP-RR-1982	Mamta Sharma IPS-W.B.-RR-1982
6. N.V. Surendra Babu IPS-AP-RR-1987	A.R. Anuradha IPS-AP-RR-1987
7. Pranab Nanda IPS-AGMU-RR-1988	Sivagami Sundari Nanda IPS-AGMU-RR-1988
8. D.M. Mitra IPS-MP-RR-1983	Rina Mitra IPS-MP-RR-1983
9. A.P. Maheshwari IPS-Gujarat-UP-RR-1984	Sutapa Sanyal PS-UP-RR-1984
10. Ashish Gupta IPS-UP-RR-1989	Tilottama Verma IPS-UP-RR-1990
11. Shafi Ahsan Rizvi IPS-UP-RR-1989	Anju Gupta IPS-UP-RR-1990
12. Aditya Misra IPS-UP-RR-1989	S.Renuka Shastry IPS-UP-RR-1990
13. A.K. Srivastav IPS-Rajasthan-RR-1994	Smitha Srivastava IPS-Rajasthan-RR-1994
14. Kumar Vishwajeet IPS-AP-RR-1994	Abhilasha Bisht IPS-WB-AP-RR-1994
15. Praveen Kumar Sinha IPS-Punjab-RR-1994	Anita Punj IPS-Kerala-Punjab-RR-1994

(Contd. . .)

(Contd. . .)

	Husband	Wife
16.	Navdeep Singh Virk IPS-Haryana-RR-1994	Ramchandran Kala IPS-TN/Haryana-RR-1994
17.	Ajai Singh IPS-Bihar-RR-1993	Anupam Saxena IPS-Bihar-RR-1995
18.	S.Ravindran IPS-Bihar-RR-1995	Malar Vizhi IPS-Bihar-RR-1995
19.	Sanjeeb Panda IPS-Orissa-RR-1994	Santosh Bala IPS-Haryana-RR-1995
20.	Vijai Kumar IPS-J & K -RR-1997	Shikha Goel IPS-J & K- RR-1995

Father, Son/Daughter, Son-in-Law

Father	Son/Daughter	Son-in-law
1. K.R. Bhatnagar IPS-UP-1948 (EROM)	Rajiv Bhatnagar UP-RR-1983	A.C. Verma IPS-Bihar-RR-1979
2. Ram Ratan IPS-MP-RR-1959	Deepak Ratan IPS-AP-1997	Mahan Bharat Sagar IPS-MP-RR-1985
3. Y.N. Saxena IPS-UP-RR-1959	Anupam Saxena IPS-Bihar-RR-1995	Ajai Singh IPS-Bihar-RR-1993
4. S.R. Arun IPS-UP-RR-1963	Asim Kumar Arun IPS-UP-RR-1994	Sanjeev Shami IPS-MP-RR-1993

Fathers-in-Law and Sons-in-Law

These names are of U.P. cadre officers only. The names of other States are not known, hence not being mentioned.

Father-in-Law	Son-in-Law
1. Onkar Singh (Expired) SPS/IP 1936	Lal Singh Verma (Expired) IPS-UP-RR-1948
2. H.K. Kerr SPS/IPS-UP-1941 (Retired as DGP,UP)	(1) Ashish Kumar Mitra IPS-UP-RR-1970 (2) Abhijit Mitra IPS-UT-RR-1961
3. N.C. Dutta IPS-Rajasthan-1944	Dr. Dharam Veer Mehta IPS-UP-RR-1964
4. M.L. Khare SPS/IPS-1948-UP	Anand Kumar Srivastava IPS-UP-RR-1963 (IAS-MP-1966)
5. J.N. Chaturvedi IPS-UP-RR-1951 (Retired as DGP,UP)	Ranjan Dwivedi IPS-UP-RR-1979
6. Radhey Shyam Sharma SPS/IPS-1951(Expired)	M.C. Dewedy IPS-UP-RR-1963
7. Sarvendra Vikram Singh SPS-IPS-1953	Suresh Pal Singh IPS-UP-RR-1968 (Expired)
8. D.K. Agrawal IPS-UP-RR-1953	Anil Kumar Gupta IPS-WB-RR-1972
9. G.S. Bajpai IPS-UP-RR-1954 Former Director RAW	Sanjeev Tripathi IPS-UP-RR-1972
10. M.K. Joshi SPS-IPS-1955 (Expired)	J.S. Pandey IPS-UP-RR-1976
11. G.N. Sinha IPS-UP-RR-1958	Vikram Srivastava IPS-UP-RR-1973

(Contd. . .)

(Contd. . .)

	Father-in-Law	Son-in-Law
12.	B.S. Bedi IPS-UP-RR-1961	Rajendra Pal Singh IPS-UP-RR-1987
13.	R.P. Saroj IPS-UP-RR-1964	Abhaya Kumar Prasad IPS-UP-RR-1991
14.	R.B. Singh SPS/IPS-1968	(1) Yogesh Pratap Singh IPS-Maharashtra-RR-1985 (2). Rajiv Krishna IPS-UP-RR-1991
15.	Satrughan Prasad Misra SPS-IPS-1968	Suvrat Tripathi IPS-UP-RR-1977

12

Introspection

Self introspection exercise by the retired and serving I.P./I.P.S. and other senior police officers has been going on since long through debates, various seminars, workshops and media, etc. The *Indian Police Journal* published in 1961 on the eve of centenary of Indian Police and the *Indian Police Journal* (Jan.-June,1998) published by Bureau of Police Research and Development (BPR&D) about "Indian Police After 50 Years of Independence" have carried several articles of senior Police leaders highlighting the changes, challenges, achievements and failures in policing from time to time . The S.V.P. National Police Academy, Hyderabad, have also been conducting evaluation exercises regarding IPS leadership and they have been publishing material in this respect in their magazines. Here we examine various issues which this service has encountered since India's independence and also see as to what our stalwarts have to say.

Sacrifices and Achievements

Shri G.S. Pandher, IPS, Director, BPR&D, in his message in *Indian Police Journal*-1998 said: "Since Independence, Indian Police drew mixed response from the countrymen. They have been the focal point of criticism from various quarters without any regard to the serious limitations under which they function. The sacrifices and achievements made during the last five decades in maintaining internal security especially in Punjab , J & K and North-Eastern States where they exhibited great sense of dedication to duty to maintain the unity and integrity of our country have been largely ignored. It is not known to public that as many as 18,217 police officers and men have laid down their lives on active duty for the nation since 1961. I take this opportunity to pay homage to those policemen who have sacrificed their lives for this great cause".

Role of I.P. in Independent India

After the departure of European I.P. officers on the eve of India's independence, the Indian I.P. officers continued and directed the police forces of the country. Dr. S.M. Diaz, former Director-NPA, in his article 'Senior Service of the Police in India, Before and After Independence' says, "I.P. men as such continued for about thirty years after Independence and occupied all the top positions of the Police at the Centre and in each one of the states. As I have already stated, during the British days their main concerns were maintenance of the public peace and order and investigation of crimes that occur inspite of their preventive efforts. With Independence naturally, the situation radically changed, but inspite of it, the new rulers bodily adopted the old system without taking into account changed circumstances of the people's aspirations and their welfare needs to which also the police of the new set up should train themselves to pay a fair amount of attention."

Dr. Diaz again observes, "all of them were stalwarts as well as extremely capable and decent men, reputed for maintaining high standards and achieving very good performance. All this was due, however, to their personal character and efficiency. But as a group, the I.P.S. officers were ostensibly better educated and better trained and this should, therefore, have reflected and did reflect of their group standards and morale, except where in latter years the political administration corrupted them totally and many of them succumbed and let the whole service down".

Highly Qualified

It is a well known fact that I.P.S. officers, particularly the new generations, have higher academic pursuits as compared to I.P. officers of the olden days. Shri D.C. Nath, former Special Director, Intelligence Bureau, in his article ' Indian Police in British India and Independent India' says, "by all reckoning, the I.P.S. officers are highly qualified and as it is known, they are known to be the 'most educated' amongst all police officers in the world. The police service in no other country can boast of officers with such high level of academic accomplishment. As is the recent trend quite a few among the IPS officers in the country are also known to have carried on academic pursuits in their profession and have successfully earned Ph.D. labels for their distinguished dissertations. How good to know this! The service should be proud of them! The difficulty or the cause for consternation arises thereafter. Barring some honourable exceptions, how many of them, whether Ph.D. degree holders or otherwise bring to bear their high level of intelligence, academic acumen or scholarship upon the service problems? On the other hand, most of them tend to forget their academic background as if that was of no use in the police service, popularly known to be served more by the brawn than by the brain. That is a pity ! The cumulative loss to the service, or should we say, even to the society, is heavy".

Public Goodwill

Dr. Diaz is of the opinion that I.P.S. officers, "because of their continued and fruitful public contacts and resultant goodwill, even after retirement they are sought after for many meaningful social service assignments. Their very orderly and disciplined mind enables the IPS men to acquit themselves very creditably in whatever job they take up, and establish a good reputation for a good job well done. Obviously, therefore the IPS provides greater public contact and various inimitable opportunities for public service. And when this is utilised in the best manner, the person concerned is respected and remembered by all around him. In such a context, one feels that he has accomplished his life's mission. And that is what really matters".

Erosion

Shri K.S. Dhillon (IPS-1953-VP/MP), former DGP, Punjab, and a prolific writer and thinker in his article 'Indian Police: 1947-97 - A Random Review ' laments by saying that " The Indian Police Service (IPS) formed in 1947 to man leadership positions in the Indian Police continued to replicate the precepts and practices of their colonial forerunners for several decades before they realised that the milieu had vastly changed. Rising governmental preoccupation with development activity resulted in considerable downgrading of crime and order concerns and a progressive marginalisation of the IPS. This coupled with growing public hostility, the escalating magnitude and frequency of political intervention in law enforcement and the low pay scales and prospects of IPS appointees tended to erode the attractiveness of the service. The poor quality of leadership would, in time, tell upon the general police performance. . . . . . The flaws which crept into the IPS eroded its leadership potential". Shri Dhillon while dwelling upon the observations of the National Police Commission (1978-81) further says, "every new generation of IPS officers do not fail to show their concern and anxiety about the physical and moral health of the police and security agencies. Their efforts in this regard though sincere and enthusiastic, do not make much of a dent in the political and bureaucratic citadel of resistance". Unhappy situation but no shortage of honest officers.

Shri N.S. Saksena, IP-1941, former Chief of U.P. Police as I.G., D.G., CRPF, Member, Union Public Service Commission, Member, National Police Commission (1977-81), and our Guru as Principal of Police Training College, Moradabad (UP), in his article ' The IPS of the Future' published in SVP NPA magazine July-Dec., 1988, about the prevailing bad situation wrote, "it would do us no good if we merely sing the praises of the I.P.S. and forget what the Indian Police Service is expected to do and what it has failed to achieve. In brief it has well served the government and the elite but not the people of India. This is mainly due to the atmosphere in which it is working at present." He adds:

> "There is a hardcore of honest and dedicated officers in the IPS, as in the IAS, who find themselves helpless. Politicians and senior officers do not even permit them to register all crimes nothing to speak of honestly investigating crimes.......... In spite of this unhappy situation it is to the credit of both the IPS and the IAS that there is no shortage of honest officers in both the services, who can join together to make India the fourth most powerful nation in the world. They can also succeed in removing the sense of helplessness, despair and cynicism, which is the prevailing mood of over 80% people in India".

Awaiting Informal Signals

While dwelling upon 'Indian Police After Fifty Years of Independence', Shri S.V.M. Tripathi (IPS-1961-UP) former DGP, UP and CRPF, expresses his concern by saying that "In Police administration the informal system has enlarged its domain to such extent that people have largely lost faith in the formal system. The effect of such an informal system has become significant in the spheres of maintenance of law and order, criminal investigation and prosecution. Police officers await informal signals before taking action in situations which are meant to be handled by them only. Instances are not wanting in which for execution of warrants issued by courts police officers act on the basis of hints from political functionaries. Even rewards and punishments to police officers depend on their affiliations." He again says that " A sensitive police officer can ensure justice and fair-play as no other public servant can. The least he should do is to prevent injustices on the poor in the society and other areas of administration, specially a police station. Upholding human rights and protection of life and property of citizens should be a matter of habit with the police rather than that of display . The sooner we accept this premise as imperative and honestly work towards achieving it, the better it would be for the society and the nation. The police leadership will have to push the limits of feasibility for this purpose".

'Commitment' and 'Nexus'

Shri Prakash Singh (Padma Shri) (IPS-UP-1959), former DGP, Assam, U.P. and B.S.F., in his article ' Indian Police: Fifty Years of Serfdom' observes, " the political leadership injected the concept of 'commitment' in administration. It caused havoc. Officers were selected and given key placements in consideration of their affinity and loyalty to the ruling party and its political philosophy. Their intrinsic merit and administrative qualifications were given secondary importance". Shri Singh again says, "what is particularly disturbing is that a large segment of police officers are getting politicised. They are identified with one political grouping or the other. This is another reason which leads to widespread displacement of officers whenever there is a change of regime. It is indeed a vicious claim. Yet another development and this truly alarming is the growing nexus between the politicians, criminals and the bureaucrats/police which, as mentioned in the Vohra Report, is 'virtually running a parallel Government, pushing the State apparatus into irrelevance'."

Get Together and Develop Pride

Dr. Diaz opened his heart by saying that " it is suggested, therefore, that in each State cadre, the IPS officers get together as a core group and systematically develop a certain pride in their personal integrity, and pride also in the essentially great service that they are systematically rendering to the people. This kind of pride will be catalystic in its effect. Persons with a good background and proper education will feel that it will be beneath their dignity to go in for disgraceful corrupt practice. That will be the right beginning to be fostered and fully developed." He adds:

> " The younger elements, the new IPS officers should be so trained that they cultivate this sense of pride as a habit, right from the beginning. It should become natural to them to shun those who are notorious for adopting questionable and corrupt practices. When this sort of thing is carefully inculcated in as a habit in an organised group, the group itself will develop a pride of its own as the basis of their group morale of integrity and character."

The parting message to the IPS officers trained by Shri Diaz was that "whatever place he was in and whatever job he took up, he should leave the place and the job better and cleaner than he found it". It is our wish that the IPS lot of the country follows this message in letter and spirit so that they become darling of the people and the police forces of the country.

The IPS Association's Self-introspection

There is a body known as 'The India Police Service Association' which was registered in Delhi on 16-7-1965. It has its branches in states which are known by their state names like the IPA (UP Branch). All the IP/IPS officers including those retired are eligible to become the members. The objects of the Association have been (1) to develop an *esprit de corps* among the members, (ii) generally to protect and to promote the interest of the service and (iii) to promote study of police subjects.

During nineties of this century, IAS Association (UP Branch) has launched a drive against corruption. Some IAS officers demanded identification of three most corrupt members of its service in U.P. This was done through a secret ballot in 1996, but the results were never made public. The dishonesty continues to worry the comparatively honest lot. Nevertheless, the beginning has been made to create climate against dishonest ones.

IPS Association (UP Branch) in its general body meeting held on 14-2-1996 at Lucknow appointed an in-house "Self Introspection Committee" (1) to study the prevailing situation about professionalism, morality and ethics of the cadre, and (2) to propose remedial measures. This committee, after studying the recommendations of the National Police Commission, other reports and deliberations with members of the service, pointed out (1) assets and strengths, (2) public expectations, (3) professionalism of the members of the service , (4) morality and ethics, (5) some issues arising out of recent developments, and ultimately suggested points for self introspection. About assets and strength, the committee noted certain observations of the National Police Commission about IPS, which are (I) they are better educated and better paid, (ii) they have better facilities like housing and health care, (iii) they have constitutional safeguards in respect of service interests, and (iv) they have sizeable human resources. The public expectations are: (1) high standard of performance commensurate with the advantages that they enjoy (2) (a) competence (b) ability, (c) character, (3) able leadership, (4) high standard of discipline, (5) high standards of integrity, (6) fair and impartial administration, (7) sensitive concern and respect for the people, and (8) prompt response, courtesy, and consideration to any representation. About professionalism, the committee while relying on the report of the National Police Commission mentioned that (1) they tend to abdicate their role, initiative and responsibility, (2) some are pessimists about resources, control, outside interference etc., (3) deficiencies of the politicians have not been made up by the senior leadership, (4) lack of delegation, trust and support to the subordinates, (5) they have no time to think, study or initiate new ideas and policies, (6) some senior officers increase their routine workload by wanting to see, monitor and approve every activity, (7) they tend to lose contact with problems and issues, (8) they are over obsessed by the fear of a possible failure and in turn adopt defensive postures, (9) they are not dynamic and performance oriented, and (10) they are isolated of command. The National Police Commission further observed that the very process of survival and of rising higher in the system exhausts and dehydrates many of them; those who win and reach the top are too tired and worn-out to be able to do much, or even want to do much and little energy that remains goes into surviving on the post, keeping the powers that be pleased, dealing with the routine paperwork and making arrangements for post retirement jobs and supplementing their incomes.

The self-introspection committee also highlighted some more issues arising out of the recent developments, which are: (1) frequent transfers and resultant problems to organisation, personal, family members and the public, (2) continuous upgradation of senior posts leading to mushroom growth of senior ranks who tend to usurp the role of their subordinates, (3) non-observance of the All India Services (Conduct) Rules, particularly regarding (i) politics and elections, (ii) gifts, (iii) valuable property — both movable and immovable, (iv) character, (v) canvassing, and (vi) consumption of intoxicating drinks and alcohol.

The committee posed certain points for consideration which included: (1) are we not better than crores of our under-privileged countrymen? If yes, then why do we tend to become corrupt and self seeking; (2) are we not the ablest, highly educated, well trained and sensitive officers? If yes, then why not prove it as a service and class in the times to come; (3) are we comparatively inferior to any other service or class? If not, then why not rise to the occasion and show to the people by our performance that we are an outstanding class and service. This committee said, (1) let us ponder over our criticisms and take remedial measures; (2) violators of code of conduct must do their heart searching; and (3) we must ensure strict adherence to prescribed code of conduct with particular reference to character, integrity and professionalism. This was approved in the general body meeting of the IPA at Lucknow.

Set High Standards

The National Police Commission were of the view that, "the standards for the conduct and performance of the IPS officers should be set at an appropriate high level. . . . . We would, therefore, like the IPS officers to be able to raise the morale of their force by their ability, qualities of leadership and by observing a high standard of personal conduct".

Lot to Be done

Shri K.F. Rustamji (Padma Bhushan) (IP-MP), founder DG of B.S.F. , former Member of National Police Commission (1977-81), in his article 'The Dangers Ahead', exhorts by saying that "I am convinced that there is an inner strength in India that defies all calamities, all distress, all disaster, even all maladministration. How else can we explain the last fifty years . We started with a partition in which millions were killed and millions uprooted and we had emerged, just a few years before from a terrible famine in Bengal. We started with politicians who were worshipped for their sacrifices in the freedom struggle, and who have now become the objects of criticism and contempt for their corruption and abuse of power. We have steadily damaged all public institutions. We even killed the most revered figure in the land, the Mahatma, who secured freedom. And yet after fifty years of freedom we are a working democracy, the country has held together, its Constitution has functioned efficiently, secularism has been upheld, the flag of Kashmir is flying high. True, poverty has continued, illiteracy and educational decline may have increased. But today we face no danger of war, no threats of disruption. Large sections of the people have prospered, the middle class has increased in size, the economic indicators are at safe levels. The dreadful hand of communal strife has been stayed. And all because India has the strength to forge ahead". Shri Rustamji exhorts all of us by saying that " there is a lot that has to be done by the security forces (police and military), by the judiciary and by all civil servants to keep the ship of Indian democracy on an even keel in the next fifty years. There are big dangers ahead, but we can meet the dangers and even transform our country if we put our faith in the rule of law". His advice to us is, " The police must set a standard of efficiency of simple living, and obedience to the law, and of integrity and compassion. If we can do that the nation will depend on us always."

Proud to Be IPS

Majority of the service members would like to join the following feelings of Dr. S.M. Diaz: "I am proud to have joined the Indian Police Service. It gave me an opportunity to serve the people in their time of suffering and injury". To a question, " If you had a second chance to reshape your career, sir, would you still have opted for the Indian Police Service ", the reply of Dr. Diaz was, "I should definitely do so". Many of us would like to say so as Dr. Diaz says, " No other service would have given me the opportunity as the IPS has done to wipe the tears of the suffering and to bind the wounds of the injured, as this service has given me".

Cherished Desire

As I come from the rural humble background, who was born in a poor down-trodden family and was educated in the village school under a banyan tree and thatch up to class VIII and subsequently in a small town upto Intermediate, I have not only seen but also shared the hunger, poverty, sufferings and miseries of the people. I, in my childhood , also used to see the *Zulum* (atrocities) of zamindars, the Thana police and other lower functionaries of the administration. Till I passed my B.A., I did not know as to what the IAS and the IPS were. I appeared in the competitive examination in 1962 and was selected in 1963. After having served in various capacities I became the Director General of Police, U.P., and had the privilege of leading the largest police force not only of the country but of the world in 1997-98. I have served for 35 years and would have retired on July 31, 1998, but for raising of retirement age by two years upto 60. Looking back I feel happy, satisfied and contented person who tried to serve the people, particularly the victims of crimes, the poor and the under privileged irrespective of their caste, sex or community. I feel that there was no other career or service which could have attracted me more than the IPS.

With all humility at my command and apologies for bringing this personal factor, I would like to say that my son and son-in-law are also in IPS. I wish that my grandchildren also join this great 'Service'.

I urge upon all the serving officers to remain scrupulously honest, be thorough professionals, perfect human beings and have compassion for the sufferers and bring name, fame and laurels to IPS so that Government and people adorn us. I am sure that honesty of mind, words and deeds at every level will take us to our goal. After all, monetarily and otherwise, we are among the first few thousands out of the crores of people of this Great Nation, and therefore, we owe everything to our motherland. As all the important services of the country, particularly IAS and IPS, are at the crossroad, let us "STOP" (introspect), "LOOK"(at the writing on the wall) and "GO"(on the right path).

APPENDIX-I

COMBINED GRADATION LIST OF IP OFFICERS (AS ON 1.1.1970)

Sl. No.	Name of Officer	Year of Allotment	State
1.	Banerjee, B B	1934	Bihar
2.	Ghosh, S N	1935	West Bengal
3.	Maswood, M A H	1935	West Bengal
4.	Bhattacharya, D G	1936	West Bengal
5.	Kr. Shamsher Singh	1936	Punjab
6.	Islam Ahmed	1936	UP
7.	Sinha R A P	1936	Bihar
8.	Ghosh, T N	1937	Bihar
9.	Sen, P K	1937	West Bengal
10.	Jia Ram	1937	UP
11.	Balbir Singh	1937	Punjab
12.	Ghosh, J C	1937	Orissa
13.	Hosali, S N	1937	Mysore
14.	Nagarvala, J D	1937	Gujarat
15.	Rustamji, K F	1938	MP
16.	Shetty, S. Balakrishnan	1938	Tamil Nadu
17.	Menon, M. Balakrishnan	1938	Tamil Nadu
18.	Imdad Ali	1938	Assam
19.	Hooja, M M L	1939	West Bengal
20.	Rama Iyer, N.	1939	Gujarat
21.	Trilok Nath	1939	Bihar
22.	Gupta, A S	1939	UP

(Contd. . .)

(Contd. . .)

Sl. No.	Name of Officer	Year of Allotment	State
23.	Rajadhyaksha, A G	1939	Maharashtra
24.	Ghosh, A K	1939	Bihar
25.	Misra, B B	1940	Orissa
26.	Wagh, M G	1940	Maharashtra
27.	Chatterjee, B	1940	West Bengal
28.	Dass, A K	1940	UP
29.	Kao, R N	1940	UP
30.	Mahadevan, R M	1940	Tamil Nadu
31.	Arul, F V	1940	Tamil Nadu
32.	Pavi, K S	1940	Gujarat
33.	Padhi, R K	1941	Orissa
34.	Saxena, N S	1941	UP
35.	Modak, B S	1941	Maharashtra
36.	Pant, P M	1942	Gujarat
37.	Dave, A K	1942	MP
38.	Gupta, R K	1942	West Bengal
39.	Ray, N K	1942	Orissa
40.	Stracey, E L	1943	Tamil Nadu
41.	Nair, K. Sankaran	1943	Tamil Nadu
42.	Kumar, A	1943	Punjab
43.	Dhar, D.	1943	West Bengal

APPENDIX-II

COMBINED GRADATION LIST OF WAR SERVICE RECRUITS APPOINTED TO THE IPS

Sl. No.	Name of Officer	Year of Allotment	State
1.	Bisht, L S	1942	Uttar Pradesh
2.	Speirs, I M S	1942	Uttar Pradesh
3.	Nair, V P	1943	Kerala
4.	Dey, L B K	1943	Assam
5.	Chhabra, J R	1943	Punjab
6.	Shenai, K R	1944	Madras
7.	Gopal, R C	1944	Uttar Pradesh
8.	Tandon, S	1944	Uttar Pradesh
9.	Sethna, N H	1944	Bombay
10.	Satur, S P	1945	Andhra Pradesh
11.	Midha, A S	1945	Punjab
12.	De Cunha, M E	1945	Uttar Pradesh
13.	Suntook, N R	1946	Mysore
14.	Writer, P M	1947	Bombay

APPENDIX-III

COMBINED GRADATION LIST OF IPS OFFICERS RECRUITED THROUGH OPEN MARKET (Emergency Recruitment Scheme)

Sl. No.	Name of Officer	Year of Allotment	State
1	2	3	4
1.	G J Kharkar	1939	Bombay
2.	N C Ghosh	1939	Rajasthan
3.	Yaga Dutta	1940	Orissa
4.	B L Srivastava	1941	MP
5.	Inderjit Johar	1941	Vindhya Pradesh
6.	L R Malhotra	1942	Punjab
7.	S K Kulkarni	1942	Saurashtra
8.	K S Vankataraman	1942	Madras
9.	Sant Ram Sharma	1942	Rajasthan
10.	Ashvini Kumar	1942	Bihar
11.	B R Malhotra	1942	Hyderabad
12.	M N Chaturvedi	1942	UP
13.	H S Kohli	1942	UP
14.	E J Mukand	1942	UP
15.	C J V Miranda	1943	Bombay
16.	P A Bombawale	1943	MP
17.	R A Mundukar	1943	Hyderabad
18.	S P Marathe	1943	Bombay

(Contd. . .)

(Contd. . .)

1	2	3	4
19.	H C Saxena	1943	Punjab
20.	R D Tiwari	1943	UP
21.	P N Banerjee	1943	West Bengal
22.	D S Sahi	1943	Rajasthan
23.	Chidamber Rao Patil	1943	Hyderabad
24.	Radha Charan Dutt	1943	Assam
25.	J C Dixit	1944	MP
26.	Shanti Prasad Bhargava	1944	Rajasthan
27.	N C Dutta	1944	Rajasthan
28.	P C Rai	1944	MP
29.	S V Pandit	1944	Bombay
30.	Ram Singh	1944	UP
31.	J P Kulshreshtha	1944	UP
32.	S N Bhattacharya	1944	West Bengal
33.	N N Diwan	1944	Rajasthan
34.	I P N Menon	1944	Assam
35.	S G De Choudhary	1944	West Bengal
36.	Kailash Nath Soral	1944	Rajasthan
37.	A P Batra	1944	UP
38.	B C Bagchi	1944	West Bengal
39.	Prahlad Singh	1944	Hyderabad
40.	J K Sen	1944	Saurashtra
41.	D Jagannathan	1944	Rajasthan
42.	B K Goverdhan	1944	MP
43.	P L Dhar	1945	West Bengal
44.	L Lungalang	1945	Assam
45.	Gurcharan Das Chaddha	1945	Rajasthan

(Contd. . .)

(Contd. . .)

1	2	3	4
46.	P S Vishwanathan	1945	Madras
47.	D S Grewal	1945	Punjab
48.	E M Bede	1945	Bihar
49.	A C Madhvan Nambiar	1945	Madras
50.	R G Hazari	1945	Saurashtra
51.	S K Chakravorty	1945	West Bengal
52.	R R Harnaglay	1945	MP
53.	S G Gokhle	1945	Bombay
54.	A R Braganza	1945	Hyderabad
55.	J Dharamraj	1945	Orissa
56.	B N Muttoo	1945	Punjab
57.	P J Lewis	1946	Bombay
58.	A K Paul	1946	West Bengal
59.	B K Lokhande	1946	Bombay
60.	A K Banerjee	1946	West Bengal
61.	M A Kamble	1946	Bombay
62.	M L Puri	1946	Punjab
63.	J C Bachhar	1946	Punjab
64.	N R Bose	1946	West Bengal
65.	MP Singh	1946	Bihar
66.	J W Rodtrigues	1946	MP
67.	B N Mukheriee	1946	Vindhya Pradesh
68.	H K Chakravorty	1946	West Bengal
69.	W K Patil	1946	Bombay
70.	B R Chaddha	1946	Punjab
71.	Ranjit Singh	1946	MP
72.	Devendra Nath Vohra	1946	Assam

(Contd. . .)

(Contd. . .)

1	2	3	4
73.	L J Victor	1946	Andhra Pradesh
74.	B C Majumdar	1946	West Bengal
75.	V A Gokhle	1946	Hyderabad
76.	D Chhotray	1946	Orissa
77.	R Nainaswamy	1946	Hyderabad
78.	K L Diwan	1946	MP
79.	J M Jain	1946	UP
80.	R D Pande	1946	UP
81.	S Venugopalrao	1946	Andhra Pradesh
82.	C B Srinivasarao	1946	Hyderabad
83.	K B Chakravarty	1946	UP
84.	S C Sarkar	1947	West Bengal
85.	B L Gulati	1947	UP
86.	A C Ambwani	1947	UP
87.	S M Diaz	1947	Madras
88.	O P Grover	1947	Orissa
89.	Jacob Abrahim	1947	Assam
90.	H N Sarkar	1947	West Bengal
91.	V N Bakshi	1947	Punjab
92.	K Subramaniam	1947	Hyderabad
93.	V Sriniwasan	1947	Hyderabad
94.	B N Mukherjee	1947	West Bengal
95.	G S Das	1947	Orissa
96.	K Rajgopalan	1947	Orissa
97.	S V Tankhiwale	1947	MP
98.	D C Sharma	1947	Hyderabad
99.	D P Verma	1947	UP

(Contd. . .)

(Contd. . .)

1	2	3	4
100.	J M Shukla	1947	Bihar
101.	P S Raturi	1948	UP
102.	A B Choudhary	1948	West Bengal
103.	F S Diwan	1948	Hyderabad
104.	R N Haldipur	1948	Bombay
105.	K R Bhatnagar	1948	UP
106.	K G Ramanna	1948	Hyderabad
107.	J Lobo	1948	Bombay
108.	T K Pande	1948	UP
109.	Lalit Mohan	1948	Rajasthan
110.	H G Abhyankar	1948	Hyderavad
111.	Harish Chandra Singhji	1949	Bombay

APPENDIX-IV

TRAINEES WHO PASSED OUT OF THE ACADEMY

Training Year: 1948-49;
Batch: 1948-IPS-RR (Regular Recruits)

1.	D. Kakati	IPS
2.	P.C. Das	IPS
3.	S.P. Karnik	IPS
4.	M.S. Heble	IPS
5.	V.V. Chaubal	IPS
6.	S. Datta Chowdhury	IPS
7.	R. Lall	IPS
8.	S.K. Chatterji	IPS
9.	K.N. Prasad	IPS
10.	S.P. Sinha	IPS
11.	C.V. Narsimhan	IPS
12.	C.V. Narayanan	IPS
13.	N. Krishnaswamy	IPS
14.	K.V. Subramanian	IPS
15.	M.V. Narayana Rao	IPS
16.	V.N. Rajan	IPS
17.	V.V. Naik	IPS
18.	P.R. Rajagopal	IPS
19.	H.M. Joshi	IPS
20.	R.L. Bhinge	IPS
21.	H.K. Talwar	IPS
22.	P. A. Rosha	IPS
23.	S.N. Mathur	IPS
24.	T.S. Sachdeva	IPS

25.	B.K. Roy	IPS
26.	L.S. Verma	IPS
27.	S.N. Gupta	IPS
28.	B.S. Das	IPS
29.	Mahendra Singh	IPS
30.	R.N. Sheopory	IPS
31.	K.N. Kishita	IPS
32.	N.K. Verma	IPS
33.	Onkar Singh	IPS
34.	M.C. Sharma	IPS
35.	S.C. Chaudhri	IPS
36.	S.K. Mitra	IPS
37.	A.B. Chakravarty	IPS
38.	K.K. Dutt	IPS

Training Year- 1949;
Batch - IPS- SRB-1 (Special Recruitment Board)

39.	L. Lungalang	IPS
40.	D.N. Bora	IPS
41.	R.C. Dutt	IPS
42.	Ashwini Kumar	IPS
43.	M.P. Singh	IPS
44.	E.M. Bede	IPS
45.	M.A. Kamble	IPS
46.	C.J.V. Miranda	IPS
47.	S.G. Gokhale	IPS
48.	B.K. Lokhande	IPS
49.	W.K. Patil	IPS
50.	John Lobo	IPS
51.	P.J. Lewis	IPS
52.	S.P. Marathe	IPS
53.	B.K. Govardhan	IPS

54.	J.C. Dikshit	IPS
55.	Ranjit Singh	IPS
56.	P.A. Bambawale	IPS
57.	D. Chhotray	IPS
58.	G.S. Das	IPS

Training Year: 1949-50; Batch: 1949 - IPS - RR-2

59.	K.P. Madhekar	IPS/Bombay
60.	V.V. Nagarkar	IPS/Bombay
61.	Raj Dev Singh	IPS/Bihar
62.	Syed Fazal Ahmed	IPS/Bihar
63.	H.S. Dubey	IPS/ MP
64.	D. Khamgaonkar	IPS/MP
65.	T.M. Subramaniam	IPS/Madras
66.	A. Kandaswami	IPS/Madras
67.	K. Ramamurthy	IPS/Orissa
68.	Shivraj Bahadur	IPS/Orissa
69.	S.S. Bajwa	IPS/Punjab
70.	S.D. Agnihotri	IPS/UP
71.	R.D. Kewalramani	IPS/UP
72.	R.N. Agrawala	IPS/UP
73.	T.K. Das	SPS/WB
74.	C. Krishna Reddy	SPS/Hyderabad
75.	G. Srinivasa Reddy	SPS/Hyderabad
76.	S. Devender Rao	SPS/Hyderabad
77.	E. Sampat Rao	SPS/Hyderabad
78.	S.N. Shukla	SPS/Hyderabad
79.	Tulja Raj	SPS/Hyderabad
80.	S. Krishna Kumar	SPS/Hyderabad
81.	R.D. Bhoopal	SPS/Hyderabad
82.	Mudaliar Balraj	SPS/Hyderabad
83.	S. Ananda Ram	SPS/Hyderabad

84.	M.D. Dittia	SPS/Hyderabad
85.	A.B. Krishnaswamy	SPS/Hyderabad
86.	Mahmood Bin Muhamad	SPS/Hyderabad
87.	Syed Shamsuddin Ahmed	SPS/Hyderabad

IPS - SRB -2

88.	B.C. Bagchi	IPS
89.	A.K. Banerji	IPS
90.	P.N. Banerji	IPS
91.	S.N. Bhattacharya	IPS
92.	N.R. Bose	IPS
93.	A.B. Chowdhury	IPS
94.	S.C. De Chowdhury	IPS
95.	K.B. Chakravarti	IPS
96.	P.L. Dhar	IPS
97.	A.K. Moitra	IPS
98.	A.C. Sinha	IPS
99.	J.M. Shukla	IPS
100.	K.L. Dewan	IPS
101.	M.G. Gavai	IPS
102.	S.V. Tankhiwale	IPS
103.	S.M. Diaz	IPS
104.	S. Venugopal Rao	IPS
105.	L.J. Victor	IPS
106.	P.S. Viswanathan	IPS

Training Year: 1950; IPS - SRB-3

107.	R.N. Haldipur	IPS
108.	R.R. Harnagley	IPS
109.	P.C. Rai	IPS
110.	J.W. Rodrigues	IPS
111.	B.L. Shrivastava	IPS

112.	K.S. Venkataraman	IPS
113.	J. Dharamraj	IPS
114.	O.P. Grover	IPS
115.	I.J. Johar	IPS
116.	H.S. Kohli	IPS
117.	K. Rajgopalan	IPS
118.	Yagya Datta	IPS
119.	V.N. Bakshi	IPS
120.	B.R. Chadha	IPS
121.	B.N. Muttoo	IPS
122.	M.L. Puri	IPS
123.	H.C. Saxena	IPS
124.	J.C. Vachher	IPS
125.	A.C. Ambwani	IPS
126.	K.R. Bhatnagar	IPS
127.	M.N. Chaturvedi	IPS
128.	B.L. Gulati	IPS
129.	P.V. Hingorani	IPS
130.	J.M Jain	IPS
131.	J.P. Kulshreshta	IPS
132.	E.J. Mukand	IPS
133.	T.K. Pande	IPS
134.	R.D. Pande	IPS
135.	R. Prasad	IPS
136.	Ram Singh	IPS
137.	R.D. Tiwari	IPS
138.	S.K. Chakravorti	IPS
139.	S.N. de Silva	IPS
140.	H. Sarcar	IPS
141.	S.C. Sarcar	IPS

Training Year: 1950-51; Batch: 1950 - IPS - RR-3

142.	G. Narayan	IPS/Bihar
143.	B.P.N. Sahi	IPS/Bihar
144.	M.K. Jha	IPS/Bihar
145.	S.N. Singh	IPS/Bihar
146.	B.R. Kalyanpurkar	IPS/Bihar
147.	C.E.J. Elisha	IPS/Bombay
148.	M.S. Kasbekar	IPS/Bombay
149.	S.P.C. Joshi	IPS/Hyderabad
150.	S.K. Chaturvedi	IPS/Hyderabad
151.	S.S. Sahni	IPS/Hyderabad
152.	J.S. Saldanha	IPS/Hyderabad
153.	T.V. Rajeswar	IPS/Hyderabad
154.	G.V. Rao	IPS/Hyderabad
155.	M.N. Gadgil	IPS/MP
156.	B.P. Misra	IPS/MP
157.	B.P. Dube	IPS/MP
158.	B.N. Yadav	IPS/MP
159.	K.V. Subramaniam	IPS/Madras
160.	R. Krishnaswamy	IPS/Madras
161.	N. Swain	IPS/Orissa
162.	Harjit Singh	IPS/Pepsu
163.	Surendra Nath	IPS/Punjab
164.	Bhagwan Singh	IPS/Punjab
165.	Bhawani Mal	IPS/Rajasthan
166.	T.A.S. Iyer	IPS/Trvn.&Cochin
167.	G.S. Arya	IPS/UP
168.	G.C. Saxena	IPS/UP
169.	S.C. Dikshit	IPS/UP
170.	K.P. Agarwal	IPS/UP
171.	R.K. Kapoor	IPS/UP
172.	G.D. Mukherjee	IPS/WB

173.	R.K. Mukherjee	IPS/WB
174.	S.K. Sinha	IPS/WB
175.	A. Chakravarty	IPS/WB
176.	G. Majumdar	IPS/WB
177.	P.K. Sen	IPS/WB
178.	Iqbal Singh	IPS/Orissa

IPS - SRB -4

179	L.R. Malhotra	IPS/Punjab
180	D.S. Garewal	IPS/Punjab
181	P.S. Raturi	IPS/UP
182	A.P. Batra	IPS/UP
183	A.C.M. Nambiar	IPS/Madras

Training Year: 1951; IPS - SRB-5

184.	H.C. Singh	IPS/Bombay
185.	S.V. Pandit	IPS/Bombay
186.	D.P. Verma	IPS/UP
187.	B.N. Mukherjee	IPS/VP
188.	H.K. Chakravarti	IPS/WB
189.	B.C. Mazumdar	IPS/WB
190.	A.K. Pal	IPS/WB

Training Year: 1951-52; Batch: 1951 - IPS - RR-4

191.	R.C. Rastogi	IPS/Assam
192.	K.C. Sinha	IPS/Bihar
193.	A.R. Nath	IPS/Bihar
194.	Jagdanand	IPS/Bihar
195.	S.M. Warty	IPS/Bombay
196.	S.D. Rege	IPS/Bombay
197.	R.T. Nagrani	IPS/Hyderabad
198.	K.C.K. Raja	IPS/Hydeabad
199.	P.V.G.K. Charyulu	IPS/Hyderabad

200.	S.G. Sahasrabhojane	IPS/MP
201.	M.C. Misra	IPS/MP
202.	Baldev Singh	IPS/MP
203.	P.R. Khurana	IPS/MP
204.	K. Ravindran	IPS/Madras
205.	V.R.Lakshminarayanan	IPS/Madras
206.	S.S. Padhi	IPS/Orissa
207.	Birbal Nath	IPS/Pepsu
208.	J.S. Bawa	IPS/Punjab
209.	G.C. Singhvi	IPS/Rajasthan
210.	D.P. Gupta	IPS/Rajasthan
211.	K.S. Tripathi	IPS/UP
212.	Shiv Swarup	IPS/UP
213.	S.K. Shunglu	IPS/UP
214.	G.S. Misra	IPS/UP
215.	B.R. Kishore	IPS/UP
216.	M.D. Dikshit	IPS/UP
217.	K.L. Chhabra	IPS/UP
218.	J.N. Chaturvedi	IPS/UP
219.	S. Basu	IPS/WB
220.	N.R. De	IPS/WB
221.	N.N. Mazumdar	IPS/WB
222.	B. Mukhopadhyay	IPS/WB
223.	S.K. Mallik	IPS/WB

Training Year: 1952; IPS - SRB-6

224.	Jacob Abraham	IPS/Assam
225.	I.P.M. Menon	IPS/Assam
226.	K. Randeep Singh	IPS/Assam
227.	J.G. Kharkar	IPS/Bombay
228.	D.C. Sarma	IPS/Hyderabad
229.	C.V.S. Rao	IPS/Hyderabad

230. V. Sreenivasan IPS/Hyderabad
231. K. Subramanyam IPS/Hyderabad
232. Prahalad Singh IPS/Hyderabad
233. K.G. Ramanna IPS/Hyderabad
234. C.B. Patil IPS/Hyderabad
235. R. Narayana Swamy IPS/Hyderabad
236. R.A. Mundkur IPS/Hyderabad
237. B.R. Malhotra IPS/Hyderabad
238. V.A. Gokhale IPS/Hyderabad
239. F.S. Dewaras IPS/Hyderabad
240. A.R. Braganza IPS/Hyderabad
241. H.G. Abhyankar IPS/Hyderabad
242. J.K. Sen IPS/Saurashtra
243. S.K. Kulkarni IPS/Saurashtra
244. R.G. Hazare IPS/Saurashtra

IPS - SRB - 7th

245. D.S. Sahi IPS/Rajasthan
246. G.C.D. Chadha IPS/Rajasthan
247. K.N. Soral IPS/Rajasthan
248. Lalit Mohan IPS/Rajasthan
249. N.C. Datta IPS/Rajasthan
250. N.N. Dewan IPS/Rajasthan
251. N.C. Ghosh IPS/Rajasthan
252. S.R. Sarma IPS/Rajasthan
253. S.P. Bhargava IPS/Rajasthan
254. B.N. Mukherjee IPS/WB

Training Year: 1952-53; Batch 1952 - IPS - RR-5

255. Balraj Pabbi IPS/Assam
256. T.A. Subramanian IPS/Assam
257. A. Chandrasekhar IPS/Bihar

258.	S.B. Sahai	IPS/Bihar
259.	B.N. Sinha	IPS/Bihar
260.	T.G.L. Iyer	IPS/Bombay
261.	M.G. Katre	IPS/Bombay
262.	P.G. Nawani	IPS/Bombay
263.	S.M. Paranjepe	IPS/Bombay
264.	M.A. Saifiullah Khan	IPS/Hyderabad
265.	R. Madhava Rau	IPS/Hyderabad
266.	H.K. Pahuja	IPS/Madya Bharat
267.	S.E. Joshi	IPS/MP
268.	G.K. Kasture	IPS/MP
269.	R.N. Palit	IPS/MP
270.	J.C. Pande	IPS/MP
271.	K.G. Erady	IPS/AP
272.	K. Radhakrishnan	IPS/Madras
273.	B.N. Mishra	IPS/Orissa
274.	D. Mishra	IPS/Orissa
275.	B.K. Panigrahi	IPS/Orissa
276.	M.S. Bhatnagar	IPS/Punjab
277.	P.C. Wadhwa	IPS/Punjab
278.	D. Jagannadhan	IPS/Rajasthan
279.	M.K. Saxena	IPS/Rajasthan
280.	S.C. Tandon	IPS/Rajasthan
281.	S. Ramaiah	IPS/Saurashtra
282.	O.P. Bhutani	IPS/UP
283.	B.C. Goel	IPS/UP
284.	R.P. Govil	IPS/UP
285.	Vishambhar Nath	IPS/UP
286.	B.M. Mathur	IPS/UP
287.	M.C. Pant	IPS/UP
288.	Amar Singh	IPS/UP

289.	B. Verma	IPS/UP
290.	J.S. Kand	IPS/V.P.
291.	R.K. Bhattacharya	IPS/WB
292.	S. Gupta	IPS/WB
293.	P.G. Mukhopadhyay	IPS/WB

Training Year: 1953-54; Batch: 1953 - IPS - RR-6

294.	J.S. Pathak	IPS/Assam
295.	B.C. Sarma	IPS/Assam
296.	P.K. Jain	IPS/Bihar
297.	K. Pati	IPS/Bihar
298.	A.C. Vijaya Kumar	IPS/Bombay
299.	R.S. Parekh	IPS/Bombay
300.	J.F. Ribeiro	IPS/Bombay
301.	D.S. Soman	IPS/Bombay
302.	B.N. Garudachari	IPS/Hyderabad
303.	P.V. Pavithran	IPS/Hyderabad
304.	Mahendra Reddy	IPS/Hyderabad
305.	B.M. Saihgal	IPS/Madhya Bharat
306.	R.K. Agnihotri	IPS/MP
307.	S.S. Jog	IPS/MP
308.	A.K. Verma	IPS/MP
309.	R. Govinda Rajan	IPS/Madras
310.	T. Ponnaiah	IPS/Andhra
311.	R.K. Rajagopalan	IPS/Madras
312.	C.G. Saldana	IPS/Andhra
313.	P.S. Challappa	IPS/Mysore
314.	P.K. Joseph	IPS/Orissa
315.	G.C. Senapathi	IPS/Orissa
316.	Prakash Chand	IPS/Punjab
317.	J.K. Balani	IPS/Rajasthan

318.	H.N. Kak	IPS/Rajasthan
319.	S.D. Mehta	IPS/Saurashtra
320.	V.T. Shah	IPS/Saurashtra
321.	D.K. Agarwal	IPS/UP
322 .	P.C. Kackar	IPS/UP
323.	R.K. Kandelwal	IPS/UP
324.	S.D. Pande	IPS/UP
325.	H.C. Shah	IPS/UP
326.	K.S. Dhillon	IPS/VP
327.	H.A. Barari	IPS/WB
328.	R.N. Bhattacharya	IPS/WB
329.	P.B. Choudhary	IPS/WB
330.	Nirupom Som	IPS/WB
331.	J.L. Kapoor	DySP/Tripura
332.	R.C. Kochar	DySP/Tripura
333.	P.N. Singh	DySP/Tripura

Training Year: 1954-55; Batch: 1954 - IPS - RR-7

334.	Hari Singh	IPS/Andhra
335.	R. Swaminathan	IPS/Andhra
336.	Man Mohan Singh	IPS/Saurashtra
337.	K.V.V. Subramanian	IPS/Andhra
338.	M.K. Barooah	IPS/Assam
339.	B.S. Babar	IPS/Assam
340.	P.K. Mullick	IPS/Bihar
341.	M.H. Rashid	IPS/Bihar
342.	R.S. Kulkarni	IPS/Bombay
343.	S.K. Warrior	IPS/Bombay
344.	J.N. Mehra	IPS/Bombay
345.	G. Krishna Swamy	IPS/Bombay
346.	S.R. Sankarnarayanan	IPS/Hyderabad
347.	S.P. Singh	IPS/Hyderabad

348.	T.N. Bhargava	IPS/Madhya Bharat
349.	M.L. Jain	IPS/Madhya Bharat
350.	A.N. Banerjee	IPS/MP
351.	S.P. Banerjee	IPS/MP
352.	A.R. Nizamudin	IPS/Mysore
353.	K.C. Patnaik	IPS/Orissa
354.	J.M. Samal	IPS/Orissa
355.	V.K. Tripathi	IPS/Orissa
356.	V.K. Kalia	IPS/Punjab
357.	B.R. Sur	IPS/Punjab
358.	I.J. Verma	IPS/Punjab
359.	D.K. Dutta	IPS/Rajasthan
360.	P.C. Mishra	IPS/Rajasthan
361.	J.P. Sarma	IPS/Rajasthan
362.	M.K. Joseph	IPS/Trvn.&Cochin
363.	G.S. Bajpai	IPS/UP
364.	D.S. Bhatnagar	IPS/UP
365.	Tushar Dutt	IPS/UP
366.	R.N. Gupta	IPS/UP
367.	Hari Mohan	IPS/UP
368.	V.D. Panjani	IPS/UP
369.	Som Prakash	IPS/UP
370.	R.D. Sharma	IPS/UP
371.	C.M.R. Nair	IPS/Andhra
372.	A.M.P. Verma	IPS/VP
373.	B.K. Mukherjee	IPS/VP
374.	A.B. Bhattacharya	IPS/VP
375.	S. Basu	IPS/WB
376.	C.N. Bhattacharya	IPS/WB
377.	S. Kitson	IPS/WB
378.	D.K. Sen	IPS/WB

379.	M.M. Khajuria	DySP/J&K
380.	Amar Singh	DySP/J&K
381.	Dundy Raj	Nepal Police (Foreign)
382.	R.B. Thapa	Nepal Police (Foreign)

Training Year: 1955-56; Batch: 1955 - IPS - RR-8

383.	M.V. Thomas	IPS/Andhra
384.	P.V.R. Naidu	IPS/Andhra
385.	S.K. Das	IPS/Assam
386.	V.S. Dhaliwal	IPS/Assam
387.	S.P. Singh	IPS/Bihar
388.	S.N. Roy	IPS/Bihar
389.	A.M. Mistry	IPS/Bombay
390.	C.G. Phadke	IPS/Bombay
391.	G.R. Ramachandran	IPS/Bombay
392.	V.W. Pradhan	IPS/Bombay
393.	A. Varghese	IPS/Karnataka
394.	M.K. Narayanan	IPS/Madras
395.	R.N. Das	IPS/Orissa
396.	V.S. Scigelle	IPS/Punjab
397.	M.S. Bawa	IPS/Punjab
398.	C.K. Sawhney	IPS/Punjab
399.	I.S. Sodi	IPS/Punjab
400.	I.C. Dwivedi	IPS/UP
401.	R.N. Mathur	IPS/UP
402.	B.P. Singhal	IPS/U.P
403.	V.P. Kumar	IPS/UP
404.	R.P. Joshi	IPS/UP
405.	A.K. Banerji	IPS/UP
406.	Sushil Kumar	IPS/Hyderabad
407.	K.N. Srinivasan	IPS/Hyderabad
408.	S.V. Singh	IPS/MP

409.	M. Natarajan	IPS/MP
410.	N.S. Srinivasan	IPS/Mysore
411.	G.P. Pillania	IPS/Rajasthan
412.	W.G.A. Mudhaliar	IPS/Rajasthan
413.	A.A. Ali	IPS/MP
414.	D.N. Ahuja	IPS/MP
415.	R. Dechan	DySP/J&K
416.	M.S. Farooqi	DySP/J&K
417.	A.R. Nanda	DySP/J&K
418.	N.K. Vishwanath	DySP/Hyderabad
419.	N.S. Rana	Nepal Police (Foreign)
420.	C.S. Rana	Nepal Police (Foreign)

Training Year: 1956-57; Batch: 1956 - IPS - RR-9

421.	R.M. Rao	IPS/AP
422.	N. Radhakrishna Murthy	IPS/AP
423.	V. Sreenivas Rao	IPS/AP
424.	S. Chandrasekharan	IPS/AP
425.	D.N. Sonowal	IPS/Assam
426.	M.I.S. Iyer	IPS/Assam
427.	R.B. Subramanyam	IPS/Assam
428.	L.V. Singh	IPS/Bihar
429.	J.N. Singh	IPS/Bihar
430.	A.K. Chaudhary	IPS/Bihar
431.	S.P. Sharma	IPS/Bihar
432.	R. Balakrishnan	IPS/Bombay
433.	S.V. Bhave	IPS/Bombay
434.	V.K. Saraf	IPS/Bombay
435.	K.H. Bhaya	IPS/Bombay
436.	K. Prabhakaran	IPS/Bombay
437.	D. Ramachandran	IPS/Bombay
438.	R. Ranga Raju	IPS/Bombay

439.	A.V. Venkatachalam	IPS/Kerala
440.	V.K. Sreenivas Rao	IPS/Kerala
441.	Janak Kumar	IPS/MP
442.	J.M. Quereshi	IPS/MP
443.	Gurdarshan Singh	IPS/MP
444.	P.N. Uppal	IPS/MP
445.	K.K. Puri	IPS/MP
446.	S.S. Lamba	IPS/MP
447.	K. Mohan Das	IPS/Madras
448.	P.G. Halankar	IPS/Mysore
449.	P.C. Rathore	IPS/Orissa
450.	S. Sinha	IPS/Orissa
451.	Krishan Kumar	IPS/Punjab
452.	D.D. Kashyap	IPS/Punjab
453.	V.K. Kaul	IPS/Rajasthan
454.	H.P. Bhatnagar	IPS/Rajasthan
455.	D.R. Puri	IPS/Rajasthan
456.	T.S. Bhist	IPS/UP
457.	R.P. Mathur	IPS/UP
458.	K.L. Watts	IPS/UP
459.	Shyam Lal	IPS/UP
460.	A.P. Mukherjee	IPS/WB
461.	S.C. Mazumdar	IPS/WB
462.	D.N. Pandey	IPS/WB
463.	H.B. Johri	IPS/WB
464.	V.P. Marwah	IPS/WB
465.	R.P. Modi	DySP/M.P.
466.	D.K. Bharat	DySP/M.P.
467.	S. Misra	DySP/M.P.
468.	K.J. Thapa	Nepal Police (Foreign)
469.	D.K. Thapa	Nepal Police (Foreign)
470.	R.S. Shrestha	Nepal Police (Foreign)

471.	S.P. Sinha	Nepal Police (Foreign)
472.	I.B. Chetri	Nepal Police (Foreign)
473.	D.S. Rana	Nepal Police (Foreign)
474.	M.N.J.B. Rana	Nepal Police (Foreign)
475.	M.B. Karti	Nepal Police (Foreign)

Training Year: 1957-58; Batch: 1957 - IPS-RR-10

476.	P Jagan Mohan	IPS/AP
477.	R. Prabhakar Rao	IPS/AP
478.	D.V.L.N.R. Rao	IPS/AP
479.	K.V.H. Padmanabhan	IPS/AP
480.	K.A. Narayana Swamy	IPS/AP
481.	N. Changkakoti	IPS/Assam
482.	Bhupinder Singh	IPS/Assam
483.	K.P. S. Gill	IPS/Assam
484.	V. Pandeya	IPS/Bihar
485.	S.N. Mishra	IPS/Bihar
486.	Krithbhu Deo	IPS/Bihar
487.	Krishna Prakash Jee	IPS/Bihar
488.	Tej Pratap Singh	IPS/Bihar
489.	S.T. Raman	IPS/Bombay
490.	J.S. Bedi	IPS/Bombay
491.	Jaspal Singh	IPS/Bombay
492.	Keki Dadabhoy	IPS/Bombay
493.	T.R. Varadha Rajan	IPS/Bombay
494.	S. Ramamurthi	IPS/Bombay
495.	S.K. Varma	IPS/Bombay
496.	P.G. Nair	IPS/Kerala
497.	K. John Mathai	IPS/Kerala
498.	R.G. Narayan	IPS/Kerala
499.	J. Padmagiriswaran	IPS/Kerala
500.	K.V. Kumaraswamy	IPS/Kerala

501.	S. Chandrasekharan	IPS/Kerala
502.	M.C. Trikha	IPS/MP
503.	N.M. Virmani	IPS/MP
504.	Yogendra Rajpal	IPS/MP
505.	P.D. Malaviya	IPS/MP
506.	Puran Batria	IPS/MP
507.	S.C. Vidyardhi	IPS/MP
508.	Raja Sreedharan	IPS/MP
509.	B.P.G. Rangaswamy	IPS/Madras
510.	R.L. Handa	IPS/Madras
511.	K.U.B. Rao	IPS/Mysore
512.	N. Narasimhan	IPS/Mysore
513.	S. Misra	IPS/Orissa
514.	D.N. Singh	IPS/Orissa
515.	Roshan Sahgal	IPS/Orissa
516.	M.L. Bhanot	IPS/Punjab
517.	G.S. Mander	IPS/Punjab
518.	H.R. Swan	IPS/Punjab
519.	P.S. Shukla	IPS/Punjab
520.	K.L. Diwan	IPS/Punjab
521.	P.P. Srivastav	IPS/Rajasthan
522.	R. Shekhar	IPS/Rajasthan
523.	O.P. Tandon	IPS/Rajasthan
524.	S.S.M. Kumar	IPS/Rajasthan
525.	M.L. Kalia	IPS/Rajasthan
526.	D.P.N. Singh	IPS/Rajasthan
527.	Gurmel Mehmi	IPS/Rajasthan
528.	R.K. Saxena	IPS/UP
529.	M. Shankar	IPS/UP
530.	P.C. Prasad	IPS/UP
531.	S.K. Mukherji	IPS/UP

532.	S.S. Misra	IPS/UP
533.	S.P. Mukherjee	IPS/WB
534.	B.K.Basu	IPS/WB
535.	S.M. Chakrabarti	IPS/WB
536.	Harris James	IPS/WB
537.	Shiv Lal	IPS/WB
538.	S.K. Singh	IPS/WB
539.	S.S. Bindra	IPS/WB
540.	A.K. Datta	IPS/WB
541.	S.J. Barman	IPS/WB
542.	R.K. Trivedi	IPS/WB
543.	Viswanathan Pillai	DySP/Kerala
544.	O.N. Kaul	DySP/J&K
545.	G.J. Pandit	DySP/J&K

Training Year: 1958-59; Batch: 1958 - IPS-RR-11

546.	S. Subramanian	IPS/AP
547.	R. Vijaya Karan	IPS/UT
548.	H.K. Bhattacharya	IPS/Assam
549.	L.B. Sewa	IPS/Assam
550.	Gajendra Narain	IPS/Bihar
551.	K.D. Dubey	IPS/Bihar
552.	B.J. Misar	IPS/Bombay
553.	V.C. Vaidya	IPS/Bombay
554.	B. Ray	IPS/Bombay
555.	P.R. Parthasarathy	IPS/Bombay
556.	T. Suryanarayana Rao	IPS/Bombay
557.	C. Subramaniam	IPS/Kerala
558.	A.S. Syali	IPS/MP
559.	R.P. Sharma	IPS/MP
560.	C.Z. Ghafoor	IPS/MP
561.	P.P. Mahurkar	IPS/MP

562.	K.K. Singh	IPS/MP
563.	K. Sitaraman	IPS/Madras
564.	A.R. Sridharan	IPS/Mysore
565.	M.S. Raghuraman	IPS/Mysore
566.	T. Ananthachari	IPS/Orissa
567.	K.B. Vohra	IPS/Orissa
568.	P.S. Bhinder	IPS/Punjab
569.	J.S. Anand	IPS/Punjab
570.	R.K. Hooda	IPS/Rajasthan
571.	R.K. Baijal	IPS/Rajasthan
572.	S.K. Sarma	IPS/Rajasthan
573.	V.K. Jain	IPS/UP
574.	A.P. Misra	IPS/UP
575.	K.N. Daruwala	IPS/UP
576.	C.N. Sinha	IPS/UP
577.	Inder Bhagat Negi	IPS/UP
578.	Dipak Haldhar	IPS/WB
579.	S.J. Phillip	IPS/WB
580.	G.A. Bhatt	IPS/J&K

Training Year: 1959-60; Batch: 1959 - IPS-RR-12

581.	K.V. Rama Rao	IPS/AP
582.	G.G. Rao	IPS/AP
583.	K. Saranyan	IPS/AP
584.	G.S. Prabhakar	IPS/AP
585.	B.D. Kharkwal	IPS/Assam
586.	N. Natarajan	IPS/Assam
587.	A.J. Bahadur	IPS/Bihar
588.	Zaffar Ibrahim	IPS/Bihar
589.	N.C. Venkatachalam	IPS/Maharashtra
590.	Sudhakar Dev	IPS/Maharashtra
591.	R.V. Bahadur Desai	IPS/Maharashtra

592.	V. Balachandran	IPS/Maharashtra
593.	S.S. Vaidyanathan	IPS/Gujarat
594.	B.K. Jha	IPS/Gujarat
595.	A. Arjunan	IPS/Kerala
596.	M.S. Verma	IPS/MP
597.	C.S. Dwivedi	IPS/MP
598.	O.N. Srivastava	IPS/MP
599.	K.S. Rathore	IPS/MP
600.	Ram Ratan	IPS/M.P
601.	C.L. Ramakrishnan	IPS/Madras
602.	P. Dorai	IPS/Madras
603.	S.N. Srinivasa Murthy	IPS/Mysore
604.	P.P.R. Nair	IPS/Mysore
605.	B. Mahapatra	IPS/Orissa
606.	S.C. Misra	IPS/Orissa
607.	S.S. Brar	IPS/Punjab
608.	Dalbir Singh	IPS/Punjab
609.	K.K. Zutshi	IPS/Punjab
610.	K.C. Jatav	IPS/Punjab
611.	V.K. Tanvi	IPS/Rajasthan
612.	S.C. Mehta	IPS/Rajasthan
613.	Sankar Saran	IPS/Rajasthan
614.	Prakash Singh	IPS/UP
615.	Y.N. Saxena	IPS/UP
616.	J. Jacob	IPS/UP
617.	B.J.S. Sial	IPS/UP
618.	A.P. Verma	IPS/UP
619.	R.K. Wadhera	IPS/UP
620.	S.K. Dutta	IPS/UP
621.	S.K. Ramachandran	IPS/WB
622.	A. Ghatak	IPS/WB

Training Year: 1960-61; Batch: 1960 - IPS-RR-13

623.	D.N. Sahaya	IPS/Bihar
624.	S.N. Misra	IPS/MP
625.	G. Sundaram	IPS/AP
626.	B. Bhattacharji	IPS/WB
627.	B.K. Mishra	IPS/Assam
628.	P.P. Biswas	IPS/WB
629.	S.V. Subramanian	IPS/Assam
630.	B.K. Saha	IPS/WB
631.	B.S. Nirula	IPS/Gujarat
632.	J.N. Saxena	IPS/MP
633.	Ram Asray	IPS/UP
634.	R.K. Basisht	IPS/Gujarat
635.	A. Rajamohan	IPS/UP
636.	K.K. Mitra	IPS/Orissa
637.	C. Chakravarty	IPS/Orissa
638.	M.M. Sadanah	IPS/Assam
639.	J.N. Roy	IPS/MP
640.	B.K. Jha	IPS/Bihar
641.	S.C. Gossain	IPS/WB
642.	G.S. Mussaffir	IPS/Gujarat
643.	D.C. Nath	IPS/WB
644.	R.S. Chopra	IPS/Mysore
645.	R. J. Padikkal	IPS/Kerala
646.	B. K. Choudhary	IPS/UP
647.	Surendra Singh	IPS/MP
648.	H.D. Pillai	IPS/UP
649.	B.R. Luthra	IPS/MP
650.	D.K. Arya	IPS/MP
651.	S.D. Trivedi	IPS/UP
652.	M.F. Rasool	IPS/MP
653.	S. Sripal	IPS/Madras

654.	P. Swani	Left IPS
655.	S.K. Set	IPS/Maharashtra
656.	P.S. Yadav	IPS/Rajasthan
657.	M. Wadhwa	IPS/Maharashtra
658.	D.C. Pathak	IPS/Rajasthan
659.	P.K. Kanungo	IPS/Maharashtra
660.	Rattan Lall	IPS/Punjab
661.	K. Padmanabhan	IPS/Maharashtra
662.	V.P. Jain	IPS/Bihar
663.	R. Ramalingam	IPS/Mysore
664.	P. K. Misra	IPS/Orissa
665.	Kalyan Rudra	IPS/Punjab
666.	Sankar Sen	IPS/Orissa
667.	P.B. Rajagopalan	IPS/Maharashtra
668.	K.S. Bains	IPS/Punjab
669.	R. Kuppu Rao	IPS/AP
670.	K. J. Reddy	IPS/AP
671.	V.K. Agnihotri	DySP/M.P.
672.	R.S. Rathore	DySP/M.P.
673.	S.L. Shukla	DySP/M.P.
674.	C.S. Naidu	DySP/M.P.
675.	V.L. Taran	DySP/M.P.
676.	R.S.Verma	DySP/M.P.
677.	H.C. Mishra	DySP/M.P.
678.	U.S. Akolekar	DySP/M.P.

Training Year: 1961-62; Batch: 1961 - IPS - RR-14

679.	Ismael Pullanna	IPS/AP
680.	M.V. Bhaskaran	IPS/AP
681.	C.K. Gajanan	IPS/AP
682.	S.K. Jha	IPS/Assam

683.	J.K. Sinha	IPS/Assam
684.	H.S. Chittaranjan	IPS/Assam
685.	A.K. Sinha	IPS/Assam
686.	N.N. Singh	IPS/Bihar
687.	Maiku Ram	IPS/Bihar
688.	S.R. Gopal	IPS/Gujarat
689.	V. Subramanyam	IPS/Gujarat
690.	A.K. Tandon	IPS/Gujarat
691.	T.V. Madhusudanan	IPS/Kerala
692.	P.J. Alexander	IPS/Kerala
693.	B. Raman	IPS/MP
694.	Pratap Singh	IPS/MP
695.	S. Chandra	IPS/MP
696.	S.P. Taluqdar	IPS/MP
697.	R.C. Jha	IPS/MP
698.	V.P. Sahni	IPS/MP
699.	R.J. Khurana	IPS/MP
700.	S.N. Chaturvedi	IPS/MP
701.	S.R. Adarmi	IPS/MP
702.	K. Rajasekhara Nair	IPS/Madras
703.	V. Vaikuntam	IPS/Madras
704.	B.K.R. Rao	IPS/Madras
705.	A.Venkata Krishnan	IPS/Maharashtra
706.	S.V. Baraukar	IPS/Maharasthra
707.	R.K. Bhatia	IPS/Maharashtra
708.	Nek Ram	IPS/Maharashtra
709.	A.T. Desh Pande	IPS/Maharashtra
710.	R.M. Vasanth Kumar	IPS/Mysore
711.	F.T.R. Colaso	IPS/Mysore
712.	Joginder Singh	IPS/Mysore
713.	S.C. De	IPS/Orissa

714.	R.M. Patnaik	IPS/Orissa
715.	N.K. Singh	IPS/Orissa
716.	Ranjan Roy	IPS/Orissa
717.	H.S. Shekon	IPS/Punjab
718.	R.R. Singh	IPS/Punjab
719.	M.S. Madok	IPS/Rajasthan
720.	K.N. Thakur	IPS/Rajasthan
721.	Balwant Singh	IPS/Rajasthan
722.	Kishan Lal	IPS/Rajasthan
723.	S.V.M. Tripathi	IPS/UP
724.	G. Behari	IPS/UP
725.	V.P. Kapur	IPS/UP
726.	B.S. Bedi	IPS/UP
727.	N.L. Jatav	IPS/UP
728.	M.P. Singh	IPS/WB
729.	V.K. Jha	IPS/WB
730.	Arun Bhagat	IPS/Delhi & HP
731.	R.R. Verma	IPS/Delhi & HP
732.	A. Mitra	IPS/Delhi & HP
733.	B.N. Yugundar	IPS/AP
734.	Radhakanth Naik	IPS
735.	S.K. Basu	IPS/WB
736.	C.B. Giridhar	IPS/Gujarat
737.	V. Ganesh	IPS/MP
738.	R.K. Puri	IPS/Gujarat
739.	G.K. Kanchan	IPS/MP
740.	R. Matho	IPS/UP
741.	P.N. Khanna	IPS/Assam
742.	M.P. Singh	DySP/CRP
743.	S.N. Mathur	DySP/CRP
744.	K.R.K. Prasad	DySP/CRP

745. G.R.K. Rao DySP/CRP
746. B.B.S. Chauhan DySP/MP
747. H.P. Singh DySP/MP
748. P.L. Kaim DySP/MP
749. K.K. Saxena DySP/MP
750. Y.C. Dikshit DySP/MP
751. S.S. Gupta DySP/MP
752. A.S. Pooni DySP/CRP
753. K. Bikram Singh DySP/CRP

Training Year: 1962-63; Batch: 1962 - IPS-RR-15

754. M.K. Rethindran IPS/AP
755. M.V. Bhaskara Rao IPS/AP
756. R.K. Rao Ragala IPS/AP
757. Idusekhar Sarma IPS/Assam
758. R.K. Sharma IPS/Assam
759. R. Chogthu IPS/Assam
760. J. Biswas IPS/Assam
761. Balbir Jha IPS/Bihar
762. G.P. Dohare IPS/Bihar
763. G.D. Khemani IPS/Gujarat
764. R. Sibal IPS/Gujarat
765. K.V. Joseph IPS/Gujarat
766. S.N. Sinha IPS/Gujarat
767. M.S. Raju IPS/Gujarat
768. M.M. Mehta IPS/Gujarat
769. N.L. Kalma IPS/Gujarat
770. K.V. Rajagopalan Nair IPS/Kerala
771. R. Radhakrishnan IPS/Kerala
772. V. Krishnamoorthy IPS/Kerala
773. A. Dave IPS/MP
774. S. Dayal IPS/MP

775.	A. Gurtoo	IPS/MP
776.	D. P. Khanna	IPS/MP
777.	M.D. Sharma	IPS/MP
778.	N. Prasad	IPS/MP
779.	S. Kumar	IPS/MP
780.	V.K. Bhalla	IPS/MP
781.	Sukhlal Suchari	IPS/MP
782.	G.V. Soreng	IPS/MP
783.	L.N. Venkatesan	IPS/Madras
784.	K.V. Unnikrishnan	IPS/Madras
785.	C. Dorairaj	IPS/Madras
786.	S.M. Pathania	IPS/Maharashtra
787.	B.J.K. Tampi	IPS/Manipur
788.	S.K. Bapat	IPS/Maharashtra
789.	A.S. Samra	IPS/Maharashtra
790.	N.K. B. Bhat	IPS/Mysore
791.	R. Jagannathan	IPS/Mysore
792.	A.S. Malurkar	IPS/Mysore
793.	Chandu Lal	IPS/Mysore
794.	A.J. Anandan	IPS/Mysore
795.	A.P. Durai	IPS/Mysore
796.	M. Mukherjee	IPS/Orissa
797.	A.B. Tripathi	IPS/Orissa
798.	S.P. Mallik	IPS/Orissa
799.	Surjit Singh	IPS/Punjab
800.	Lachhman Dass	IPS/Punjab
801.	P.S. Hura	IPS/Punjab
802.	P.N. Raina	IPS/Rajasthan
803.	Devendra Singh	IPS/Rajasthan
804.	L.M. Jain	IPS/Rajasthan
805.	Ram Narain	IPS/Rajasthan

806.	V.S. Mathur	IPS/UP
807.	O.P. Sharma	IPS/UP
808.	C.M. Sharma	IPS/UP
809.	Tripuresh Tripathy	IPS/UP
810.	S.N.P. Sinha	IPS/UP
811.	B.N. Tiwari	IPS/UP
812.	C.L. Wasan	IPS/UP
813.	D. Kevichusa	IPS/UP
814.	C.L. Pradyot	IPS/UP
815.	A.K. Samanta	IPS/WB
816.	H.P. Kumar	IPS/WB
817.	K.K. Majumdar	IPS/WB
818.	R.K. Nigam	IPS/WB
819.	K.S. Bajwa	IPS/Delhi & HP
820.	G.S. Sahi	IPS/Delhi & HP
821.	Amrik Singh	IPS/Delhi & HP
822.	T.R. Kalra	IPS/J&K
823.	M.K. Khatri	DySP/MP
824.	P.G. Kekre	DySP/MP
825.	C.P. Singh	DySP/MP
826.	K.L. Thakur	DySP/MP
827.	R.K. Singh	DySP/MP
828.	Vijay C. David	DySP/MP
829.	Narayan Singhar	DySP/MP
830.	P.V. Sinari	DySP/Goa
831.	U.P. Dhaimode	DySP/Goa
832.	A.D. D'Souza	DySP/Goa
833.	D.D. Gupta	DySP/Delhi & HP
834.	R.M. Sahai	DySP/CRP
835.	C.P. Singh	DySP/CRP
836.	A.K. Bandyopadhyay	DySP/CRP

837.	R. Ohri	DySP/CRP
838.	R.B. Singh	Nepal Police (Foreign)
839.	R.S.J. Bahadur	Nepal Police (Foreign)
840.	P.S.M. Bahadur	Nepal Police (Foreign)
841.	K.B. Khatri	Nepal Police (Foreign)

Training Year: 1963; Batch: Dy Supdts CBI/ CRPF

842.	S. Sen	DySP/CBI
843.	K. Madhavan	DySP/CBI
844.	J. Trikha	DySP/CBI
845.	R.N. Sinha	DySP/CBI
846.	R.L. Vasishta	DySP/CBI
847.	P.S. Mahadevan	DySP/CBI
848.	S.P.S. Marwah	DySP/CBI
849.	R.C. Sharma	DySP/CBI
850.	S. Seshadri	DySP/CBI
851.	R.N. Sinha	DySP/CBI
852.	A.T. Thiruvengadam	DySP/Manipur
853.	V.V. Sardana	DySP/Manipur
854.	I.N. Vohra	DySP/Manipur
855.	M.N. Biswas	DySP/Tripura
856.	G.P. Joshi	DySP/Tripura
857.	S.K. Chatterjee	DySP/Tripura
858.	Chintamani Pandey	DySP/CRP
859.	K.N. Mathur	DySP/CRP
860.	B.S. Rekhi	DySP/CRP
861.	R.K. Sharma	DySP/CRP
862.	Mohinder Singh	DySP/CRP
863.	P.V. Subha Rao	DySP/CRP
864.	R.C. Roy	DySP/CRP
865.	B. Chakrabarti	DySP/CRP

866.	R. Santhanam	DySP/CRP
867.	R. Narayana	DySP/CRP
868.	N.K. Tiwary	DySP/CRP
869.	Y.P. Baxi	DySP/CRP
870.	K.L. Sachdev	DySP/CRP

Training Year: 1964; Batch: 1963 - IPS - RR-16

871.	V.S. Ravi	IPS/AP
872.	N.V. Vathsan	IPS/AP
873.	K.V. Sriram Kumar	IPS/AP
874.	M. Haridas Kachari	IPS/Assam
875.	S.K. Saxena	IPS/Bihar
876.	P.K. Datta	IPS/Gujarat
877.	K.N. Singh	IPS/Gujarat
878.	V. Kannu Pillai	IPS/Gujarat
879.	J.S. Bindra	IPS/Gujarat
880.	P.K. Bansal	IPS/Gujarat
881.	N. Krishnan Nair	IPS/Kerala
882.	M.A.S. Kunju	IPS/Kerala
883.	I. Thangaraj	IPS/Kerala
884.	S.C. Tripathi	IPS/MP
885.	Surjit Singh	IPS/MP
886.	N.K. Singh	IPS/MP
887.	S.C. Agrawal	IPS/MP
888.	A.V. Liddle	IPS/MP
889.	A.S. Bal	IPS/MP
890.	Nikhil Kumar	IPS/MP
891.	B.K. Damle	IPS/MP
892.	P.C. Mondal	IPS/MP
893.	O. Pillarswamy	IPS/MP
894.	V.K. Vohra	IPS/MP
895.	D.P. Maheshwari	IPS/MP

896.	R.K. Raghavan	IPS/Madras
897.	W.I. Davaram	IPS/Madras
898.	S.A. Harharane	IPS/Madras
899.	Satish Sahney	IPS/Maharashtra
900.	P. S. Narayanswami	IPS/Maharashtra
901.	C. Dinakar	IPS/Mysore
902.	Subhash Chandra	IPS/Mysore
903.	P.S. Uppund	IPS/Mysore
904.	J.E. George	IPS/Mysore
905.	S.N. Tewari	IPS/Orissa
906.	B.B. Panda	IPS/Orissa
907.	M.A. Balasubramanian	IPS/Orissa
908.	B.P. Saha	IPS/Orissa
909.	D.P.S. Chauhan	IPS/Orissa
910.	S.B. Jain	IPS/Orissa
911.	J.P. Atray	IPS/Punjab
912.	I.S. Bindra	IPS/Punjab
913.	Ramesh Sehgal	IPS/Punjab
914.	R.C. Sharma	IPS/Punjab
915.	Sube Singh	IPS/Punjab
916.	L.R. Bhagat	IPS/Punjab
917.	S.P. Singh	IPS/Rajasthan
918.	V.P. Bhatnagar	IPS/Rajasthan
919.	A.K. Srivastava	IPS/UP
920.	V.N. Misra	IPS/UP
921.	M.C. Dewedy	IPS/UP
922.	C.K. Mallick	IPS/UP
923.	Haridas Rao	IPS/UP
924.	B.R. Gupta	IPS/UP
925.	J.L. Varma	IPS/UP
926.	Shriram Arun	IPS/UP

927.	T.K. Talukdar	IPS/WB
928.	B.K. Singh	IPS/WB
929.	S. Bhandari	IPS/WB
930.	M.B. Kaushal	IPS/Delhi & HP
931.	K.N. Kapoor	IPS/Delhi & HP
932.	P.R. Sund	IPS/Delhi & HP
933.	K.S. Subramanian	IPS/Delhi & HP
934.	W. Damodar Singh	DySP/Manipur
935.	I.C. Singh	DySP/Manipur
936.	Ashok Chandorkar	DySP/MP
937.	M. Pathak	DySP/MP
938.	N.K. Dhoreliya	DySP/MP
939.	Bhagwant Singh	DySP/MP
940.	R.B. Pandit	DySP/MP
941.	M.C. Nigam	DySP/MP
942.	R.L. Varma	DySP/MP
943.	H.C. Trivedi	DySP/MP
944.	B.C. Sepaha	DySP/MP
945.	S.S. Warwade	DySP/MP

Training Year: 1964-65; Batch: 1964 - IPS-RR-17

946.	V.P. Bahuleyan Nair	IPS/AP
947.	A.P. Rajan	IPS/AP
948.	Ranju Das	IPS/Assam
949.	D.N.S. Shrivastava	IPS/Assam
950.	I.T. Longkumar	IPS/Assam
951.	S.K. Sinha	IPS/Bihar
952.	R.C. Mehta	IPS/Gujarat
953.	T.S. Viswanathan	IPS/Gujarat
954.	R.D. Tamhane	IPS/Gujarat
955.	P.G.J. Nampoothiri	IPS/Gujarat
956.	P.S. Ingty	IPS/Gujarat

957.	C.A. Chaly	IPS/Kerala
958.	B.S. Sastry	IPS/Kerala
959.	D. Das Gupta	IPS/MP
960.	S.N. Tiwari	IPS/MP
961.	Chaman Lal	IPS/MP
962.	A.N. Pathak	IPS/MP
963.	O.C. Sharma	IPS/MP
964.	R. Sehgal	IPS/MP
965.	G.S. Sahota	IPS/MP
966.	Bani Singh	IPS/MP
967.	A.S. Inamdar	IPS/MP
968.	K. Sreenivasan	IPS/Mysore
969.	D.R. Karthikeyan	IPS/Mysore
970.	T. Srinivasulu	IPS/Mysore
971.	P. Kodandaramaiah	IPS/Mysore
972.	S.C. Barman	IPS/Mysore
973.	A.K. Pattanayak	IPS/Orissa
974.	Sridhar Misra	IPS/Orissa
975.	V. Appa Rao	IPS/AP
976.	S.K. Chatopadhyay	IPS/Orissa
977.	B.B. Nandy	IPS/Orissa
978.	B.S. Varma	IPS/Punjab
979.	S.R. Sharma	IPS/Punjab
980.	R.L. Wadhwa	IPS/Punjab
981.	V.K. Wadhwa	IPS/Punjab
982.	J.C. Gogoi	IPS/Punjab
983.	Budh Ram	IPS/Punjab
984.	Amitabh Gupta	IPS/Rajasthan
985.	V. Nath	IPS/Rajasthan
986.	S.P.S. Rathore	IPS/Rajasthan
987.	D.V. Mehta	IPS/UP

988.	R.C. Dikshit	IPS/UP
989.	G.B.S. Sidhu	IPS/UP
990.	B.P. Singh	IPS/UP
991.	J.K.P. Singh	IPS/UP
992.	R.P. Saroj	IPS/UP
993.	M.K. Dhar	IPS/WB
994.	S.K. Mukherjee	IPS/WB
995.	T.P.S. Rajan	IPS/WB
996.	K.L.S. Baidwan	IPS/WB
997.	Kamalesh Roy	IPS/WB
998.	M.N. Sabharwal	IPS/J&K
999.	A.K. Kapoor	IPS/J&K
1000.	Rajendra Mohan	IPS/Delhi & HP
1001.	R.C. Sharma	IPS/Delhi & HP
1002.	R.K. Srivastava	IPS/Delhi & HP
1003.	P.S. Bawa	IPS/Delhi & HP
1004.	A.K. Singh	IPS/Delhi & HP
1005.	Lashkari Ram	IPS/Delhi & HP
1006.	Prakash Singh	IPS/Delhi & HP
1007.	S.K. Singh	DySP/Delhi & HP
1008.	V. Vaidyanathan	DySP/Delhi & HP
1009.	Gopi Ram Gupta	DySP/Delhi & HP
1010.	K. Panchapagesan	DySP/Delhi & HP
1011.	Nungshiliba Ao	DySP/Nagaland
1012.	Mangkholian Sitlthu	DySP/Nagaland
1013.	Nungsangkaba	DySP/Nagaland
1014.	A.B. Singh	Nepal Police (Foreign)
1015.	R.S. Thapa	Nepal Police (Foreign)

Training Year: 1965-66; Batch - 1965 -IPS-RR-18

1016.	H.J. Dora	IPS/AP
1017.	M.M. Sagar	IPS/Assam

1018.	D.K. Das	IPS/Assam
1019.	E.N. Rammohan	IPS/Assam
1020.	B.N. Jha	IPS/Assam
1021.	P.K. Misra	IPS/Assam
1022.	F.L.R. Siama	IPS/Assam
1023.	K. Chakravarti	IPS/Gujarat
1024.	R.P.C. Nair	IPS/Gujarat
1025.	M.A. Nomani	IPS/J&K
1026.	P.R. Chandran	IPS/Kerala
1027.	W.J. Dawson	IPS/Kerala
1028.	V.P. Singh	IPS/MP
1029.	A.K. Babbar	IPS/MP
1030.	Y.S. Patro	IPS/MP
1031.	N.R. Deo	IPS/MP
1032.	P.V. Rajagopal	IPS/MP
1033.	R. Sivaswamy	IPS/MP
1034.	Mohan Shukla	IPS/MP
1035.	G. Veeraraghavan	IPS/Madras
1036.	A. Ravindranath	IPS/Madras
1037.	A.A. Khan	IPS/Maharashtra
1038.	Gian Chand	IPS/Maharashtra
1039.	V.K. Talwar	IPS/Maharashtra
1040.	G.N. Ubale	IPS/Maharashtra
1041.	V.V. Bhaskar	IPS/Mysore
1042.	L. Revannasiddaiah	IPS/Mysore
1043.	B.M. Yashvantgol	IPS/Mysore
1044.	D.K. Mahapatra	IPS/Orissa
1045.	B. B. Nanda	IPS/Orissa
1046.	R.C. Mohanty	IPS/Orissa
1047.	Janardhan Singh	IPS/Orissa
1048.	K.D. Bajpai	IPS/Orissa

1049.	S.M. Mathur	IPS/Orissa
1050.	John Nayak	IPS/Orissa
1051.	Sarabjit Singh	IPS/Punjab
1052.	R.P. Rai	IPS/Punjab
1053.	S. Kumar	IPS/Punjab
1054.	S.P.S. Rathore	IPS/Punjab
1055.	A.S. Dulat	IPS/Rajasthan
1056.	Trinath Misra	IPS/UP
1057.	A.C. Sharma	IPS/UP
1058.	Kanhaiya Lal	IPS/UP
1059.	J.P. Roy	IPS/UP
1060.	Lakshman Prasad	IPS/UP
1061.	A.K. Sharan	IPS/UP
1062.	Ram Rakha	IPS/UP
1063.	M.K. Raju	IPS/UP
1064.	S.C. Mishra	IPS/WB
1065.	K.K. Kalia	IPS/WB
1066.	A.R. Khan	IPS/WB
1067.	S. Datta	IPS/WB
1068.	Suman Sanyal	IPS/WB
1069.	D.K. Sanyal	IPS/WB
1070.	S. Laskar	IPS/WB
1071.	T. Misao	IPS/WB
1072.	Tilak Raj	IPS/Delhi & HP
1073.	Kishan Singh	IPS/Delhi & HP
1074.	I.N.S. Sandhu	IPS/Delhi & HP
1075.	Kulbir Singh	IPS/Delhi & HP
1076.	Gautam Kaul	IPS/Delhi & HP
1077.	P.S. Kumar	IPS/Delhi & HP
1078.	S. Johia	IPS/Delhi & HP
1079.	Kartar Singh	IPS/Delhi & HP

1080.	K.K. Bhargava	IPS/Delhi & HP
1081.	W.M. Keishing	DySP/Manipur
1082.	T.K. Singh	DySP/Manipur
1083.	R.K. Niyogi	DySP/Delhi & HP
1084.	P.R.S. Brar	DySP/Delhi & HP
1085.	R.P. Misra	DySP/Delhi & HP
1086.	O.S. Singh	DySP/Delhi & HP
1087.	Kali Caran	DySP/Delhi & HP
1088.	M.V. Prasad	DySP/Delhi & HP
1089.	V. Rai	DySP/Delhi & HP
1090.	R. Tewari	DySP/Delhi & HP
1091.	Lalbahadur Basnet	Bhutan Police (Foreign)
1092.	K.G. Paljor	Bhutan Police (Foreign)

Training Year: 1966-67; Batch - 1966 -IPS-RR-19

1093.	S.C. Dwivedi	IPS/AP
1094.	C.A. Reddy	IPS/AP
1095.	Janak Raj	IPS/AP
1096.	P.K. Mahanta	IPS/Assam
1097.	Gautam Barooah	IPS/Assam
1098.	P.C. Sharma	IPS/Assam
1099.	N. Ramakrishnan	IPS/Assam
1100.	V.N. Sharma	IPS/Assam
1101.	Gopal Achari	IPS/Bihar
1102.	Y.N. Srivastava	IPS/Bihar
1103.	T.P. Sinha	IPS/Bihar
1104.	Shiv Murti Rai	IPS/Bihar
1105.	S. Banerjee	IPS/Gujarat
1106.	J.R. Ahir	IPS/Gujarat
1107.	R. Bhattacharya	IPS/Gujarat
1108.	K.S. Chaturvedi	IPS/Gujarat
1109.	B. Guha	IPS/Gujarat

1110.	Y.S. Harishankar	IPS/Haryana
1111.	Veeranna Aivalli	IPS/J&K
1112.	R. Padmanabhan	IPS/Kerala
1113.	A.V. Subba Rao	IPS/Kerala
1114.	A. Kshetrapal	IPS/MP
1115.	V. K. Das	IPS/MP
1116.	K.P. Singh	IPS/MP
1117.	M.K. Shukla	IPS/MP
1118.	U.M. Joshi	IPS/MP
1119.	A.N. Singh	IPS/MP
1120.	D.C. Jugran	IPS/MP
1121.	S.P. Dangwal	IPS/MP
1122.	D.C. Mohan	IPS/MP
1123.	R.L.S. Negi	IPS/MP
1124.	R.S. Yadav	IPS/MP
1125.	P.C. Pant	IPS/Madras
1126.	S.K.K. Iyengar	IPS/Maharasthra
1127.	R.H. Mendonca	IPS/Maharasthra
1128.	D.C. Malhotra	IPS/Maharasthra
1129.	B. Akashi	IPS/Maharasthra
1130.	P.S. Ramanujam	IPS/Mysore
1131.	R. Viswanathan	IPS/Mysore
1132.	B.R. Das	IPS/Orissa
1133.	P.C. Padhi	IPS/Orissa
1134.	B.B. Singh	IPS/Orissa
1135.	J.P. Varma	IPS/Orissa
1136.	A. Ramudu	IPS/Orissa
1137.	Gurbachan Jagat	IPS/Punjab
1138.	L.M. Mehta	IPS/Punjab
1139.	B.S. Pawar	IPS/Punjab
1140.	J.P. Aswal	IPS/Punjab

1141.	Shantanu Kumar	IPS/Rajasthan
1142.	A.K. Bhandari	IPS/Rajasthan
1143.	Y.K. Mishra	IPS/UP
1144.	M. Ahmed	IPS/UP
1145.	S.C. Chaube	IPS/UP
1146.	A.R. Sharma	IPS/UP
1147.	R.S. Pushkar	IPS/UP
1148.	Sunder Lal	IPS/UP
1149.	M.K. Chakrabarti	IPS/WB
1150.	D. Banerjee	IPS/WB
1151.	S.K. Ghosh	IPS/WB
1152.	R. Sharma	IPS/WB
1153.	K.P. Bandhopadhyay	IPS/WB
1154.	D.C. Vajpai	IPS/WB
1155.	I. Sangtam	IPS/WB
1156.	S. Sundarajan	IPS/Delhi & HP
1157.	R.C. Kohli	IPS/Delhi & HP
1158.	V.M. Singh	IPS/Delhi & HP
1159.	V.S. Sandhu	IPS/Delhi & HP
1160.	Y.R. Dhuriya	IPS/Delhi & HP
1161.	V.K. Malik	IPS/Delhi & HP
1162.	B.C. Negi	DySP/Delhi & HP
1163.	Balwant Singh	DySP/Delhi & HP
1164.	B. Pandit	DySP/Delhi & HP
1165.	H.S. Vir.	DySP/Delhi & HP
1166.	B. Dubey	DySP/CBI
1167.	G. Singh	DySP/CBI
1168.	R.N. Kaul	DySP/CBI
1169.	Sang Kwon Kim	Korean Police (Foreign)
1170.	Jin Mo Kang	Korean Police (Foreign)

Training Year: 1967-68; Batch - 1967 -IPS-RR-20

1171.	Ramulu Pervar	IPS/AP
1172.	S.K. Sukumara	IPS/AP
1173.	S. Kodali Rao	IPS/AP
1174.	B. Barthakur	IPS/Assam
1175.	P.V. Sumant	IPS/Assam
1176.	Leslie David	IPS/Assam
1177.	G.N. Das	IPS/Assam
1178.	J.K. Sinha	IPS/Bihar
1179.	A.K. Pandey	IPS/Bihar
1180.	W.H. Khan	IPS/Bihar
1181.	D.P. Ojha	IPS/Bihar
1182.	Santosh Kumar	IPS/Bihar
1183.	S.M. Cairae	IPS/Bihar
1184.	Baljit Singh	IPS/Bihar
1185.	V.S. Ghuman	IPS/Gujarat
1186.	S.K. Saha	IPS/Gujarat
1187.	S.H. Mohan	IPS/Haryana
1188.	B.R. Lall	IPS/Haryana
1189.	Ram Prakash	IPS/J&K
1190.	S.S. Ali	IPS/J&K
1191.	T.S.V. Pillai	IPS/Kerala
1192.	R.S. Mooshahary	IPS/Kerala
1193.	G.K. Sinha	IPS/MP
1194.	Anand Kumar	IPS/MP
1195.	R. Pandey	IPS/MP
1196.	A.K. Kar	IPS/MP
1197.	Amar Bhushan	IPS/MP
1198.	S. Raza	IPS/MP
1199.	G.P. Dubey	IPS/MP
1200.	S. Ramakrishnan	IPS/Madras

1201.	B.P. Nailwal	IPS/Madras
1202.	S. Ganapathy	IPS/Madras
1203.	V.K. Rajagopal	IPS/Madras
1204.	Y.S. Jafa	IPS/Maharashtra
1205.	M.N. Singh	IPS/Maharashtra
1206.	R.S. Negi	IPS/Maharashtra
1207.	M.R. Reddy	IPS/Maharashtra
1208.	S.S. Puri	IPS/Maharashtra
1209.	O.P. Bali	IPS/Maharashtra
1210.	T. Singaravel	IPS/Maharashtra
1211.	B.N. Misra	IPS/Maharashtra
1212.	U.D. Rajwade	IPS/Maharashtra
1213.	R.C. Dembla	IPS/Maharashtra
1214.	M.G. Narvane	IPS/Maharashtra
1215.	C.S. Azad	IPS/Maharashtra
1216.	C.D. Sahay	IPS/Mysore
1217.	K.U. Shetty	IPS/Mysore
1218.	S. Krishnamurthy	IPS/Mysore
1219.	H.T. Sangliana	IPS/Mysore
1220.	B.P. Misra	IPS/Orissa
1221.	A.A. Shahed	IPS/Orissa
1222.	P.K. Senapati	IPS/Orissa
1223.	S. Singh	IPS/Orissa
1224.	L.C. Amaranathan	IPS/Orissa
1225.	S.S. Mann	IPS/Punjab
1226.	R.P. Joshi	IPS/Punjab
1227.	S.V. Singh	IPS/Punjab
1228.	S.K. Verma	IPS/Punjab
1229.	B.P. Tiwari	IPS/Punjab
1230.	B.S. Rathore	IPS/Rajasthan
1231.	Prabhat Narain	IPS/Rajasthan

1232.	S.S. Darbari	IPS/Rajasthan
1233.	R.M. Shukla	IPS/UP
1234.	K.K. Bansal	IPS/UP
1235.	G. Jha	IPS/UP
1236.	M. Lalka	IPS/UP
1237.	Radhey Shyam	IPS/UP
1238.	T.A. Khan	IPS/WB
1239.	Sunder Singh	IPS/WB
1240.	H.A. Safwi	IPS/WB
1241.	B.P. Singh	IPS/WB
1242.	V. Sahai	IPS/WB
1243.	R.K. Handa	IPS/WB
1244.	M.K. Singh	IPS/WB
1245.	S.K. Sarkar	IPS/WB
1246.	G.C. Pander	IPS/DHANI
1247.	A.K. Murarka	IPS/DHANI
1248.	A.K. Puri	IPS/DHANI
1249.	S. Ramakrishnan	IPS/DHANI
1250.	R.L. Verma	IPS/DHANI
1251.	R.K. Sharma	IPS/DHANI
1252.	D.K. Kasyap	IPS/DHANI
1253.	D.S. Amist	DySP/DHANI
1254.	Puram Singh	DySP/DHANI
1255.	B.N. Ghosh	DySP/CBI
1256.	D. Bagchi	DySP/CBI
1257.	S. Mukherjee	DySP/CBI
1258.	Kepon Tan Dorji	Bhutan Police (Foreign)
1259.	Harish Kumar Gurung	Bhutan Police (Foreign)

Training Year: 1968-69; Batch: 1968 -IPS-RR-21

1260.	E.S.L. Narasimhan	IPS/AP
1261.	P.A. Reddy	IPS/AP

1262.	C. Ramaswamy	IPS/AP
1263.	H. Deka	IPS/Assam
1264.	J.D. Singh	IPS/Assam
1265.	K. Hrishikesan	IPS/Assam
1266.	K. Lalchhunga	IPS/Assam
1267.	Anil Kumar	IPS/Bihar
1268.	R.C. Khan	IPS/Bihar
1269.	K. Abraham Jacob	IPS/Bihar
1270.	J.S. Mehta	IPS/Bihar
1271.	B. Srinivasan	IPS/Bihar
1272.	R.H. Das	IPS/Bihar
1273.	B.B. Bhasin	IPS/Gujarat
1274.	Hiralal	IPS/Gujarat
1275.	Ram Mohan Ambat	IPS/J&K
1276.	A.K. Doval	IPS/Kerala
1277.	P.K.H. Tharankan	IPS/Kerala
1278.	Tapeshwar Sharma	IPS/Kerala
1279.	D.S. Gill	IPS/MP
1280.	N.C. Padhi	IPS/MP
1281.	A. Darbari	IPS/MP
1282.	Ajit P.K. Jogi	IPS/MP
1283.	B.R. Nirmal	IPS/MP
1284.	S.K. Saxena	IPS/MP
1285.	S. Kumaraswamy	IPS/TN
1286.	F.C. Sharma	IPS/TN
1287.	Taj Prakash	IPS/TN
1288.	R.B. Sharma	IPS/Maharashtra
1289.	R.D. Tyagi	IPS/Maharashtra
1290.	R. Srinivasan	IPS/Maharashtra
1291.	S.M. Shangari	IPS/Maharashtra
1292.	K.M. Singh	IPS/Maharashtra

1293.	P.K. Joshi	IPS/Maharashtra
1294.	A.K. Agarwal	IPS/Maharashtra
1295.	Sudhir Kumar	IPS/Maharashtra
1296.	N.V. Lungalang	IPS/Maharashtra
1297.	H.N. Sambharya	IPS/Maharashtra
1298.	S.A. Subbiah	IPS/Mysore
1299.	S.K. Bajerjee	IPS/Mysore
1300.	M.D. Singh	IPS/Mysore
1301.	S. Prasad	IPS/Mysore
1302.	I.J. Jachuck	IPS/Orissa
1303.	Umashankar Misra	IPS/Orissa
1304.	K.M. Lal	IPS/Orissa
1305.	M.M.R. Batra	IPS/Punjab
1306.	Puran Chand	IPS/Punjab
1307.	Anil Prakash Bhatnagar	IPS/Punjab
1308.	K.K. Sharma	IPS/Punjab
1309.	V.B. Singh	IPS/Rajasthan
1310.	R.S. Sahaya	IPS/UT
1311.	Gurcharan Singh	IPS/UT
1312.	S.C. Malik	IPS/UT
1313.	R.D. Gupta	IPS/UT
1314.	T.R. Kakkar	IPS/UT
1315.	D. Prasad	IPS/UT
1316.	D.S. Grewal	IPS/UT
1317.	R.P. Kureel	IPS/UT
1318.	S.K. Sharma	IPS/UP
1319.	R.C. Agarwal	IPS/UP
1320.	S.P. Singh	IPS/UP
1321.	S.R. Aiyangar	IPS/UP
1322.	R.S. Dhatt	IPS/UP
1323.	P. S. V. Prasad	IPS/UP

1324. S.M. Nasim IPS/UP
1325. C.D. Premi IPS/UP
1326. R.K. Sharma IPS/WB
1327. T.K. Mitra IPS/WB
1328. V. Kumar IPS/WB
1329. Sultan Singh IPS/WB
1330. Madan Gopal IPS/WB
1331. S.K. Dutt IPS/WB
1332. U. Biswas IPS/WB
1333. B.B. Negi IPS/WB
1334. Indrajit Kumar DySP/UT
1335. Hang Singh Chemiong Nepal Police (Foreign)
1336. Indrabahadur Sher Chand Nepal Police (Foreign)

Training Year: 1969-70; Batch; 1969 -IPS-RR-22

1337. A. Subhas Chandra Bose IPS/AP
1338. B. Danam IPS/AP
1339. Anil Chowdhry IPS/Assam
1340. J.K. Sinha IPS/Bihar
1341. R. R. Prasad IPS/Bihar
1342. A.N. Singh IPS/Bihar
1343. Narayan Mishra IPS/Bihar
1344. R.B. Ram IPS/Bihar
1345. Ram Swaroop IPS/Bihar
1346. S.K. Sood IPS/UT
1347. A.K. Srivastava IPS/UT
1348. Mathew John IPS/UT
1349. T. Dawa IPS/UT
1350. S.P. Mehta IPS/UT
1351. A.C. Bhargava IPS/Gujarat
1352. C.P. Singh IPS/Gujarat
1353. A.K. Suri IPS/J&K

1354.	O.P. Bhaskar	IPS/J&K
1355.	K.J. Joseph	IPS/Kerala
1356.	Chandra Pal	IPS/Kerala
1357.	V.K. Deuskar	IPS/MP
1358.	S.K. Banerjee	IPS/MP
1359.	Yatish Chandra	IPS/MP
1360.	R. Chaturvedi	IPS/MP
1361.	Sukhpal Singh	IPS/MP
1362.	S.K. Das	IPS/MP
1363.	R.V. Subramanian	IPS/TN
1364.	R.K. Gupta	IPS/TN
1365.	R. Rajagopalan	IPS/TN
1366.	I.K. Govind	IPS/TN
1367.	V.C. Kishore	IPS/TN
1368.	K.K. Kashyap	IPS/Maharashtra
1369.	Y.S. Rao	IPS/Mysore
1370.	Jai Prakash	IPS/Mysore
1371.	B.N.P. Albuquerque	IPS/Mysore
1372.	B.K. Swain	IPS/Orissa
1373.	A.S. Atwal	IPS/Punjab
1374.	J.S. Chahal	IPS/Punjab
1375.	Purshottam Lal	IPS/Punjab
1376.	V.N. Mathur	IPS/Punjab
1377.	Gurdial Singh	IPS/Punjab
1378.	S.B. Panwar	IPS/Rajasthan
1379.	Arun Dugar	IPS/Rajasthan
1380.	M.S. Pareek	IPS/Rajasthan
1381.	S.N. Jairath	IPS/Rajasthan
1382.	N.N. Meena	IPS/Rajasthan
1383.	R.N. Sharma	IPS/UP
1384.	A.A. Kurian	IPS/UP

1385.	H. Kumar	IPS/UP
1386.	Jangi Singh	IPS/UP
1387.	S.K. Chakrabarti	IPS/WB
1388.	K.J. Singh	IPS/WB
1389.	Uday Veer	IPS/WB
1390.	J.M. Hakim	IPS/WB
1391.	Ajay Prasad	IPS/WB
1392.	M. Tumsanga	IPS/WB
1393.	K.K. Das	IPS/WB
1394.	Shiv Kumar	DySP/DHANI
1395.	K. Kannan	DySP/Manipur
1396.	N.K. Mukhopadhyay	DySP/Manipur
1397.	Krishna Pal Singh	DySP/Manipur
1398.	B.P. Mishra	DySP/Manipur
1399.	Balasubramanian	DySP/CBI
1400.	R.M. Singh	DySP/CBI

Training Year: 1970-71; Batch - 1970 -IPS-RR-23

1401.	Bharath Chandra	IPS/AP
1402.	Jaspal Singh	IPS/AP
1403.	Swatantra Singh	IPS/AP
1404.	Shyam Ratan Mehta	IPS/Assam
1405.	P.G. Haldar	IPS/Bihar
1406.	S.C. Jha	IPS/Bihar
1407.	R.R. Prasad	IPS/Bihar
1408.	Amber Sen	IPS/Bihar
1409.	G.S. Aujla	IPS/Punjab
1410.	M.S. Aulakh	IPS/Punjab
1411.	P.C. Pande	IPS/Gujarat
1412.	Vikas	IPS/Haryana
1413.	Ajit Narayan	IPS/HP
1414.	N.C. Joshi	IPS/HP

1415.	Anjan Ghosh	IPS/J&K
1416.	A.C. Chaturvedi	IPS/J&K
1417.	R. Tikoo	IPS/J&K
1418.	K.J. Thomas	IPS/Kerala
1419.	A. Chaturvedi	IPS/MP
1420.	A.X. Alexander	IPS/TN
1421.	S. Ramani	IPS/TN
1422.	C.S. Munzni	IPS/TN
1423.	S.S. Virk	IPS/Maharashtra
1424.	P.S. Pasricha	IPS/Maharashtra
1425.	V.B. Sasnur	IPS/Mysore
1426.	R.P. Gadegawanlia	IPS/Mysore
1427.	R.K. Sachar	IPS/Orissa
1428.	P.C. Mishra	IPS/Orissa
1429.	Lalit Bhatia	IPS/Punjab
1430.	S.C. Jain	IPS/Punjab
1431.	D.R. Bhatti	IPS/Punjab
1432.	Ajai Singh	IPS/Rajasthan
1433.	K.K. Chaturvedi	IPS/UP
1434.	A.K. Mitra	IPS/UP
1435.	R.K. Pandit	IPS/UP
1436.	R.C. Sharma	IPS/UP
1437.	R.K. Das	IPS/UP
1438.	Choote Lal	IPS/UP
1439.	V.K. Jha	IPS/UP
1440.	P.K. Vinayak	IPS/WB
1441.	T. Chatopadhyay	IPS/WB
1442.	S.C. Awasti	IPS/WB
1443.	R.K. Mohanti	IPS/WB
1444.	S.I.S. Ahmed	IPS/WB
1445.	B.K. Sharma	IPS/WB

1446.	D. Tshering	IPS/WB
1447.	K.K. Paul	IPS/UT
1448.	R. Sundararaj	IPS/UT
1449.	S.K. Kain	IPS/UT
1450.	T.N. Tenzing	IPS/UT
1451.	K.G. Vidyasagar	DySP/CBI
1452.	A.W. Degwekar	DySP/CBI
1453.	K.C. Kanungo	DySP/CBI
1454.	H.R. Mina	DySP/CBI
1455.	J. Changkika	DySP/Nagaland
1456.	N.N. Walling	DySP/Nagaland
1457.	N. Aonochet	DySP/Nagaland
1458.	Kalikant Jha	DySP/Tripura
1459.	R.S. Bajaj	DySP/Tripura

Training Year: 1971-72; Batch: 1971 -IPS-RR-24

1460.	B.M.R. Rao	IPS/AP
1461.	K.K. Srivastava	IPS/AP
1462.	D.N. Dutt	IPS/Assam
1463.	M.K. Sinha	IPS/Bihar
1464.	K.K. Attri	IPS/Bihar
1465.	K.C. Verma	IPS/Bihar
1466.	V.K. Joshi	IPS/Bihar
1467.	Mani Ram	IPS/Gujarat
1468.	R.B.Sreekumar	IPS/Gujarat
1469.	B. Mahapatra	IPS/HP
1470.	K.G. Mahalingam	IPS/J&K
1471.	M.K. Mohanty	IPS/J&K
1472.	T.P. Gopinathan	IPS/Kerala
1473.	Upendra Verma	IPS/Kerala
1474.	R.K. Diwaker	IPS/MP
1475.	Basudeo Dubey	IPS/MP

1476.	G.S. Mathur	IPS/MP
1477.	Avtar Singh	IPS/MP
1478.	P.K.B. Chakravarty	IPS/Maharashtra
1479.	V.K. Jain	IPS/Maharashtra
1480.	Rahul Gopal	IPS/Maharashtra
1481.	T. Madiyal	IPS/Mysore
1482.	B.S. Sial	IPS/Mysore
1483.	Suchit Das	IPS/Orissa
1484.	S.R. Shangpliang	IPS/Orissa
1485.	M.S. Bhullar	IPS/Punjab
1486.	G.S. Bhullar	IPS/Punjab
1487.	S.P. Sharma	IPS/Punjab
1488.	R. Kumar	IPS/Rajasthan
1489.	V.K. Hansuka	IPS/Rajasthan
1490.	G.S. Rajagopal	IPS/Rajasthan
1491.	C. Babu Rajeev	IPS/Rajasthan
1492.	A. Sahasranaman	IPS/TN
1493.	D. Mukherjee	IPS/TN
1494.	C. Prakash	IPS/UT
1495.	A.K. Agarwal	IPS/UT
1496.	K.T. Chacko	IPS/UT
1497.	Rewari Lal (Ashok Kumar Singh)	IPS/UP
1498.	M.S. Yadav	IPS/UP
1499.	D.K. Panda	IPS/UP
1500.	Tilak Kak	IPS/UP
1501.	C.D. Kainth	IPS/UP
1502.	V.K. B. Nair	IPS/UP
1503.	S.K. Guha	IPS/WB
1504.	R.K. Majumdar	IPS/WB
1505.	S. Zosangliana	IPS/WB
1506.	J.K. Dutt	IPS/WB

1507.	V.K. Mehta	IPS/WB
1508.	Hem Chand	IPS/WB
1509.	D. Mishra	DySP/Manipur
1510.	Eric Ekka	DySP/Manipur
1511.	P.C. Sharma	DySP/Manipur
1512.	N. Rajendran	DySP/Tripura
1513.	P.K. Pradhan	Sikkim Police(Foreign)
1514.	K.W. Tshering	Bhutan Police(Foreign)
1515.	K.R. Thinlay	Bhutan Police(Foreign)

Training Year: 1972-73; Batch: 1972 -IPS-RR-25

1516.	P.V. Naidu	IPS/AP
1517.	M.L. Kumawat	IPS/AP
1518.	S.S.P. Yadav	IPS/AP
1519.	C.H.K. Rao	IPS/AP
1520.	G.M. Srivastava	IPS/Assam
1521.	L. Sailo	IPS/Assam
1522.	A.R. Singh	IPS/Bihar
1523.	J.B. Mahapatra	IPS/Bihar
1524.	R. Oraon	IPS/Bihar
1525.	Gurinder Singh	IPS/Gujarat
1526.	K.K. Shahi	IPS/Gujarat
1527.	K.R. Kaushik	IPS/Gujarat
1528.	G.C. Raiger	IPS/Gujarat
1529.	Lachhman Das	IPS/Haryana
1530.	Gopal Sharma	IPS/J&K
1531.	S.C. Mina	IPS/J&K
1532.	Rajan Baxi	IPS/J&K
1533.	M.G.A. Ramen	IPS/Kerala
1534.	Avtar Krishan	IPS/MP
1535.	A.R. Pawar	IPS/MP
1536.	O.P. Garg	IPS/MP

1537.	D.R. Bains	IPS/MP
1538.	A.N. Roy	IPS/Maharashtra
1539.	J.D. Virkar	IPS/Maharashtra
1540.	S. Chakravarty	IPS/Maharashtra
1541.	K.R. Srinivasan	IPS/Mysore
1542.	S. Mariswamy	IPS/Mysore
1543.	B.B. Mahanty	IPS/Orissa
1544.	R.N. Gupta	IPS/Orissa
1545.	R.K. Sharma	IPS/Punjab
1546.	N.S. Aulakh	IPS/Punjab
1547.	D.P. Sinha	IPS/Punjab
1548.	R.S. Chalia	IPS/Punjab
1549.	M.L. Sharma	IPS/Rajasthan
1550.	A.S. Gill	IPS/Rajasthan
1551.	P.K. Tiwari	IPS/Rajasthan
1552.	P.N. Rachhoya	IPS/Rajasthan
1553.	I.R. Arumugam	IPS/TN
1554.	Deepak Samal	IPS/TN
1555.	S.P. Mathur	IPS/TN
1556.	P. Kalimuthu	IPS/TN
1557.	K.P. Bedi	IPS/UT
1558.	Rajeev Mathur	IPS/UP
1559.	S.K. Tripathi	IPS/UP
1560.	G.L. Sharma	IPS/UP
1561.	Y.P. Singh	IPS/UP
1562.	Ajai Singh	IPS/UP
1563.	S.S. Banerjee	IPS/UP
1564.	Govind Vyas	IPS/UP
1565.	Harmol Singh	IPS/UP
1566.	J.S. Ghungesh	IPS/UP
1567.	K.C. Singh	IPS/UP

1568.	C.B. Satpathy	IPS/UP
1569.	Sarvan Ram	IPS/UP
1570.	A.B. Vohra	IPS/WB
1571.	P. Bhattacharya	IPS/WB
1572.	R.P. Singh	IPS/WB
1573.	Sarvesh Chandra	IPS/WB
1574.	A.K. Abrol	IPS/WB
1575.	A.K. Gupta	IPS/WB
1576.	D. Sarangi	IPS/WB
1577.	Nikhilesh Das	IPS/WB
1578.	S.K. Sarkar	IPS/WB
1579.	G.C. Murmu	IPS/WB
1580.	C. Kiko	DySP/Nagaland
1581.	V. Peseyie	DySP/Nagaland
1582.	T. Jamir	DySP/Nagaland
1583.	T.M. Wati	DySP/Nagaland
1584.	Murari Lal	DySP/CBI
1585.	A.K. Suri	DySP/CBI
1586.	M.K. Chetri	Sikkim Police (Foreign)
1587.	E.S. Lesita	Lesotha Police (Foreign)

Training Year: 1973-74; Batch: 1973 -IPS-RR-26

1588.	A.K. Srivastava	IPS/AP
1589.	Ramavatar Yadav	IPS/AP
1590.	Swaranjit Sen	IPS/AP
1591.	Ram Pratap Singh	IPS/AP
1592.	Sharda Prasad	IPS/A&M
1593.	Ravindra Nath Mathur	IPS/A&M
1594.	Manoje Nath	IPS/Bihar
1595.	Birendra Kumar Sinha	IPS/Bihar
1596.	Vishnu Dayal Ram	IPS/Bihar
1597.	Nehchal Sandhu	IPS/Bihar

1598.	Ajit Datt	IPS/Bihar
1599.	Ram Singh	IPS/Bihar
1600.	S.S. Khandwawala	IPS/Gujarat
1601.	Gurdial Singh	IPS/Gujarat
1602.	Ashok Sinha	IPS/Gujarat
1603.	A.K. Bhargava	IPS/Gujarat
1604.	Hari Chand Solanki	IPS/Gujarat
1605.	A.S. Bhatotia	IPS/Haryana
1606.	Koshy Koshy	IPS/Haryana
1607.	Nirmal Singh	IPS/Haryana
1608.	Ashwani Kumar	IPS/HP
1609.	K. Sukumaran Nair	IPS/Kerala
1610.	Raman Srivastava	IPS/Kerala
1611.	Pramod Kumar Sharma	IPS/MP
1612.	S.K. Puri	IPS/MP
1613.	Vishwa Ranjan	IPS/MP
1614.	C.P.G. Unni	IPS/MP
1615.	Raman Kakar	IPS/MP
1616.	Om Prakash Rathor	IPS/MP
1617.	Banwari Lal	IPS/MP
1618.	T.K. Choudhary	IPS/Maharashtra
1619.	J.Y. Umranikar	IPS/Maharashtra
1620.	D.N. Jadhav	IPS/Maharashtra
1621.	R.G. Bansod	IPS/Maharashtra
1622.	R.S. Sharma	IPS/Maharashtra
1623.	Gurcharan Singh	IPS/Maharashtra
1624.	Pramod Chandra Bisaria	IPS/Maharashtra
1625.	Bir Singh	IPS/Maharashtra
1626.	Rajan Homchandra Gupta	IPS/Karnataka
1627.	Virendra Diwan	IPS/Karnataka
1628.	S. Bhaskara Rao	IPS/Karnataka

1629.	Amarananda Pattanayak	IPS/Orissa
1630.	Ajit Singh	IPS/Punjab
1631.	Rajdeep Singh Gill	IPS/Punjab
1632.	Sadhu Singh Nahar	IPS/Punjab
1633.	Girish Chandra Varma	IPS/Punjab
1634.	A.A. Siddiqui	IPS/Punjab
1635.	R.S. Chauhan	IPS/Rajasthan
1636.	Hari Narayan Meena	IPS/Rajasthan
1637.	Arun Sharan	IPS/Rajasthan
1638.	Ajit Kumar Saxena	IPS/Rajasthan
1639.	Ms. S. Mitra Kumari	IPS/TN
1640.	K. Natarajan	IPS/TN
1641.	P. Rajendran	IPS/TN
1642.	R.R.P. Narayan Sahi	IPS/TN
1643.	K.N.V.R.M. Gopala Krishna	IPS/TN
1644.	Deepak Samal	IPS/TN
1645.	Seva Dass	IPS/UT
1646.	Suresh Roy	IPS/UT
1647.	Padam Singh	IPS/UT
1648.	Vikram Srivastava	IPS/UP
1649.	Sunil Krishna	IPS/UP
1650.	Syed Khalid Rizvi	IPS/UP
1651.	Rakesh Mittal	IPS/UP
1652.	Vijay Shankar	IPS/UP
1653.	R.S. Sirohi	IPS/UP
1654.	Prem Dutt Raturi	IPS/UP
1655.	Kanchan Choudhary (Ms.)	IPS/UP
1656.	R. Srikumar	IPS/UP
1657.	Hakam Singh	IPS/UP
1658.	Thangjamang Gwite	IPS/UP
1659.	Bua Singh	IPS/UP

1660.	Chaman Lal	IPS/UP
1661.	Prasun Mukherjee	IPS/WB
1662.	K.K. Mandal	IPS/WB
1663.	Balkar Singh	IPS/WB
1664.	M.P. Malhotra	IPS/WB
1665.	Niraj Ranjan Das	IPS/WB
1666.	Vinod Kumar Sharma	IPS/WB
1667.	Jose Jacob Tharayil	IPS/WB
1668.	Raj Kamal Johri	IPS/WB
1669.	S.C. Agarwal	IPS/WB
1670.	Sankaran Ramarkishnan	IPS/WB
1671.	H. Upadhyay	IPS/WB
1672.	J.R. Bhagat	IPS/WB
1673.	Bijan Kumar Dey	IPS/WB
1674.	Chhajoo Ram Meena	IPS/WB
1675.	Lanumenan Ao	DySP/Nagaland
1676.	A.K. Majumdar	DySP/CBI
1677.	Samsteu Dorji	Bhutan Police(Foreign)
1678.	Karma Tenzin	Bhutan Police(Foreign)

Training Year: 1974-75; Batch: 1974 -IPS-RR-27

1679.	Agarwal R.	IPS
1680.	Ahluwalia V.K.	IPS
1681.	Ahmad N.	IPS
1682.	Ajitlal	IPS
1683.	Akhilesh A.K.S.	IPS
1684.	Alam M.I.	IPS
1685.	Alind Jain	IPS
1686.	Ansari J.	IPS
1687.	Anup Kumar	IPS
1688.	Awasthi S.K.	IPS
1689.	Bahadur R.	IPS

1690.	Bakshi Ram	IPS
1691.	Bansal C.P.	IPS
1692.	Bansal U.K.	IPS
1693.	Basith M.A.	IPS
1694.	Barua S.	IPS
1695.	Baskar N.B.	IPS
1696.	Bhatia R.K.	IPS
1697.	Bhattacharya P.	IPS
1698.	Bhatt C.M.	IPS
1699.	Bhola B.K.	IPS
1700.	Bhupinder Singh	IPS
1701.	Biswas D.N.	IPS
1702.	Borkar S.N.	IPS
1703.	Chak S.N.	IPS
1704.	Correya T.	IPS
1705.	Dadwal Y.S.	IPS
1706.	Dalal R.S.	IPS
1707.	Das S.	IPS
1708.	Das S.C.	IPS
1709.	Dhatt S.S.	IPS
1710.	Diwakar V.M.	IPS
1711.	D. Souza K.	IPS
1712.	Earyil A.L.	IPS
1713.	Gafoor K.H.	IPS
1714.	Gahot H.R.	IPS
1715.	Gangadharan R.	IPS
1716.	Gavi S.M.	IPS
1717.	Gautam D.N.	IPS
1718.	Gill G.S.	IPS
1719.	Gill P.S.	IPS
1720.	Iqbal Z.	IPS
1721.	Jitendra Kumar	IPS

1722.	Kanth A.K.	IPS
1723.	Katna U.K.	IPS
1724.	Khanna J.K.	IPS
1725.	Khoda K.	IPS
1726.	Lakra I.	IPS
1727.	Lalthara	IPS
1728.	Luke A.K.	IPS
1729.	Mahapatra J.	IPS
1730.	Malhi G.S.	IPS
1731.	Malik R.L.	IPS
1732.	Mathur R.K.	IPS
1733.	Mehra I.S.	IPS
1734.	Meena R.	IPS
1735.	Meena R.N.	IPS
1736.	Menon M.D.	IPS
1737.	Mishra J.P.	IPS
1738.	Mitra Kumari S. (Ms.)	IPS
1739.	Nagia I.J.	IPS
1740.	Nair B.N.	IPS
1741.	Nanda G.C.	IPS
1742.	Nghinglova B.T.	IPS
1743.	Palanivel A.	IPS
1744.	Pandey A.P.	IPS
1745.	Pandey S.P.	IPS
1746.	Panna Lal	IPS
1747.	Paramvir Singh	IPS
1748.	Prem Singh	IPS
1749.	Ram S.P.	IPS
1750.	Rai B.	IPS
1751.	Raj Kumar	IPS
1752.	Rachpal Singh	IPS
1753.	B.P. Rao	IPS

1754.	M.V.K. Rao	IPS
1755.	R.U. Rey	IPS
1756.	K.C. Reddy	IPS
1757.	S.K. Rout	IPS
1758.	P.K. Sahay	IPS
1759.	S. Shujauddin	IPS
1760.	A.P. Singh	IPS
1761.	T.D. Singh Kumar	IPS
1762.	R.K. Singh	IPS
1763.	R. Sinha	IPS
1764.	Sohan Singh	IPS
1765.	Suraj Kaur Mehta (Smt.)	IPS
1766.	A. Thapan	IPS
1767.	B.S. Thind	IPS
1768.	Tripathi N.K.	IPS
1769.	S.V. Venkata Krishna	IPS
1770.	T.R. Verma	IPS
1771.	R.P. Verma	IPS
1772.	Vikram Singh	IPS
1773.	K.S. Vyas	IPS
1774.	S.N. Achhunni	DySP/Nagaland
1775.	V. Angami	DySP/Nagaland
1776.	M.O. Ao	DySP/Nagaland
1777.	Giri C.B.	DySP/Nagaland
1778.	K. Kaire	DySP/Nagaland
1779.	Z. Lotha	DySP/Nagaland
1780.	H.K. Rengma	DySP/Nagaland
1781.	M. Yanthan	DySP/Nagaland
1782.	G.K. Rengma	DySP/Nagaland
1783.	L. Hrangnawna	DySP/Mizoram
1784.	F. Hranglira	DySP/Mizoram

1785.	Saizela	DySP/Mizoram
1786.	Hmingdailova Khiangte	DySP/Mizoram
1787.	T. Chongthu	DySP/Mizoram
1788.	Lalsang Sualasailo	DySP/Mizoram
1789.	Raj Mohinder Singh Brar	DySP/CBI

Training Year: 1975-76; Batch: 1975 -IPS-RR-28

1790.	K.R. Nandan	IPS/AP
1791.	P. Gautam Kumar	IPS/AP
1792.	M.V.P.C. Sastry	IPS/AP
1793.	Ajit Kumar Mohanty	IPS/AP
1794.	Chawngthu Dothanga	IPS/AP
1795.	Hanuman Ram Kataria	IPS/AP
1796.	William Richmond Marbania	IPS/A&M
1797.	M. Mohan Raj	IPS/A&M
1798.	Jagdish Ramaswamy Saligra	IPS/A&M
1799.	Asoka Kumar Sahu	IPS/A&M
1800.	Anand Shankar	IPS/Bihar
1801.	Sanjay Narayan	IPS/Bihar
1802.	Raj Kishore Mishra	IPS/Bihar
1803.	Yashwant Malhotra	IPS/Bihar
1804.	Neel Mani	IPS/Bihar
1805.	Prakash Satyen Natarajan	IPS/Bihar
1806.	Balbir Chand	IPS/Bihar
1807.	Bishan Singh Jayant	IPS/Bihar
1808.	Raj Mohinder Singn Brar	IPS/Gujarat
1809.	Om Prakash Mathur	IPS/Gujarat
1810.	Vipin Kumar	IPS/Haryana
1811.	Ram Kishan Rang	IPS/Haryana
1812.	John V. George	IPS/Haryana
1813.	Sharad Chandra Sinha	IPS/Haryana
1814.	Norbu Gyeltsan Negi	IPS/HP

1815.	Deepak Bagai	IPS/HP
1816.	Madan Lal	IPS/J&K
1817.	Radhavinod Raju	IPS/J&K
1818.	Subhas Bhrani	IPS/Karnataka
1819.	Ms. Jija P. Madhavan	IPS/Karnataka
1820.	Jacob Punnoose	IPS/Kerala
1821.	Rajan Krishnanath Medheka	IPS/Kerala
1822.	C.V.Singh Juneja	IPS/Kerala
1823.	M.P. George	IPS/MP
1824.	Heimant Kumar Sarin	IPS/MP
1825.	Vijay Raman	IPS/MP
1826.	Kalika Prasad	IPS/MP
1827.	R.S. Gupta	IPS/Maharashtra
1828.	Hari Shankar Joshi	IPS/Maharashtra
1829.	P.P. Srivastava	IPS/Maharashtra
1830.	C. P. Ngahanyui	IPS/M&T
1831.	Pranay Sahay	IPS/M&T
1832.	Avadesh Behari Mathur	IPS/M&T
1833.	Vijay Kumar Sharma	IPS/M&T
1834.	Ramesh Charan Behera	IPS/Orissa
1835.	Jogishwar Singh	IPS/Punjab
1836.	Gobind Ram	IPS/Punjab
1837.	Anil Kaushik	IPS/Punjab
1838.	Navin Sharma	IPS/Rajasthan
1839.	R. Natarajan	IPS/TN
1840.	K.V.S. Gopalakrishna	IPS/TN
1841.	T.N. Mannen	IPS/TN
1842.	Jagan M. Seshadri	IPS/TN
1843.	K.Vijaya Kumar	IPS/TN
1844.	Narendra Singh Rana	IPS/UT
1845.	Anil Kumar Seth	IPS/UT

1846.	P. Deepak Sudhakar	IPS/UT
1847.	Brijesh Kumar Gupta	IPS/UT
1848.	Syed Murtuza Hasan	IPS/UP
1849.	Aloke Behari Lal	IPS/UP
1850.	Rajiv	IPS/UP
1851.	Karamvir Singh	IPS/UP
1852.	Babu Lal Yadava	IPS/UP
1853.	Vikram Chandra Goel	IPS/UP
1854.	Vibuti Narain Rai	IPS/UP
1855.	Om Prakash Singh Malik	IPS/UP
1856.	Pyare Lal	IPS/UP
1857.	Pritam Pal Singh Sidhu	IPS/UP
1858.	Bidhan Chandra Nayak	IPS/UP
1859.	Rajinder Singh Dhillon	IPS/UP
1860.	Rajiv Verma	IPS/UP
1861.	Dinesh Kumar Sharma	IPS/UP
1862.	Bishnu Pada Chakraborty	IPS/UP
1863.	Dhirendra Narayan Samal	IPS/UP
1864.	Subir Hari Singh	IPS/UP
1865.	Dharan Chand Lakha	IPS/UP
1866.	Anup Kumar Chanda	IPS/WB
1867.	Rajatava Bagchi	IPS/WB
1868.	Anil Kumar	IPS/WB
1869.	Om Prakash Kala	IPS/WB
1870.	Ranbir Singh Rawat	IPS/WB
1871.	J. Bendangtoshi	DySP/Nagaland
1872.	Rajinder Kumar Sharma	DySP/CBI
1873.	S. Dhendup	Bhutan Police (Foreign)
1874.	G.B. Pradhan	Bhutan Police (Foreign)
1875.	A.Q. Muhboobi	Afghanistan Police (Foreign)
1876.	N. Nazark	Afghanistan Police (Foreign)

1877.	A. Wahab	Afghanistan Police (Foreign)
1878.	M. Qassim	Afghanistan Police (Foreign)

Training Year: 1976-77; Batch: 1976 -IPS-RR-29

1879.	Parvez Dewan	IPS/AP
1880.	R.R. Girish Kumar	IPS/AP
1881.	Balvinder Singh	IPS/AP
1882.	O. Chaya Devi (Ms.)	IPS/AP
1883.	Kulbir Krishan	IPS/A&M
1884.	Sibabrata Kakati	IPS/A&M
1885.	Daulat Singh	IPS/A&M
1886.	Madan Mohan Jha	IPS/Bihar
1887.	Anil Kumar	IPS/Bihar
1888.	Rakesh Jaruhar	IPS/Bihar
1889.	Ramesh C. Prasad	IPS/Bihar
1890.	Uday Shankar Dutt	IPS/Bihar
1891.	Sittal Dass	IPS/Bihar
1892.	Ram Kumar Kataria	IPS/Bihar
1893.	Kuldip N. Sharma	IPS/Gujarat
1894.	Ram Niwas Gupta	IPS/Gujarat
1895.	Deepak Swaroop	IPS/Gujarat
1896.	Jagan Mathews	IPS/Gujarat
1897.	Sudhir Kumar Sinha	IPS/Gujarat
1898.	Murli Dhar Meena	IPS/Gujarat
1899.	Swaranjit Singh	IPS/Haryana
1900.	Rakesh Malik	IPS/Haryana
1901.	Ravikant Sharma	IPS/Haryana
1902.	Alok Joshi	IPS/Haryana
1903.	Virendra Bahadur Singh	IPS/Haryana
1904.	R.N. Chahalia	IPS/Haryana
1905.	Manjari Sen Ms.	IPS/HP
1906.	Anirudh Uppal	IPS/HP

1907.	Ashok Thakur	IPS/HP
1908.	Ashok Kumar Bhan	IPS/J&K
1909.	S.T. Ramesh	IPS/Karnataka
1910.	Sharat Chander Saxena	IPS/Karnataka
1911.	D.V. Guruprasad	IPS/Karnataka
1912.	K.M. Shiva Kumar	IPS/Karnataka
1913.	N. Atchutta Rao	IPS/Karnataka
1914.	K.P. Somarajan	IPS/Kerala
1915.	G. Premshanker	IPS/Kerala
1916.	Ramesh Chandra Bhanu	IPS/Kerala
1917.	Ravindera Narayan Ravi	IPS/Kerala
1918.	Subhash Chander Negi	IPS/Kerala
1919.	P. Mahendru	IPS/MP
1920.	Asha Gopal (Ms.)	IPS/MP
1921.	Dilip G. Kapdeo	IPS/MP
1922.	Nandan Dube	IPS/MP
1923.	Yashovardhan Azad	IPS/MP
1924.	Gorekh Govind Megh	IPS/MP
1925.	Shridhar Vagal	IPS/Maharashtra
1926.	Ajit Vasant Parasnis	IPS/Maharashtra
1927.	D. Sivanandan	IPS/Maharashtra
1928.	K. Subramanyam	IPS/Maharashtra
1929.	Pratap V. Joshi	IPS/Maharashtra
1930.	Subhash Kumar	IPS/Maharashtra
1931.	Subhash Chandra Gadhe	IPS/Maharashtra
1932.	Yajakumar Y. Singh	IPS/M&T
1933.	Dileep Shivpuri	IPS/M&T
1934.	Bevis A. Couthinho	IPS/M&T
1935.	Rajendra Kumar Shukla	IPS/M&T
1936.	William K. Lengen	IPS/M&T
1937.	Manmohan Prah Raj	IPS/Orissa

1938.	Ajit Singh Bedi	IPS/Orissa
1939.	Arun Kumar Upadhyay	IPS/Orissa
1940.	Om Prakash	IPS/Punjab
1941.	K.S. Sankaranarayanan	IPS/Punjab
1942.	Mohinder Singh	IPS/Punjab
1943.	Kuljit Singh Bains	IPS/Rajasthan
1944.	Smt. G. Thilakavathi Amma	IPS/TN
1945.	V. Balachandran	IPS/TN
1946.	Kum. Letika Dhar	IPS/TN
1947.	Bhola Nath	IPS/TN
1948.	Sanjiv Kumar Upadhyay	IPS/TN
1949.	K.V.S. Murthy	IPS/TN
1950.	G. Nanchil Kumaran	IPS/TN
1951.	V. Raja Gopal	IPS/UT
1952.	Shamshe B. Deol	IPS/UT
1953.	Neeraj Kumar	IPS/UT
1954.	Rumal Singh Dinkar	IPS/UT
1955.	Alok Rawat	IPS/UP
1956.	Jyoti Swaroop Pandey	IPS/UP
1957.	Subhash Joshi	IPS/UP
1958.	Manoj Kumar	IPS/UP
1959.	Rajendra Kumar Tiwari	IPS/UP
1960.	Satya Vrat Bansal	IPS/UP
1961.	Shailendra Sagar	IPS/UP
1962.	Kum. Renuka Bhatia	IPS/UP
1963.	Atul	IPS/UP
1964.	Deo Raj Nagar	IPS/UP
1965.	Padam Singh	IPS/UP
1966.	Ramnath Jha	IPS/UP
1967.	Mahabir Singh Bali	IPS/UP
1968.	Prem Chander Sabarwal	IPS/UP

1969.	Alexander Daniel	IPS/UP
1970.	Udayan Parmar	IPS/UP
1971.	Kavi Raj Negi	IPS/UP
1972.	Ram Lal Ram	IPS/UP
1973.	Harbhajan Singh	IPS/UP
1974.	Hoshiar Singh Balwaria	IPS/UP
1975.	Prakash Singh	IPS/UP
1976.	Rati Ram	IPS/UP
1977.	Shitala P. Srivastava	IPS/UP
1978.	Sushant K. Bhattacharya	IPS/WB
1979.	Chittaranjan Singh	IPS/WB
1980.	Naparajit Mukherjee	IPS/WB
1981.	Dilip Mitra	IPS/WB
1982.	Bharat V. Wanchoo	IPS/WB
1983.	Jagbahadur S. Negi	IPS/WB
1984.	Harish Chandra Meena	IPS/WB
1985.	T.D. Burghungpa	Sikkim Police (Foreign)
1986.	A. Datta	Sikkim Police (Foreign)
1987.	T.D. Thinzing	Sikkim Police (Foreign)
1988.	A.K. Shrestha	Sikkim Police (Foreign)
1989.	O.H. Subba	Sikkim Police (Foreign)
1990.	Dorji L	Bhutan Police (Foreign)
1991.	Wangdi T	Bhutan Police (Foreign)

Training Year: 1977-78; Batch: 1977 -IPS-RR-30

1992.	K. Arvinda Rao	IPS/AP
1993.	V. Dinesh Reddy	IPS/AP
1994.	Umesh Kumar	IPS/AP
1995.	Alok Srivastava	IPS/AP
1996.	A. Siva Sankar	IPS/AP
1997.	M. Bhaskaraiah	IPS/AP
1998.	M. Alagar	IPS/AP

1999.	Anil Pradhan	IPS/A&M
2000.	Subhas Goswami	IPS/AA&M
2001.	A.K. Gupta	IPS/Bihar
2002.	P.K. Sharma	IPS/Bihar
2003.	Shafi Alam	IPS/Bihar
2004.	R.C. Sinha	IPS/Bihar
2005.	Rajesh Nandan Prasad	IPS/Bihar
2006.	Abhayanand	IPS/Bihar
2007.	Arun Chaudhary	IPS/Bihar
2008.	Gouri Shankar Rath	IPS/Bihar
2009.	V. Narayanan	IPS/Bihar
2010.	Ratan Lal Kanojia	IPS/Bihar
2011.	C. Lima Imchen	IPS/Bihar
2012.	R.C. Kaithal	IPS/Bihar
2013.	V.K. Gupta	IPS/Gujarat
2014.	Amitabh Pathak	IPS/Gujarat
2015.	K. Nityanandan	IPS/Gujarat
2016.	S.K. Sakia	IPS/Gujarat
2017.	Upendra Singh	IPS/Gujarat
2018.	Harish Kumar	IPS/Haryana
2019.	V.N. Rai	IPS/Haryana
2020.	Rajiv Sagar Sharma	IPS/Haryana
2021.	Kum. Deepa Kaicker	IPS/Haryana
2022.	P.V. Rathee	IPS/Haryana
2023.	Resham Singh	IPS/Haryana
2024.	Ravinder Kumar	IPS/HP
2025.	D.S. Manhas	IPS/HP
2026.	G.C. Kaushal	IPS/HP
2027.	M.K. Srivastava	IPS/Karnataka
2028.	A.R. Infant	IPS/Karnataka
2029.	Lalrokhuma Pachuan	IPS/Karnataka

2030.	Siby Mathews	IPS/Kerala
2031.	V.R. Rajivan	IPS/Kerala
2032.	Arvind Ranjan	IPS/Kerala
2033.	S. Pulikesi	IPS/Kerala
2034.	P.B. D'Cruz	IPS/MP
2035.	V.M. Kanwar	IPS/MP
2036.	P.K. Patanaik	IPS/MP
2037.	P.K. Mehta	IPS/MP
2038.	Syed Asif Ibrahim	IPS/MP
2039.	V.K. Panwar	IPS/MP
2040.	R.N. Amrawanshi	IPS/MP
2041.	Sanjeev Dayal	IPS/Maharashtra
2042.	S.P.S. Yadav	IPS/Maharashtra
2043.	C. Prabhakar	IPS/Maharashtra
2044.	P.N. Dixit	IPS/Maharashtra
2045.	K.B.G. Chandran	IPS/Maharashtra
2046.	R.P. Khilwani	IPS/Maharashtra
2047.	K.S. Shinde	IPS/Maharashtra
2048.	P.M. Sawant	IPS/M&T
2049.	Amitabh Mathur	IPS/M&T
2050.	J.C. Dabas	IPS/M&T
2051.	M.K. Das	IPS/M&T
2052.	Shailja Kant Misra	IPS/M&T
2053.	Ashok Raj Maheepathi	IPS/M&T
2054.	A.K. Patnaik	IPS/Orissa
2055.	Prakash Mishra	IPS/Orissa
2056.	D.R. Meena	IPS/Orissa
2057.	Shashi Kant	IPS/Punjab
2058.	Chander Shekhar	IPS/Punjab
2059.	Jyoti Trehan	IPS/Punjab
2060.	J.P. Birdi	IPS/Punjab

2061.	Omendra Bharadwaj	IPS/Rajasthan
2062.	Bhanwar Sigh Chauhan	IPS/Rajasthan
2063.	D.S. Misra	IPS/Rajasthan
2064.	M. Tandon	IPS/Rajasthan
2065.	M.K. Devarajan	IPS/Rajasthan
2066.	Kanhaiya Lal	IPS/Rajasthan
2067.	C.M. Ravindran	IPS/Sikkim
2068.	S. Sridevi	IPS/Maharashtra
2069.	S. Machendra Nathan	IPS/TN
2070.	K.R. Shyamsundar	IPS/TN
2071.	P.R. Thapa	IPS/TN
2072.	Vibhakar Sharma	IPS/TN
2073.	R. Sawani	IPS/TN
2074.	P. Thangarajan	IPS/TN
2075.	R.M. Srivastava	IPS/UT
2076.	Bhim Sain	IPS/UT
2077.	Ajay Chadha	IPS/UT
2078.	Ahmad Saeed Khan	IPS/UT
2079.	B.S. Brar	IPS/UT
2080.	T.C. Lalduhawma	IPS/UT
2081.	Kanwaljit Deol(Smt)	IPS/UT
2082.	V.K. Singh	IPS/UP
2083.	Om Prakash Dikshit	IPS/UP
2084.	Ramesh Sehgal	IPS/UP
2085.	Ambrish Chandra Sharma	IPS/UP
2086.	S. Tripathi	IPS/UP
2087.	B.M. Saraswat	IPS/UP
2088.	Balaji S.	IPS/UP
2089.	Mumtaz Ahmed	IPS/UP
2090.	K.S. Rao	IPS/UP
2091.	V.R. Sampath	IPS/UP

2092.	Arun Kumar Gupta	IPS/UP
2093.	Brij Lal	IPS/UP
2094.	Rameshwar Dayal	IPS/UP
2095.	Bansi Lal	IPS/UP
2096.	Malkiat Ram	IPS/UP
2097.	Abdullais Khan	IPS/WB
2098.	Rajendra Singh	IPS/WB
2099.	Nawal Kishore Singh	IPS/WB
2100.	Vagesh Misra	IPS/WB
2101.	S. Jayaraman	IPS/WB
2102.	C.S. Paarcha	IPS/WB
2103.	Ramji Lal Meena	IPS/WB
2104.	N.N. Ngullir	DySP/Nagaland
2105.	T.P. Chakhesong	DySP/Nagaland
2106.	Toshi Aier	DySP/Nagaland
2107.	J.S. Gurung	DySP/Bhutan (Foreign)
2108.	T. Wangda	DySP/Bhutan (Foreign)
2109.	J. Basnett	DySP/Sikkim (Foreign)
2110.	S.D. Bhutia	DySP/Sikkim (Foreign)
2111.	T.T. Lachungpa	DySP/Sikkim (Foreign)
2112.	T.T. Tamang	DySP/Sikkim (Foreign)
2113.	B. Thapa	DySP/Sikkim (Foreign)

Training Year: 1978-79; Batch: 1978 -IPS-RR-31

2114.	Vidya Nand Garg	IPS/A. P.
2115.	K. Jayachandra Subbarayal	IPS/AP
2116.	Mallela Babu Rao	IPS/AP
2117.	Musnipally Ratan	IPS/AP
2118.	Jayanto Choudhury	IPS/A&M
2119.	N. Ramachandran	IPS/A&M
2120.	Besosayo Kezo	IPS/A&M
2121.	Prem Singh	IPS/A&M

2122.	R.R. Verma	IPS/Bihar
2123.	P. Madhusudanan Nair	IPS/Bihar
2124.	Arvind Verma	IPS/Bihar
2125.	Suprebhat Das	IPS/Bihar
2126.	K. Kumarasamy	IPS/Gujarat
2127.	I.K. Abraham	IPS/J&K
2128.	S. Mahadev Bidari	IPS/Karnataka
2129.	Kuchanna Srinivasan	IPS/Karnataka
2130.	N.D. Anthony Issac	IPS/Kerala
2131.	K.S. Balasubramanian	IPS/Kerala
2132.	K.S. Jangpangi	IPS/Kerala
2133.	Anil M. Navaney	IPS/MP
2134.	Ramesh Sharma	IPS/MP
2135.	Ranjan Mukerjee	IPS/Maharashtra
2136.	P.P.P. Sharma	IPS/Maharashtra
2137.	Amba Lal Verma	IPS/Maharashtra
2138.	Sanjay Sinha	IPS/M&T
2139.	K. Saleem Ali	IPS/M&T
2140.	Rajinder Khanna	IPS/Orissa
2141.	Rajan Gupta	IPS/Punjab
2142.	Parash Moni Das	IPS/Punjab
2143.	Arvind Kumar Jain	IPS/Rajasthan
2144.	Bhasker Chaterjee	IPS/Rajasthan
2145.	Kanhaiyalal	IPS/Rajasthan
2146.	Jasbir Singh	IPS/Sikkim(Foreign)
2147.	Amir Chand Negi	IPS/Sikkim(Foreign)
2148.	Kuppusamy Ramanujam	IPS/TN
2149.	Amit Verma	IPS/TN
2150.	Ranjit Narayan	IPS/UT
2151.	Satish Chandra	IPS/UT
2152.	Vimla Mehra(Mrs)	IPS/UT

2153.	Dilip Trivedi	IPS/UP
2154.	Vijay Raghav Pant	IPS/UP
2155.	Rizwan Ahmad	IPS/UP
2156.	Rajiv Kapoor	IPS/UP
2157.	Suresh Chandra Panda	IPS/UP
2158.	Shekhar Sinha	IPS/UP
2159.	Kashmir Singh	IPS/UP
2160.	Bijendra Singh	IPS/UP
2161.	V.V. Thambi	IPS/WB
2162.	G.M. Chakrabarti	IPS/WB
2163.	Onensuja Ao	DySP/Nagaland
2164.	L.T. Lotho	DySP/Nagaland
2165.	K. Lakshman Mohan	DySP/AP
2166.	Tshering Bhutia	DySP/Sikkim(Foreign)
2167.	Wangyal Tobden	DySP/Sikkim(Foreign)
2168.	S.P. Singh	DySP/CBI
2169.	H.C. Singh	DySP/CBI
2170.	J.S. Waraich	DySP/CBI

Training Year: 1979-80; Batch: 1979 -IPS-RR-32

2171.	Syed Anwarul Huda	IPS/AP
2172.	Aruna M. Bahuguna(Mrs)	IPS/ A. P.
2173.	Tarini Prasad Das	IPS/AP
2174.	Ashok Prasad	IPS/AP
2175.	B. Prasada Rao	IPS/AP
2176.	D.T. Naik	IPS/AP
2177.	Suresh Bahuguna	IPS/AP
2178.	D.K. Pathak	IPS/A&M
2179.	Mrutunjay Sahoo	IPS/A&M
2180.	Anil Kumar Mallick	IPS/A&M
2181.	P.J.P. Hanaman	IPS/A&M
2182.	Anil Kumar Sinha	IPS/Bihar

2183.	Krishna Chaudhary	IPS/Bihar
2184.	Arun Chandra Verma	IPS/Bihar
2185.	Amrik Singh Nimbran	IPS/Bihar
2186.	Jagdish Raj	IPS/Bihar
2187.	C.B.S.Venkata Ramana	IPS/Gujarat
2188.	Pritam Chand Thakur	IPS/Gujarat
2189.	Satyendra Kumar	IPS/Haryana
2190.	Sharad Kumar	IPS/Haryana
2191.	Susant Mahapatra	IPS/Karnataka
2192.	Dharam Pal Negi	IPS/Karnataka
2193.	Venugopal K Nair	IPS/Kerala
2194.	Dineshwar Sharma	IPS/Kerala
2195.	Ramesh Chander Arora	IPS/MP
2196.	Sant Kumar Paswan	IPS/MP
2197.	Heble Dilip Madhukar	IPS/Maharashtra
2198.	Anup Mohan Patnaik	IPS/Maharashtra
2199.	Divya Prakash Sinha	IPS/M&T
2200.	Shahid Ahmad	IPS/M&T
2201.	Raghunath Behura	IPS/M&T
2202.	Rajinder Kumar	IPS/M&T
2203.	T. Thangthuam	IPS/M&T
2204.	A. Ch. Rama Rao	IPS/M&T
2205.	Avinder Singh Brar	IPS/Punjab
2206.	Suresh Chowdhary	IPS/Rajasthan
2207.	Sarabjit Singh	IPS/TN
2208.	Alok Kumar Verma	IPS/UT
2209.	Deep Chand	IPS/UT
2210.	Anand Lal Banerjee	IPS/UP
2211.	Ranjan Dwivedi	IPS/UP
2212.	Arvind Kumar Jain	IPS/UP
2213.	Venkatesh Rajagopal	IPS/UP

2214. B.S. Sidhu IPS/UP
2215. Rajdeep Singh IPS/UP
2216. Gian Singh IPS/UP
2217. Shiva Narayan Singh IPS/UP
2218. Utpal Kumar Dutta IPS/WB
2219. K.P. Prabhakara Rao IPS/WB
2220. S.N. Sarkar IPS/WB
2221. Burkumzuk DySP/Nagaland
2222. L.L. Doungel DySP/Nagaland
2223. S.T. Sangtam DySP/Nagaland
2224. Lamchung Bhutan Police (Foreign)
2225. N.M. Pradhan Bhutan Police (Foreign)

Training Year: 1980-81; Batch: 1980 -IPS-RR-33

2226. Lokendra Sharma IPS/AP
2227. Navneet Rajan Wasan IPS/AP
2228. Ambati Siva Narayana IPS/AP
2229. Madanlal IPS/AP
2230. Romesh Chand Tayal IPS/A&M
2231. Atul Kumar Mathur IPS/A&M
2232. Rajender Kumar IPS/A&M
2233. Rajyabardhan Sharma IPS/Bihar
2234. Promot Kumar Thakur IPS/Bihar
2235. Sunit Kumar IPS/Bihar
2236. Rajiv Jain IPS/Bihar
2237. Nirmal C Dhoundial IPS/Bihar
2238. Kumud Sahu(Ms) IPS/Bihar
2239. Prithvi Pal Pandey IPS/Gujarat
2240. Harjeshwar Paul Singh IPS/Gujarat
2241. R.P. Priyadarshee IPS/Gujarat
2242. Udayan Mukerji IPS/Karnataka
2243. Prem Lal Pandey IPS/MP

2244.	Surendra Singh	IPS/MP
2245.	Ahmed Javed	IPS/Maharashtra
2246.	Satya Pal Singh	IPS/Maharashtra
2247.	R.P. Raghuvanshi	IPS/Maharashtra
2248.	B. Natthuji Raut	IPS/Maharashtra
2249.	V. Ratnakar Kamble	IPS/Maharashtra
2250.	Surinder Mohan Sharma	IPS/Punjab
2251.	Satya Narain Jain	IPS/Rajasthan
2252.	Ravinder Singh Dhillon	IPS/Rajasthan
2253.	M. Ganesan	IPS/TN
2254.	Anoop Jaiswal	IPS/TN
2255.	Archana Mishra(Ms)	IPS/TN
2256.	Narinder Pal Singh	IPS/TN
2257.	K. Muthukkaruppan	IPS/TN
2258.	Himmat Singh	IPS/UP
2259.	Sulkhan Singh	IPS/UP
2260.	Darshan Dass	IPS/UP
2261.	Shanti Kumar Jain	IPS/UT
2262.	K.K. Maheshwari	IPS/UT
2263.	Prahlad Rai Meena	IPS/UT
2264	Banshi Dhar Sharma	IPS/WB
2265.	Surender Singh	IPS/WB
2266.	J.C. Chattopadhyay	IPS/WB
2267.	Dilip Kumar, N	DySP/Goa
2268.	Sanjeev Thapar	DySP/Goa
2269.	Kipchu Namgyel	DySP/Bhutan(Foreign)

Training Year: 1981-82; Batch: 1981 -IPS-RR-34

2270.	A. Mahadeorao Dalavai	IPS/AP
2271.	Vivek Dube	IPS/AP
2272.	Abdul Khayum Khan	IPS/AP
2273.	K. Durga Prasad	IPS/AP

2274.	J. Venkata Ramudu	IPS/AP
2275.	R.P. Meena	IPS/AP
2276.	C.N. Gopinatha Reddy	IPS/AP
2277.	Gunottam Bhuyan	IPS/A&M
2278.	Rajiv Mehta	IPS/A&M
2279.	Ravi Solanki	IPS/A&M
2280.	Satish Chandra Jha	IPS/Bihar
2281.	A. Radhakrishsna Kini	IPS/Bihar
2282.	Rajeev Kumar	IPS/Bihar
2283.	D.A. Bawa	IPS/Gujarat
2284.	Ramesh Manhot	IPS/Gujarat
2285.	Ambalal M. Chauhan	IPS/Gujarat
2286.	Shri Niwas	IPS/Haryana
2287.	Rupak Kumar Dutta	IPS/Karnataka
2288.	B.E. Umapathy	IPS/Karnataka
2289.	Om Prakash	IPS/Karnataka
2290.	Kampaiah	IPS/Karnataka
2291.	Anand Kumar	IPS/MP
2292.	R.P.S. Kahlon	IPS/MP
2293.	A.K. Dhasmana	IPS/MP
2294.	Sudarshan Kumar	IPS/MP
2295.	Prem Kishan Jain	IPS/Maharashtra
2296.	Satish Chand Mathur	IPS/Maharashtra
2297.	Rahul Sur	IPS/Maharashtra
2298.	Ashok Kumar Sharma	IPS/Maharashtra
2299.	Maria H.K. Rakesh	IPS/Maharashtra
2300.	Manohar Lal	IPS/Maharashtra
2301.	K. Ramachandran	IPS/Maharashtra
2302.	Meeran C. Borwankar	IPS/Maharashtra
2303.	Khinya Ram	IPS/M&T
2304.	Pradeep Kumar Sinha	IPS/M&T

2305.	C. Balasubramanian	IPS/M&T
2306.	Jagat Bahadur Negi	IPS/M&T
2307.	Sanjeev Marik	IPS/Orissa
2308.	V. Thiagarajan	IPS/Orissa
2309.	Ganesh Dutt Pandey	IPS/Punjab
2310.	Manoj Bhatt	IPS/Rajasthan
2311.	Navdeep Singh	IPS/Rajasthan
2312.	Anil Khanna	IPS/Rajasthan
2313.	Jaswant Sampatram	IPS/Rajasthan
2314.	R. Sekar	IPS/TN
2315.	T. Radhakrishnan	IPS/TN
2316.	Mahboob Alam	IPS/TN
2317.	A. Subramanian	IPS/TN
2318.	P.N. Agarwal	IPS/UT
2319.	Aditya Arya	IPS/UT
2320.	Yogendra Pal Singh	IPS/UP
2321.	Vipin Kumar	IPS/UP
2322.	Malay Kumar Sinha	IPS/UP
2323.	Kamlendra Prasad	IPS/UP
2324.	Vijay Singh	IPS/UP
2325.	Nazrul Islam	IPS/WB
2326.	Vijoy Kumar	IPS/WB
2327.	R.K. Srivastava	IPS/WB
2328.	Kishan Lal Meena	IPS/WB

Training Year: 1982-83; Batch: 1982 -IPS-RR-35

2329.	Shree Ram Tewari	IPS/AP
2330.	Anurag Sharma	IPS/AP
2331.	S. Ramanamurti	IPS/AP
2332.	Khagen Sharma	IPS/A&M
2333.	Dilip Kumar Borah	IPS/A&M
2334.	Watisangba Ao	IPS/A&M

2335.	Asha Sinha (Smt)	IPS/Bihar
2336.	Paras Nath Rai	IPS/Bihar
2337.	Ranjit Raj William	IPS/Gujarat
2338.	C.V. Geetha (Ms)	IPS/Gujarat
2339.	Surendra Prasad Chitturi	IPS/Gujarat
2340.	Anil Dawra	IPS/Haryana
2341.	Parminder Rai	IPS/Haryana
2342.	Ishwar Dev	IPS/HP
2343.	Kamal Kumar Boddupalli	IPS/HP
2344.	K. Ilango	IPS/J&K
2345.	Bipin Gopalkrishna	IPS/Karnataka
2346.	Prabha H. Rao(Ms)	IPS/Karnataka
2347.	Alexander Jacob	IPS/Kerala
2348.	Mahesh Kumar Singla	IPS/Kerala
2349.	Ram Niwas	IPS/MP
2350.	Alok Tandon	IPS/MP
2351.	Shiv Sankar Lal	IPS/MP
2352.	Shri D.D. Padasalgikar	IPS/Maharashtra
2353.	Hemant Kamlakar Karkare	IPS/Maharashtra
2354.	Kakani Lakshmi Prasad	IPS/Maharashtra
2355.	Ajay Kumar Jain	IPS/Maharashtra
2356.	A. Ghinabaaji Dhanvijay	IPS/Maharashtra
2357.	Kishore Jha	IPS/M&T
2358.	Ratnakar Baral	IPS/M&T
2359.	R. Reddappa Reddy	IPS/M&T
2360.	Baviskar Pradip Ramdas	IPS/M&T
2361.	Shovan Lal Mukherjee	IPS/Orissa
2362.	Binoy Kumar Behara	IPS/Orissa
2363.	Sudesh Kumar	IPS/Orissa
2364.	Sanjiv Gupta	IPS/Punjab
2365.	Kanwal Ranbir Singh	IPS/Punjab

2366.	Sumedh Singh	IPS/Punjab
2367.	Suresh Arora	IPS/Punjab
2368.	Rajender Singh	IPS/Punjab
2369.	Ajit Sigh	IPS/Rajasthan
2370.	Krishan Kumar Sharma	IPS/Rajasthan
2371.	Laxman Lal Meena	IPS/Rajasthan
2372.	Ashok Kumar	IPS/TN
2373.	Satish Kumar Dogra	IPS/TN
2374.	K. Rajendran	IPS/TN
2375.	Jatinder Kumar Sharma	IPS/UT
2376.	Surendra Kumar Bhagat	IPS/UP
2377.	Praveen Singh	IPS/UP
2378.	Surya Kumar	IPS/UP
2379.	Vijay Kumar Gupta	IPS/UP
2380.	Ram Deo	IPS/UP
2381.	Ravinder Jit Singh Nalwa	IPS/WB
2382.	G.M.P. Reddy	IPS/WB
2383.	M. Mamatha (Ms)	IPS/WB
2384.	Anil Kumar	IPS/WB
2385.	Raj Kanojia	IPS/WB

Training Year: 1983-84; Batch: 1983 -IPS-RR-36

2386.	Tej Deep Pratihast (Mrs)	IPS/AP
2387.	D. Boobathi Babu	IPS/AP
2388.	Satyendra Pratihast	IPS/AP
2389.	Bibhuti Bhusana Mishra	IPS/A&M
2390.	Rajender Kumar Sharma	IPS/A&M
2391.	Jatin Mipun	IPS/A&M
2392.	Sanjiv Nandan Sahai	IPS/Bihar
2393.	Rituraj	IPS/Bihar
2394.	Sunil Kumar Sinha	IPS/Bihar
2395.	Ashok Sinha	IPS/Bihar

2396.	Ashok Kumar Seth	IPS/Bihar
2397.	Nirmal Kaur (Ms)	IPS/Bihar
2398.	Suresh Kumar Bhardwaj	IPS/Bihar
2399.	Ashok Kumar Patnaik	IPS/Gujarat
2400.	Parmod Kumar	IPS/Gujarat
2401.	Vipul Vijoy	IPS/Gujarat
2402.	Shivanand Jha	IPS/Gujarat
2403.	M. Sekar	IPS/Gujarat
2404.	Yash Pal Singal	IPS/Haryana
2405.	Mohinder Lal	IPS/Haryana
2406.	Rajeev Kumar Singh	IPS/HP
2407.	Harshavardhan Raju	IPS/Karnataka
2408.	Neelmani Srivastav (Miss)	IPS/Karnataka
2409.	Chandrasekharan P	IPS/Kerala
2410.	T.P. Senkumar	IPS/Kerala
2411.	Rina Mukherjee (Ms)	IPS/MP
2412.	Surya Pratap Singh Pariha	IPS/MP
2413.	Rishi Kumar Shukla	IPS/MP
2414.	Giridhari Nayak	IPS/MP
2415.	Durga Madhab Mitra (Ms)	IPS/MP
2416.	Kaushal Kumar Pathak	IPS/Maharashtra
2417.	Kamble Udhav Sahebrao	IPS/Maharashtra
2418.	K. Nagaraj	IPS/M&T
2419.	Harjit Singh Sandhu	IPS/M&T
2420.	Shashi Shekhar Sharma	IPS/M&T
2421.	Vanupa Zathang	IPS/M&T
2422.	C. Chandramouli	IPS/Orissa
2423.	Satish Kumar Sharma	IPS/Punjab
2424.	Prabhat Kumar	IPS/Punjab
2425.	Abraham Mathai N.	IPS/Punjab
2426.	Shrikant Baldi	IPS/Rajasthan

2427.	Sudhir Pratap Singh	IPS/Rajasthan
2428.	Kapil Garg	IPS/Rajasthan
2429.	T. Rajendran	IPS/TN
2430.	K. Radhakrishnan	IPS/TN
2431.	Sauvik Chakraverti	IPS/UT
2432.	Jag Mohan Yadav	IPS/UP
2433.	Gopal Gupta	IPS/UP
2434.	Ram Narayan Singh	IPS/UP
2435.	Rajeev Rai Bhatnagar	IPS/UP
2436.	Om Prakash Singh	IPS/UP
2437.	Gurbachan Lal	IPS/UP
2438.	Kanhaiya Lal Meena	IPS/UP
2439.	Banibrata Basu	IPS/WB
2440.	Durgapada Tarenia	IPS/WB
2441.	Ranjit Kumar Pachnanda	IPS/WB
2442.	Arvind Kumar Maliwal	IPS/WB
2443.	Kezang Choedon (Ms)	Bhutan Police (Foreign)
2444.	Ugyen Pema (Ms)	Bhutan Police (Foreign)

Training Year: 1984-85; Batch -1984-IPS-RR-37

2445.	Nanduri Sambasiva Rao	IPS/AP
2446.	Sudeep Lakhtakia	IPS/AP
2447.	T. Krishna Raju	IPS/AP
2448.	Sunil Kumar Jain	IPS/A&M
2449.	Prit Pal Singh	IPS/A&M
2450.	Arvinda Kumar	IPS/A&M
2451.	Mukesh Sahey	IPS/A&M
2452.	Yogesh Chander Modi	IPS/A&M
2453.	Umesh Kumar	IPS/A&M
2454.	Pradeep Kumar	IPS/A&M
2455.	Rajeev Mohan Singh	IPS/A&M
2456.	Ram Niwas Meena	IPS/A&M

2457.	Rajesh Ranjan	IPS/Bihar
2458.	Parvez Hayet	IPS/Bihar
2459.	Dinesh Kumar Pandey	IPS/Bihar
2460.	Abhay Kumar Upadhyay	IPS/Bihar
2461.	Krishna Swaroop Dwivedi	IPS/Bihar
2462.	Ravinder Kumar	IPS/Bihar
2463.	Tirth Raj	IPS/Gujarat
2464.	Anand Prakash Maheshwari	IPS/Gujarat
2465.	Rakesh Asthana	IPS/Gujarat
2466.	Prem Singh Mehra	IPS/Gujarat
2467.	Laik Ram	IPS/Haryana
2468.	Mohinder Singh Mann	IPS/Haryana
2469.	Surjeet Singh Deswal	IPS/Haryana
2470.	Baljeet Singh Sandhu	IPS/Haryana
2471.	Somesh Goyal	IPS/HP
2472.	Kondaveeti Rajendra Kumar	IPS/J&K
2473.	Pitamber Lal Gupta	IPS/J&K
2474.	Malagaveli Narayana Reddy	IPS/Karnataka
2475.	H.C. Kishore Chandra	IPS/Karnataka
2476.	Prem Shankar Meena	IPS/Karnataka
2477.	Vinson M. Paul	IPS/Kerala
2478.	Arun Kumar Sinha	IPS/Kerala
2479.	M.N. Krishnamurthy	IPS/Kerala
2480.	Vijay Kumar Singh	IPS/MP
2481.	Maithili Sharon Gupta	IPS/MP
2482.	Mohd. Wazir Ansari	IPS/MP
2483.	Vivek Kumar Johri	IPS/MP
2484.	Sanjay Choudhary	IPS/MP
2485.	Sukhraj Singh	IPS/MP
2486.	Prabhat Ranjan	IPS/Maharashtra
2487.	Vishnu Dev Misra	IPS/Maharashtra

2488.	Francis J.A. Aranha	IPS/Maharashtra
2489.	P. Mallana Goud	IPS/M&T
2490.	Santosh Macherla	IPS/M&T
2491.	Narinder Sharma	IPS/M&T
2492.	P.V. Krishna Reddy	IPS/M&T
2493.	Gurbachan Singh	IPS/Orissa
2494.	Ramesh Prasad Singh	IPS/Orissa
2495.	Samant Kumar Goel	IPS/Punjab
2496.	Anil Kumar Sharma	IPS/Punjab
2497.	Swami Singh	IPS/Punjab
2498.	Pradeep Kumar Vyas	IPS/Rajasthan
2499.	Nand Kishor	IPS/Rajasthan
2500.	Arun Kumar Arora	IPS/Rajasthan
2501.	C. Venkateswara Rao	IPS/TN
2502.	P. Magendran	IPS/TN
2503.	S. George	IPS/TN
2504.	K. Rajendran	IPS/TN
2505.	P.C. Lallawmsanga	IPS/TN
2506.	I. Raja	IPS/TN
2507.	Dharmendra Kumar	IPS/UT
2508.	Deepak Kumar Mishra	IPS/UT
2509.	Karnal Singh	IPS/UT
2510.	Ajay Kumar Singh	IPS/UT
2511.	Harish Chandra Singh	IPS/UP
2512.	Rajni Kant Mishra	IPS/UP
2513.	Sutapa Sanyal (Ms)	IPS/UP
2514.	Aloke Prasad	IPS/UP
2515.	S. Javeed Ahmad	IPS/UP
2516.	Subesh Kumar Singh	IPS/UP
2517.	Gurdarshan Singh	IPS/UP
2518.	Dharmendra Bhatnagar	IPS/WB

2519. C. Venkata Muralidhar IPS/WB
2520. Amar Kanti Sarkar IPS/WB
2521. Chimi Dorgi Bhutan Police(Foreign)
2522. Gep Tshering Bhutan Police(Foreign)

Training Year: 1985-86; Batch: 1985-IPS-RR-38

2523. Mannam Malakondiah IPS/AP
2524. Rajwant Singh IPS/AP
2525. Ajit Prasad Rout IPS/A&M
2526. Kuladhar Saikia IPS/A&M
2527. Raghvendra Awasthi IPS/A&M
2528. Prithvi Singh Purohit IPS/A&M
2529. Desh Pal Singh IPS/A&M
2530. Kumar Rajesh Chandra IPS/Bihar
2531. Amitabh Choudhary IPS/Bihar
2532. Ajay Kumar Verma IPS/Bihar
2533. Bibhuti Bhushan Pradhan IPS/Bihar
2534. Ashish Bhati IPS/Gujarat
2535. Mohan Jha IPS/Gujarat
2536. Tejpal Singh Bisht IPS/Gujarat
2537. Anupam Kumar Surollia IPS/Gujarat
2538. Anup Kumar Singh IPS/Gujarat
2539. Kantilal Dahyabhai Patadi IPS/Gujarat
2540. Meera Verma (Ms) IPS/Gujarat
2541. Anant Kumar Dhul IPS/Haryana
2542. K. Selvaraj IPS/Haryana
2543. Sheel Madhur IPS/Haryana
2544. Kushal Pal Singh IPS/Haryana
2545. Ramchander Jowel IPS/Haryana
2546. Sanjay Kumar IPS/HP
2547. S. Gopal Reddy IPS/J&K
2548. Ram Lubhaya IPS/J&K

2549.	Ashit Mohan Prasad	IPS/Karnataka
2550.	H.N.Satyanarayana Rao	IPS/Karnataka
2551.	Lokanath Behera	IPS/Kerala
2552.	Rishi Raj Singh	IPS/Kerala
2553.	Jacob Thomas	IPS/Kerala
2554.	Bandi Maria Kumar	IPS/MP
2555.	Sarbjit Singh	IPS/MP
2556.	Keshav Chander Verma	IPS/MP
2557.	Uma Kant Lal	IPS/MP
2558.	Rajendra Kumar	IPS/MP
2559.	Metta Radha Krishna	IPS/MP
2560.	Amar Nath Upadhyaya	IPS/MP
2561.	Ashok Dohare	IPS/MP
2562.	Swarn Singh	IPS/MP
2563.	Mahan Bharat	IPS/MP
2564.	Kanchan Lal Meena	IPS/MP
2565.	Ashok Kumar Dhamija	IPS/Maharashtra
2566.	Subodh Kumar Jaiswal	IPS/Maharashtra
2567.	Yogesh Pratap Singh	IPS/Maharashtra
2568.	Krishan Lal Bishnoi	IPS/Maharashtra
2569.	Surinder Kumar	IPS/Maharashtra
2570.	Ish Kumar	IPS/M&T
2571.	Kuldeep Kumar	IPS/M&T
2572.	Lallianmang Khaute	IPS/M&T
2573.	Kunwar Brajesh Singh	IPS/Orissa
2574.	Ravinder Paul Singh	IPS/Punjab
2575.	Mohd. Mustafa	IPS/Punjab
2576.	Hemant Kumar Purohit	IPS/Rajasthan
2577.	Sunil Kumar Mehrotra	IPS/Rajasthan
2578.	Om Prakash	IPS/Rajasthan
2579.	Sudhakar Jauhari	IPS/Rajasthan

2580.	Thandi Lal Meena	IPS/Rajasthan
2581.	Avinash Mohananey	IPS/Sikkim
2582.	Sanga Ram Jangid	IPS/TN
2583.	Jalada Kumar Tripathy	IPS/TN
2584.	C.K. Gandhirajan	IPS/TN
2585.	Ajay Kashyap	IPS/UT
2586.	Amulya Kumar Patnaik	IPS/UT
2587.	Sachidanand Shrivastava	IPS/UT
2588.	Sudhir Singh Yadav	IPS/UT
2589.	Kishan Kumar	IPS/UT
2590.	Parbat Singh	IPS/UT
2591.	Bhanu Pratap Singh	IPS/UP
2592.	Rajesh Pratap Singh	IPS/UP
2593.	Hitesh Chandra Awasthy	IPS/UP
2594.	Ashok Kumar Dhar Dwivedi	IPS/UP
2595.	Arun Kumar	IPS/U.P
2596.	Sukhdev Singh	IPS/UP
2597.	Girish Prasad Sharma	IPS/UP
2598.	Harish Chander	IPS/UP
2599.	Sachin Shridhar	IPS/WB
2600.	Sivaji Ghosh	IPS/WB
2601.	Virendra	IPS/WB
2602.	Surajit Kar Purkayastha	IPS/WB
2603.	K. Hari Rajan	IPS/WB
2604.	M. Harisena Varma	IPS/WB
2605.	Arun Kumar Gupta	IPS/WB
2606.	Kundan Lal Tamta	IPS/WB
2607.	D.D. Wangchuk	Bhutan Police(Foreign)
2608.	Kesang Rinzim	Bhutan Police(Foreign)

Training Year- 1986-88; Sandwich Pattern Course - Passing Out Parade after Second Phase; Batch: 1986 - IPS - RR - 39

2609.	M. Mahendar Reddy	IPS/AP
2610.	Prabhakar Aloka	IPS/AP
2611.	Ram Prawesh Thakur	IPS/AP
2612.	Vijay Ranjan Ray	IPS/AP
2613.	Varun Sindhu Kul Kumudi	IPS/AP
2614.	Rajiv Trivedi	IPS/AP
2615.	T. Krishna Prasad	IPS/AP
2616.	Damodar Gautam Sawang	IPS/AP
2617.	Anil Kumar Jha	IPS/A&M
2618.	Pallabh Bhattacharyya	IPS/A&M
2619.	Jyotirmay Chakravarty	IPS/A&M
2620.	Ram Prakash Agarwal	IPS/A&M
2621.	Swaraj Bir Singh	IPS/A&M
2622.	R. Chandra Nathan	IPS/A&M
2623.	Kamal Nayan Choubey	IPS/Bihar
2624.	Rakesh Kumar Mishra	IPS/Bihar
2625.	Sheel Vardhan Singh	IPS/Bihar
2626.	Ajoy Kumar	IPS/Bihar
2627.	Ashok Kumar Verma	IPS/Bihar
2628.	V.H.R. Deshmikh	IPS/Bihar
2629.	Kishan Singh Meena	IPS/Bihar
2630.	Keshav Kumar	IPS/Gujarat
2631.	Satish Kumar Sharma	IPS/Gujarat
2632.	Satish Chandra Verma	IPS/Gujarat
2633.	Pramod Kumar Jha	IPS/Gujarat
2634.	E. Radha Krishnaiah	IPS/Gujarat
2635.	Vinod Kumar Mall	IPS/Gujarat
2636.	Kulyash Kumar Sharma	IPS/Haryana

2637.	Binay Kumar Sinha	IPS/Haryana
2638.	Krishan Kumar Sindhu	IPS/Haryana
2639.	Prabhat Ranjan Deo	IPS/Haryana
2640.	Sanjay Bhatia	IPS/Haryana
2641.	Seetharama Mardi	IPS/HP
2642.	Shishir Kumar Mishra	IPS/J&K
2643.	Shesh Paul Vaid	IPS/J&K
2644.	Navind Agarwal	IPS/J&K
2645.	Dyuti Rani Doley (Ms)	IPS/J&K
2646.	Praveen Sood	IPS/Karnataka
2647.	Padma Kumar Garg	IPS/Karnataka
2648.	K.V. Gagan Deep	IPS/Karnataka
2649.	Nirmal Chandra Asthana	IPS/Kerala
2650.	Rajesh Dewan	IPS/Kerala
2651.	N. Sankar Reddy	IPS/Kerala
2652.	Md. B.S. Yasin	IPS/Kerala
2653.	A. Hemachandran	IPS/Kerala
2654.	Gajanand Meena	IPS/Kerala
2655.	P. Vijayanand	IPS/Kerala
2656.	Alok Kumar Pateria	IPS/MP
2657.	Kailash Nath Tiwari	IPS/MP
2658.	Purshottam Sharma	IPS/MP
2659.	Ranjeev Kumar Garg	IPS/MP
2660.	Sanjay Rana	IPS/MP
2661.	Durgesh Madhav Awasthi	IPS/MP
2662.	Shailendra Kumar Srivastava	IPS/MP
2663.	Anil Kumar	IPS/MP
2664.	Parashuram Mathur	IPS/MP
2665.	Deepak Suryakant Jog	IPS/Maharashtra
2666.	Sharda Prasad Yadava	IPS/Maharashtra
2667.	Sanjay Pandey	IPS/Maharashtra

2668.	Jawahar Singh	IPS/Maharashtra
2669.	Pramod Asthana	IPS/M&T
2670.	Ranjit Kumar Sahay	IPS/M&T
2671.	Shambhu Nath Singh	IPS/M&T
2672.	Akhil Kumar Shukla	IPS/M&T
2673.	Abhay	IPS/Orissa
2674.	Rajendra Prasad Sharma	IPS/Orissa
2675.	Bijay Kumar Sharma	IPS/Orissa
2676.	Pradeep Kapur	IPS/Orissa
2677.	M. Nageshwar Rao	IPS/Orissa
2678.	Shyam S. Hansdah	IPS/Orissa
2679.	Siddharth Chattopadhyaya	IPS/Punjab
2680.	Jasminder Singh	IPS/Punjab
2681.	Dalpat Singh Dinkar	IPS/Rajasthan
2682.	Bhupendra Singh	IPS/Rajasthan
2683.	N. Ravindra Kumar Reddy	IPS/Rajasthan
2684.	Alok Tripathi	IPS/Rajasthan
2685.	Amarjit Singh	IPS/Rajasthan
2686.	N. Tamilselvan	IPS/TN
2687.	M.S. Jaffar Sait	IPS/TN
2688.	Ashutosh Shukla	IPS/TN
2689.	Mithilesh Kumar Jha	IPS/TN
2690.	Sanjeev Kumar	IPS/TN
2691.	C. Srilakshmi Rao (Ms)	IPS/TN
2692.	Chhotu Ram Meena	IPS/TN
2693.	Ashish Bhengra	IPS/TN
2694.	T.N. Mohan	IPS/UT
2695.	Rajesh Malik	IPS/UT
2696.	S. Vasudeva Rao	IPS/UT
2697.	S. Nithyanandam	IPS/UT
2698.	Pramod Kumar Tiwari	IPS/UP

2699.	M.A. Ganapathy	IPS/UP
2700.	Mahendra Modi	IPS/UP
2701.	Md. Javed Akhtar	IPS/UP
2702.	Nasir Kamal	IPS/UP
2703.	Jawahar Lal Tripathi	IPS/UP
2704.	Sujan Vir Singh	IPS/UP
2705.	Gaurav Chandra Dutt	IPS/WB
2706.	Kuldeep Singh	IPS/WB
2707.	Rakesh Kumar Gupta	IPS/WB
2708.	Shashi Bhushan SinghTomar	IPS/WB
2709.	Manoj Malaviya	IPS/WB
2710.	R. Thyagaraju	IPS/WB
2711.	C.R. Gurung	Bhutan Police (Foreign)
2712.	Nimzar Dorji	Bhutan Police (Foreign)
2713.	Lal Bahadur Pradhan	Bhutan Police (Foreign)
2714.	Rinzin Dorji	Bhutan Police (Foreign)

Training Year: 1987-89; Batch: 1987 -IPS-RR-40

2715.	Gokle Paradesh Naidu	IPS/AP
2716.	H.V. Surendra Babu	IPS/AP
2717.	Vinoy Kumar Singh	IPS/AP
2718.	Tusaraditya Tripathi	IPS/AP
2719.	Santosh Mehra	IPS/AP
2720.	M. Gopal Krishna	IPS/AP
2721.	B.L. Meena	IPS/AP
2722.	Satya Narayan	IPS/AP
2723.	A.R. Anuradha (Mrs)	IPS/AP
2724.	A.K. Sinha Casshyap	IPS/A&M
2725.	V.K. Bhawra	IPS/A&M
2726.	Ravi Kant Singh	IPS/A&M
2727.	B.L. Buam	IPS/A&M
2728.	Neeraj Sinha	IPS/Bihar

2729.	Gupteshwar Pandey	IPS/Bihar
2730.	Md. Taj Hassan	IPS/Bihar
2731.	A. Sermarajan	IPS/Bihar
2732.	Sunil Kumar	IPS/Bihar
2733.	P.R.K. Naidu	IPS/Bihar
2734.	Dinesh Bist	IPS/Bihar
2735.	M. Vishnuvardhana Rao	IPS/Bihar
2736.	Rezi Dung Dung	IPS/Bihar
2737.	A.K. Sharma	IPS/Gujarat
2738.	Kamal Kumar Ojha	IPS/Gujarat
2739.	Sanjay Srivastava	IPS/Gujarat
2740.	Chimanlal R. Parmar	IPS/Gujarat
2741.	P.S. Gondia	IPS/Gujarat
2742.	K.K. Mishra	IPS/Haryana
2743.	V. Kamaraja	IPS/Haryana
2744.	Manpreet Vohra	IPS/HP
2745.	V.K. Singh	IPS/J&K
2746.	Shiv Murari Sahai	IPS/J&K
2747.	M.S. Saravade	IPS/J&K
2748.	Dilbagh Singh	IPS/J&K
2749.	Raghavendra H. Auradhker	IPS/Karnataka
2750.	Alok Mohan	IPS/Karnataka
2751.	N.S. Magharikh	IPS/Karnataka
2752.	Tomin J. Thachankary	IPS/Kerala
2753.	R. Sreelekha (Ms)	IPS/Kerala
2754.	Rajvir Pratap Sharma	IPS/Kerala
2755.	Arun Kumar Sinha	IPS/Kerala
2756.	Bharat Asarsa	IPS/Kerala
2757.	Sudesh Kumar	IPS/Kerala
2758.	Pavan Kumar Jain	IPS/MP
2759.	S.K. Saxena	IPS/MP

2760.	Vijay Yadav	IPS/MP
2761.	Sanjeev Kumar Singh	IPS/MP
2762.	R.K. Mishra	IPS/MP
2763.	Binay Kumar Singh	IPS/MP
2764.	M.R. Aruna (Ms)	IPS/MP
2765.	Swagat Das	IPS/MP
2766.	P.M. Mohan	IPS/MP
2767.	Vijay Kumar	IPS/MP
2768.	C.V. Muni Raju	IPS/MP
2769.	Shailesh Singh	IPS/MP
2770.	S.S. Barve	IPS/Maharashtra
2771.	S.N. Pandey	IPS/Maharashtra
2772.	Bipin Bihari	IPS/Maharashtra
2773.	D. Kannaka Ratnam	IPS/Maharashtra
2774.	Hemant N Nagrale	IPS/Maharashtra
2775.	Dalbir Singh	IPS/Maharashtra
2776.	S. Srinivas Prasad	IPS/M&T
2777.	M. Madana Mohan	IPS/M&T
2778.	Vandana Malik (Ms)	IPS/M&T
2779.	Vijay SinghYadav	IPS/M&T
2780.	P. Doungel	IPS/M&T
2781.	Thianghlima	IPS/M&T
2782.	Anand Prakash	IPS/M&T
2783.	Manoj Kumar	IPS/Orissa
2784.	Sunil Kumar Bansal	IPS/Orissa
2785.	Sunil Roy	IPS/Orissa
2786.	Surendra Panwar	IPS/Orissa
2787.	Dinkar Gupta	IPS/Punjab
2788.	C. Sita Rami Reddy	IPS/Punjab
2789.	Rajpal Meena	IPS/Punjab
2790.	Rajeev Kumar Dasot	IPS/Rajasthan

2791.	Akshaya Kumar Mishra	IPS/Rajasthan
2792.	Mohan Lal Lather	IPS/Rajasthan
2793.	M.C. Meena	IPS/Rajasthan
2794.	Ram Pal Singh	IPS/Rajasthan
2795.	A. Shankar Rao	IPS/Sikkim
2796.	Sanam Dubikey Negi	IPS/Sikkim
2797.	C. Sylendra Babu	IPS/TN
2798.	Karan Singha	IPS/TN
2799.	P.V. Philip	IPS/TN
2800.	G.U.G. Sastry	IPS/TN
2801.	S. Rajendran	IPS/TN
2802.	R.C. Kudawla	IPS/TN
2803.	Vijay Kumar	IPS/TN
2804.	Pradeep Kumar Bhardwaj	IPS/UT
2805.	S.K. Garg	IPS/UT
2806.	P. Kamaraj	IPS/UT
2807.	Anil K. Raturi	IPS/UP
2808.	Mukul Goel	IPS/UP
2809.	Rajender Pal Singh	IPS/UP
2810.	Nitin R. Gokaran	IPS/UP
2811.	Biswajit Mahapatra	IPS/UP
2812.	B.K. Singh	IPS/UP
2813.	Virendra Kumar	IPS/UP
2814.	Gopal Lal Meena	IPS/UP
2815.	Suman Bala (Ms)	IPS/WB
2816.	M.K. Singh	IPS/WB
2817.	B.B. Dash	IPS/WB
2818.	Pandeya Nirajnayan	IPS/WB
2819.	Adhir Sharma	IPS/WB
2820.	Sanjay Chander	IPS/WB
2821.	L.L. Doungel	IPS/WB

2822. Gangeshwar Singh IPS/WB
2823. Hemang Gurung Bhutan Police (Foreign)
2824. Sanjiv R. Bhatt IPS/Gujarat

Training Year: 1988-90; Batch: 1988 -IPS-RR-41

2825. J. Purna Chandra Rao IPS/AP
2826. Bhasker Jyoti Mahanta IPS/A&M
2827. Binay Kumar Mishra IPS/A&M
2828. M.R.V. Kumar IPS/A&M
2829. Arvind Pandey IPS/Bihar
2830. Sanjeev Kumar Singhal IPS/Bihar
2831. R. Manjunath Swamy IPS/Bihar
2832. Manmohan Singh IPS/Bihar
2833. Atul Karwal IPS/Gujarat
2834. Praveen Sinha IPS/Gujarat
2835. Vechatbhai M. Pargi IPS/Gujarat
2836. Prashanta Kumar Agarwal IPS/Haryana
2837. Ram Singh Yadav IPS/Haryana
2838. Tapan Kumar Deka IPS/HP
2839. Bhagnand Singh Negi IPS/HP
2840. Y. Anil Kumar IPS/Kerala
2841. B. Sandhya (Ms) IPS/Kerala
2842. Anil Kant IPS/Kerala
2843. Mukesh Gupta IPS/MP
2844. Rajeev Kumar Tandon IPS/MP
2845. Rajinder Kumar Vij IPS/MP
2846. Umesh Chandra Sarangi IPS/MP
2847. Surendra Kumar Pandey IPS/MP
2848. Avnesh Mangalam IPS/MP
2849. Kailash Makwana IPS/MP
2850. Sujoy Lal Thaosen IPS/MP
2851. Param Bir Singh IPS/Maharashtra

2852.	K. Venkateshan	IPS/Maharashtra
2853.	Rashmi Awasthi (Ms)	IPS/Maharashtra
2854.	Rajnish Seth	IPS/Maharashtra
2855.	Jagan Nath	IPS/Maharashtra
2856.	Gopabandhu Mallik	IPS/Orissa
2857.	Satyajit Mohanty	IPS/Orissa
2858.	M. Akhaya	IPS/Orissa
2859.	Santosh Kumar Upadhayaya	IPS/Orissa
2860.	Binayanand Jha	IPS/Orissa
2861.	Manoj Kumar Chhabra	IPS/Orissa
2862.	M.K. Tiwari	IPS/Punjab
2863.	Gurdev Singh	IPS/Punjab
2864.	Prabodh Kumar	IPS/Punjab
2865.	Rohit Choudhary	IPS/Punjab
2866.	Iqbal Preet Singh Sahota	IPS/Punjab
2867.	Hardeep Singh	IPS/Punjab
2868.	Bhagwan Lal Soni	IPS/Rajasthan
2869.	Pankaj Kumar Singh	IPS/Rajasthan
2870.	Nand Kumar Mishra	IPS/Sikkim
2871.	M.V.N. Surya Prasad	IPS/TN
2872.	Sanjay Arora	IPS/TN
2873.	Sunil Kumar	IPS/TN
2874.	Arvind Deep	IPS/AGMUT
2875.	Pranab Nanda	IPS/AGMUT
2876.	Uday Sahay	IPS/AGMUT
2877.	S.B.K. Singh	IPS/AGMUT
2878.	Muktesh Chander	IPS/AGMUT
2879.	N.Sivagami Sundari(Ms)	IPS/AGMUT
2880.	Kamal Saksena	IPS/UP
2881.	Devendra Singh Chauhan	IPS/UP
2882.	Rajkumar Vishwakarma	IPS/UP

2883.	Anil Kumar Agarwal	IPS/UP
2884.	Ashit Kumar Panda	IPS/UP
2885.	Vijay Kumar	IPS/UP
2886.	Brij Raj	IPS/UP
2887.	Soumesh Mitra	IPS/WB
2888.	Ram Phal	IPS/WB
2889.	B.N. Ramesh	IPS/WB
2890.	Herman Prit Singh	IPS/WB
2891.	Vivek Sahay	IPS/WB
2892.	Sudhir Mishra	IPS/WB
2893.	Zulfiquar Hassan	IPS/WB

Training Year: 1989-91; Batch -1989-IPS-RR-42

2894.	Umesh Sharraf	IPS/AP
2895.	Archana Sondawale (Ms)	IPS/AP
2896.	K.R.M. Kishore Kumar	IPS/AP
2897.	Agarwal Mukesh	IPS/A&M
2898.	Kumar Vijay Singh Deo	IPS/A&M
2899.	Pradhan Satya Narayan	IPS/Bihar
2900.	Alok Raj	IPS/Bihar
2901.	Ajay Kumar Singh	IPS/Bihar
2902.	Pratham Anil Kumar	IPS/Gujarat
2903.	Vikas Sahay	IPS/Gujarat
2904.	Ajay Kumar	IPS/Gujarat
2905.	Sudhir Choudhary	IPS/Haryana
2906.	Manoj Yadava	IPS/Haryana
2907.	Sanjay Kundu	IPS/HP
2908.	Sanjeev Ranjan Ojha	IPS/HP
2909.	Laltendu Mohanti	IPS/J&K
2910.	Baghel U.S.	IPS/Karnataka
2911.	Sanjay Vir Singh	IPS/Karnataka
2912.	Amar Kumar Pandey	IPS/Karnataka

2913.	Sanjay Sahay	IPS/Karnataka
2914.	Pavanjeet Singh Sandhu	IPS/Karnataka
2915.	S. Ananthakrishnan	IPS/Kerala
2916.	K. Padmakumar	IPS/Kerala
2917.	Arvind Kumar	IPS/MP
2918.	Sanjay Kumar Pillay	IPS/MP
2919.	Sudhir Kumar Shahi	IPS/MP
2920.	Ravi Sinha	IPS/MP
2921.	M. Kanaskar	IPS/MP
2922.	Mane S.V.	IPS/MP
2923.	Ashok Juneja	IPS/MP
2924.	Sushovan Banerjee	IPS/MP
2925.	Phalnikar Pramod Shripad	IPS/MP
2926.	Sanjay Kumar Jha	IPS/MP
2927.	Mukesh Kumar Jain	IPS/MP
2928.	Sushma Singh	IPS/MP
2929.	Dasondi H.P.	IPS/Maharashtra
2930.	Rajender Singh	IPS/Maharashtra
2931.	Bhushan Kumar Upadhyay	IPS/Maharashtra
2932.	Sanjay Kumar	IPS/Maharashtra
2933.	Ashok M. Kamte	IPS/Maharashtra
2934.	Amitabh Ranjan	IPS/M&T
2935.	Anish Dayal Singh	IPS/M&T
2936.	Nina Rani (Ms)	IPS/M&T
2937.	T. Suneel Kumar	IPS/M&T
2938.	Satya Sunder Tripathy	IPS/Nagaland
2939.	Ved Prakash	IPS/Nagaland
2940.	Ray Arun Kumar	IPS/Orissa
2941.	Pranabindu Acharya	IPS/Orissa
2942.	S.M. Narvane	IPS/Orissa
2943.	B. Radhika	IPS/Orissa

2944.	Ramesh Chandra Singh	IPS/Punjab
2945.	Sanjeev Kumar Kalra	IPS/Punjab
2946.	Parag Jain	IPS/Punjab
2947.	Lall M.K.	IPS/Rajasthan
2948.	Narasimha Rao K	IPS/Rajasthan
2949.	Utkal Ranjan Sahoo	IPS/Rajasthan
2950.	Dak B.K.	IPS/Rajasthan
2951.	Indu Kumar Bhushan	IPS/Rajasthan
2952.	A. Sudhakara Rao	IPS/Sikkim
2953.	Suneel Kumar Singh	IPS/TN
2954.	Md. Akhter Shakeel	IPS/TN
2955.	P. Kandaswamy	IPS/TN
2956.	Ravi Braj Kishore	IPS/TN
2957.	K.C. Mahali	IPS/TN
2958.	Balaji Srivastava	IPS/AGMUT
2959.	Sanjay Baniwal	IPS/AGMUT
2960.	Krishnia R.S.	IPS/AGMUT
2961.	Anand Kumar	IPS/UP
2962.	Ashok Kumar	IPS/UP
2963.	Ram Singh Meena	IPS/UP
2964.	Chandra Prakash	IPS/UP
2965.	Kailash Chandra Meena	IPS/WB
2966.	Pattapu Ravi	IPS/WB
2967.	Pradnya Bhosale (Mrs)	IPS/WB

Training Year: 1990-92; Batch: 1990 -IPS-RR-43

2968.	A.B. Venkateswara Rao	IPS/AP
2969.	Ch. D. Tirumala Rao	IPS/AP
2970.	Anjani Kumar	IPS/AP
2971.	Daljit Singh Chowdhary	IPS/AP
2972.	Govind Singh	IPS/AP
2973.	Yatendra Kumar Gautam	IPS/A&M

2974.	Lungriading	IPS/A&M
2975.	Ajay Bhatnagar	IPS/Bihar
2976.	Anil Palta	IPS/Bihar
2977.	Rajwinder Singh Bhatti	IPS/Bihar
2978.	Anurag Gupta	IPS/Bihar
2979.	Vivek Srivastava	IPS/Gujarat
2980.	P.V. Rama Sastry	IPS/Gujarat
2981.	Muhammed Akhil	IPS/Haryana
2982.	Ramesh Chandra Mishra	IPS/Haryana
2983.	B. Srinivas	IPS/J&K
2984.	P. Ravindranath	IPS/Karnataka
2985.	Bhaskar Rao	IPS/Karnataka
2986.	Savita J Dharmadhikari	IPS/Karnataka
2987.	Kamal Pant	IPS/Karnataka
2988.	Nitin Agrawal	IPS/Kerala
2989.	Hari Nath Mishra	IPS/Kerala
2990.	Govind Pratap Singh	IPS/MP
2991.	Ajay Kumar Sharma	IPS/MP
2992.	Rajesh Chawla	IPS/MP
2993.	Sajjad Wasi Naqvi	IPS/MP
2994.	Mulchand Bajaj	IPS/MP
2995.	Syed Mohd Afzal	IPS/MP
2996.	Ashok Awasthi	IPS/MP
2997.	Vipin Kumar Maheshwari	IPS/MP
2998.	B.B. Sharma	IPS/MP
2999.	Rajesh Kumar Mishra	IPS/MP
3000.	Vijay Kataria	IPS/MP
3001.	Anuradha Shankar (Ms)	IPS/MP
3002.	G.R. Meena	IPS/MP
3003.	Vivek Phansalkar	IPS/Maharashtra
3004.	Sandeep Bishnoi	IPS/Maharashtra

3005.	Jai Jeet Singh	IPS/Maharashtra
3006.	V.V. Lakshmi Narayana	IPS/Maharashtra
3007.	Rakesh Ranjan	IPS/Tripura
3008.	Rahul Rasgotra	IPS/Manipur
3009.	Shyam Sunder Chaturvedi	IPS/Tripura
3010.	Amrit Mohan Prasad	IPS/Orissa
3011.	Yogesh Bahadur Khurania	IPS/Orissa
3012.	Desh Raj Singh	IPS/Orissa
3013.	Umesh Mishra	IPS/Rajasthan
3014.	Babu N. Marris	IPS/Rajasthan
3015.	Janga Srinivas Rao	IPS/Rajasthan
3016.	Rajeev Kumar Sharma	IPS/Rajasthan
3017.	Amrendra Kumar Singh	IPS/Sikkim
3018.	Rajesh Dass	IPS/TN
3019.	Pramod Kumar	IPS/TN
3020.	A.K. Viswanathan	IPS/TN
3021.	Seema Agarwal (Mrs)	IPS/TN
3022.	Sandeep Goel	IPS/AGMUT
3023.	Sunil Kumar Gautam	IPS/AGMUT
3024.	Mukesh Kumar Meena	IPS/AGMUT
3025.	Tajinder Singh Luthra	IPS/AGMUT
3026.	Dependra Pathak	IPS/AGMUT
3027.	Sanjay Singh	IPS/AGMUT
3028.	Ashish Gupta	IPS/UP
3029.	Safi Ahsan Rizvi	IPS/UP
3030.	Aditya Mishra	IPS/UP
3031.	Avinash Chandra	IPS/UP
3032.	V. Vinay Kumar	IPS/UP
3033.	S. Renuka Sastry (Ms)	IPS/UP
3034.	Sandeep Salunke	IPS/UP
3035.	Satya Narayana Sabat	IPS/UP

3036.	Satish Kumar Mathur	IPS/UP
3037.	M. Mohan Kumar Bashal	IPS/UP
3038.	Tanuja Srivastava (Ms)	IPS/UP
3039.	D.L. Ratnam	IPS/UP
3040.	Subhash Chander	IPS/UP
3041.	Anju Gupta	IPS/UP
3042.	Sanjay Mukherjee	IPS/WB
3043.	Rajeev Kumar	IPS/WB
3044.	Ranvir Kumar	IPS/WB
3045.	Rajesh Kumar	IPS/WB
3046.	Debasish Roy	IPS/WB
3047.	Tshering Penjore	Bhutan Police (Foreign)
3048.	Phub Dorjee	Bhutan Police (Foreign)

Training Year: 1991-93; Batch -1991-IPS-RR-44

3049.	Chadalawada Umesh C	IPS/AP
3050.	Gupta Ravi	IPS/AP
3051.	Reza Md. Ahsan	IPS/AP
3052.	Madireddy Pratap	IPS/AP
3053.	Rajiv Ratan	IPS/AP
3054.	Bishnoi Lajja Ram	IPS/A&M
3055.	Singh Gyanendra Pratap	IPS/A&M
3056.	Singh S. Narayan	IPS/A&M
3057.	Natarajan A	IPS/Bihar
3058.	Dhatkar Shobe (Ms)	IPS/Bihar
3059.	Sinha Neeraj	IPS/Bihar
3060.	Agarwal Manoj	IPS/Gujarat
3061.	Raman Prakash	IPS/Gujarat
3062.	Singh Shamsher	IPS/Gujarat
3063.	Jain Sanjeev Kumar	IPS/Haryana
3064.	Kapoor Shatrujeet Singh	IPS/Haryana
3065.	Shyam Bhagat	IPS/HP

3066.	Siddiqui, Payam Ahmad	IPS/HP
3067.	Choudhary, Arun Kumar	IPS/J&K
3068.	Agarwal Sunil	IPS/Karnataka
3069.	Parashiva Murthy, S	IPS/Karnataka
3070.	Reddy C.P.	IPS/Karnataka
3071.	Shiva Kumar, N	IPS/Karnataka
3072.	Patjoshi, Sanjeeb Kumar	IPS/Kerala
3073.	Shaik Darvesh Saheb	IPS/Kerala
3074.	V. Madhukumar	IPS/MP
3075.	Long Kumar T.J.	IPS/MP
3076.	Rao K. Babu	IPS/MP
3077.	Singh Ravindra Nath	IPS/MP
3078.	Vaiphei Khailianthang	IPS/MP
3079.	Pragya Richa (Ms)	IPS/MP
3080.	Date Sadanand Vasant	IPS/Maharashtra
3081.	Fernandes Marie Low (Ms)	IPS/Maharashtra
3082.	Jaganathan, S	IPS/Maharashtra
3083.	Kargaonkar, Vinay M	IPS/Maharashtra
3084.	Kulkarni, Athuchandra M	IPS/Maharashtra
3085.	Kulwant Kumar	IPS/Maharashtra
3086.	Padmanabhan R.K.	IPS/Maharashtra
3087.	Raghavendra, T.P.	IPS/Maharashtra
3088.	Singh Bipin Kumar	IPS/Maharashtra
3089.	Verma Sanjay Kumar	IPS/Maharashtra
3090.	Doungel Christopher	IPS/M&T
3091.	Nayakjoydeep	IPS/M&T
3092.	Sunil Achaya, A.	IPS/Nagaland
3093.	Mahendra Pratap	IPS/Orissa
3094.	Panigrahi Debasis	IPS/Orissa
3095.	Sarangi Arun Kumar	IPS/Orissa
3096.	Sarangi Sudhanshu	IPS/Orissa
3097.	Singh Jaswinder	IPS/Orissa

3098.	Uppal Barjinder Kumar	IPS/Punjab
3099.	Jain Dharam Chand	IPS/Rajasthan
3100.	Maherda Ravi Prakash	IPS/Rajasthan
3101.	Muthusamy Ponnuchamy	IPS/Rajastan
3102.	Srivastava Saurabh	IPS/Rajasthan
3103.	Sachdeva Akshay	IPS/Sikkim(Foreign)
3104.	Abhash Kumar	IPS/TN
3105.	Jayanth Murali, K.	IPS/TN
3106.	Jiwal Shankar	IPS/TN
3107.	Prashant Kumar	IPS/TN
3108.	Pujari Amaresh	IPS/TN
3109.	Ravichandran, T.V.	IPS/TN
3110.	Ravi, M.	IPS/TN
3111.	Sagar Karuna	IPS/TN
3112.	Roy, Anita (Ms)	IPS/AGMUT
3113.	Singh Virender	IPS/AGMUT
3114.	Upadhyaya Rajender Pal	IPS/AGMUT
3115.	Khan Nuzhat (Ms)	IPS/AGMUT
3116.	Braj Bhushan	IPS/UP
3117.	Kiran Jadhav	IPS/UP
3118.	Maurya Bijaya Kumar	IPS/UP
3119.	Piyush Anand	IPS/UP
3120.	Rajeev Krishna	IPS/UP
3121.	Sharma Alok	IPS/UP
3122.	Tarade, Sanjay M	IPS/UP
3123.	Verma Rajeev Ranjan	IPS/UP
3124.	Babu N. Ramesh	IPS/WB
3125.	Basu Jayanta Kumar	IPS/WB
3126.	Das, Madhuparna (Ms)	IPS/WB
3127.	Jag Mohan	IPS/WB
3128.	Joshi B Nichiket	IPS/WB

3129.	Sharma Anuj	IPS/WB

Training Year: 1992-94; Batch: 1992 -IPS-RR-45

3130.	Anand C.V.	IPS/AP
3131.	Anjaneyulu P. Sita Rama	IPS/AP
3132.	Gupta Harish Kumar	IPS/AP
3133.	Kasireddy R.N. Reddy	IPS/AP
3134.	Prabhat Nalin	IPS/AP
3135.	Jitender	IPS/AP
3136.	Nongrang Idashisha (Ms)	IPS/A&M
3137.	Singh Harmeet	IPS/A&M
3138.	Ambedkar Amrendra Kumar	IPS/Bihar
3139.	Mallick Raj Kumar	IPS/Bihar
3140.	Singh Prashant	IPS/Bihar
3141.	Vashista Praveen	IPS/Bihar
3142.	Verma Preeta (Ms)	IPS/Bihar
3143.	Vinay Kumar	IPS/Bihar
3144.	Ansari Samiullah	IPS/Gujarat
3145.	K. Laxminarayana Rao	IPS/Gujarat
3146.	Sharma Rahul	IPS/Gujarat
3147.	Rai Rajnish Kumar	IPS/Gujarat
3148.	Roy Alok Kumar	IPS/Haryana
3149.	Singh Om Prakash	IPS/Haryana
3150.	Singhal Ajay	IPS/Haryana
3151.	Varma Atul	IPS/HP
3152.	Sharma Rupin	IPS/HP
3153.	Lohia Hemant Kumar	IPS/J&K
3154.	Swain Rashmi Ranjan	IPS/J&K
3155.	Murty, A.S.N.	IPS/Karnataka
3156.	Thakur Prashant Kumar	IPS/Karnataka
3157.	R.A. Chandra Sekhar	IPS/Kerala
3158.	Rawat Neera (Ms)	IPS/Kerala

3159.	Vinod Kumar T.K.	IPS/Kerala
3160.	Deo Pawan	IPS/MP
3161.	Dewangan Raj Kumar	IPS/MP
3162.	Gautam Arun Dev	IPS/MP
3163.	Gupta Rajesh	IPS/MP
3164.	Jain Upendra Kumar	IPS/MP
3165.	Janardhan G.	IPS/MP
3166.	Kapoor Varun	IPS/MP
3167.	Ranjan Alok	IPS/MP
3168.	Rao Sreenivasa, D.	IPS/MP
3169.	Sema Akheto G.	IPS/MP
3170.	Sharma Manish	IPS/MP
3171.	Srivastava Pawan Kumar	IPS/MP
3172.	Arvind Kumar	IPS/M&T
3173.	Hopingson R.N.	IPS/M&T
3174.	Das Lalit	IPS/Orissa
3175.	Mudgel Yogesh	IPS/Orissa
3176.	Tewari Sapna (Mrs)	IPS/Orissa
3177.	Oraon Arun Kumar	IPS/Punjab
3178.	Sidhu Harpreet Singh	IPS/Punjab
3179.	Singh Kuldeep	IPS/Punjab
3180.	Yadav Gaurav	IPS/Punjab
3181.	Guite Thangkhanlal	IPS/Rajasthan
3182.	Manjunatha M.N.	IPS/TN
3183.	Rajeev Kumar	IPS/TN
3184.	Rathore Sandeep Rai	IPS/TN
3185.	Vanniaperumal, K.	IPS/TN
3186.	Garg Sunil	IPS/AGMUT
3187.	Gogia Vivek	IPS/AGMUT
3188.	Golchha Satish	IPS/AGMUT
3189.	Anand Ajay	IPS/UP

3190.	Juneja Dipesh	IPS/UP
3191.	Jogdand B.P.	IPS/UP
3192.	Meena Prem Chand	IPS/UP
3193.	Pandey Ashutosh	IPS/UP
3194.	Prasad Abhay Kumar	IPS/UP
3195.	Sherpa Dawa	IPS/UP
3196.	Thakur Amitabh	IPS/UP
3197.	Agarwal Manish Kumar	IPS/WB
3198.	Gupta Siddh Nath	IPS/WB
3199.	Singh Sanjay	IPS/WB
3200.	Pema Dodo Dorji	Bhutan Police (Foreign)
3201.	Tilak Sharma	Bhutan Police (Foreign)
3202.	Bijay Lal Kayastha	Nepal Police (Foreign)
3203.	Devendra Subedi	Nepal Police (Foreign)
3204.	Rajendra Man Shrestha	Nepal Police (Foreign)

Training Year: 1993-95; Batch: 1993 -IPS-RR-46

3205.	Oberoi Madan Mohan	IPS/AGMUT
3206.	Ranjan Praveer	IPS/AGMUT
3207.	Dixit Mahesh Shantaram	IPS/AP
3208.	Shandilya Sandeep	IPS/AP
3209.	Garg Amit	IPS/AP
3210.	Raju G.H.P.	IPS/AP
3211.	Sunil Kumar P.V.	IPS/AP
3212.	Mohammed Suresh Kunhi	IPS/Karnataka
3213.	Malini Krishnamoorthy (Ms)	IPS/Karnataka
3214.	K.S.R. Charan Reddy	IPS/Karnataka
3215.	Abdulla Saleem M.	IPS/Karnataka
3216.	Gupta Yogesh	IPS/Kerala
3217.	Thomas Vinode	IPS/Kerala
3218.	Joy Ajit	IPS/Kerala
3219.	Singh Abhay Kumar	IPS/TN

3220.	Yadava Shailesh Kumar	IPS/TN
3221.	Das Ashoka Kumar	IPS/TN
3222.	Chawla Arshinder Singh	IPS/Haryana
3223.	Mittal Alok Kumar	IPS/Haryana
3224.	Garg Anurag	IPS/HP
3225.	Tewari Ashok	IPS/HP
3226.	Saxena Pankaj	IPS/J&K
3227.	Kumar Deepak	IPS/J&K
3228.	Chouhan Sharad Satya	IPS/Punjab
3229.	Deo Gurpreet Kaur (Ms)	IPS/Punjab
3230.	Kumar Varinder	IPS/Punjab
3231.	Jain Jitendra Kumar	IPS/Punjab
3232.	Asthana Satish Kumar	IPS/Punjab
3233.	Singh Ishwar	IPS/Punjab
3234.	Srinivasan Brighu	IPS/Bihar
3235.	Jha Sunil Kumar	IPS/Bihar
3236.	Kumar Arvind	IPS/Bihar
3237.	Bhatia Manvinder Singh	IPS/Bihar
3238.	Gangwar Jitendra Singh	IPS/Bihar
3239.	Kumar Jitendra	IPS/Bihar
3240.	Anand Swaroop	IPS/UP
3241.	Singh Jasvir	IPS/UP
3242.	Kaul Satyendra Kumar	IPS/UP
3243.	Zaki Ahmad	IPS/UP
3244.	Singhal Sanjay	IPS/UP
3245.	Gupta Sunil Kumar	IPS/UP
3246.	S. Shripad Bhagwanrao	IPS/UP
3247.	Jyoti S. Belur (Ms)	IPS/UP
3248.	Kumar Vitul	IPS/UP
3249.	Sharma Hari Ram	IPS/UP
3250.	Sabharwal Rajeev	IPS/UP

3251.	Prem Prakash	IPS/UP
3252.	Sagar Dinesh Chand	IPS/MP
3253.	Katiyar Adarsh	IPS/MP
3254.	Srivastava Pankaj Kumar	IPS/MP
3255.	Mishra Sonali (Ms)	IPS/MP
3256.	Gupta Anil Kumar	IPS/MP
3257.	Meena Roop Singh	IPS/MP
3258.	Priyadarshy Hemant	IPS/Rajasthan
3259.	Nirwan Rajesh	IPS/Rajasthan
3260.	Amrit Kalash	IPS/Rajasthan
3261.	Lohia Prakash Kumar	IPS/Assam
3262.	Meena Ram Prasad	IPS/Assam
3263.	Agarwal Sanjay Kumar	IPS/M&T
3264.	Singh Rajiv	IPS/M&T
3265.	Mishra Vinaytosh	IPS/Orissa
3266.	Koche Raosaheb Punjabrao	IPS/Orissa
3267.	Meghwal Bhagwanaram	IPS/WB
3268.	Singh Gyanwant	IPS/WB
3269.	Pujari Shashikant	IPS/WB
3270.	Kumar Praveen	IPS/WB
3271.	Patel Hasmukhkumar N.	IPS/Gujarat
3272.	Malik Gyanender Singh	IPS/Gujarat
3273.	Gotru Neeraja (Ms)	IPS/Gujarat
3274.	Gupta Amitabh	IPS/Maharashtra
3275.	Singhal Sanjeev Kumar	IPS/Maharashtra
3276.	Kumar Ritesh	IPS/Maharashtra
3277.	Kumar Prabhat	IPS/Maharashtra
3278.	Saxena Sanjay	IPS/Maharashtra
3279.	Tyagi Archana (Ms)	IPS/Maharashtra
3280.	Burde Prashant	IPS/Maharashtra
3281.	Dhananjay Dattatraya	IPS/Maharashtra

3282.	Shukla, D.S.	DySP. CBI
3283.	Ramnish	DySP. CBI

Training Year: 1994-96 - Passing Out Parade after First Phase; Batch: 1994 - IPS - RR - 47

3284.	Neeraj Thakur	IPS/AGMUT
3285.	Anurag Kumar	IPS/AGMUT
3286.	Kumar Vishwajeet	IPS/AGMUT
3287.	Rajesh Khurana	IPS/AGMUT
3288.	Robin Hibu	IPS/AGMUT
3289.	Abhilasha Bisht (Ms)	IPS/AGMUT
3290.	Anand Mohan	IPS/AGMUT
3291.	K.N. Tripathi Ujela	IPS/AP
3292.	B. Shiv Dhar Reddy	IPS/AP
3293.	K. Sreenivasa Reddy	IPS/AP
3294.	Ravishankar Ayyanar	IPS/AP
3295.	Soumya Mishra (Ms)	IPS/AP
3296.	N. Balasubramanyam	IPS/AP
3297.	Vinayak Prabhakar Apte	IPS/AP
3298.	Kumar Deepak	IPS/A&M
3299.	Rithwik Rudra	IPS/Bihar
3300.	Nirmal Kumar Azad	IPS/Bihar
3301.	Anupama S. Nilekar (Ms)	IPS/Bihar
3302.	Tadasha Mishra (Ms)	IPS/Bihar
3303.	Murari Lal Meena	IPS/Bihar
3304.	Amit Kumar	IPS/Bihar
3305.	Kundan Krishnan	IPS/Bihar
3306.	Amitabh Kumar Das	IPS/Bihar
3307.	Navdeep Singh Vierk	IPS/Haryana
3308.	Kala Ramachandran (Ms)	IPS/Haryana
3309.	Shrikant Jadhav Atmaram	IPS/Haryana
3310.	S. Zahur H. Zaidi	IPS/HP

3311.	Rakesh Aggarwal	IPS/HP
3312.	S.J. Mujtaba Gillani	IPS/J&K
3313.	Pronob Mohanty	IPS/Karnataka
3314.	Alok Kumar	IPS/Karnataka
3315.	K. Ramachandra Rao	IPS/Karnataka
3316.	Manoj Abraham	IPS/Kerala
3317.	Ashutosh Roy	IPS/MP
3318.	Raja Babu Singh	IPS/MP
3319.	Manmeet Singh Narang	IPS/MP
3320.	Anil Kumar	IPS/MP
3321.	Ravi Kumar Gupta	IPS/MP
3322.	Kalluri Siva Rama Prasad	IPS/MP
3323.	Gurjinder Pal Singh	IPS/MP
3324.	Deo Prakash Gupta	IPS/MP
3325.	Sanjeev Shami	IPS/MP
3326.	Anant Kumar Singh	IPS/MP
3327.	Sukhwinder Singh	IPS/Maharashtra
3328.	Sunil Bharma Ramanand	IPS/Maharashtra
3329.	Anup Kumar	IPS/Maharashtra
3330.	Devan Bharti	IPS/Maharashtra
3331.	Vineet Agarwal	IPS/Maharashtra
3332.	Anjana Singh (Ms)	IPS/Nagaland
3333.	Ashutosh Kumar	IPS/Manipur
3334.	Lupheng Kailun	IPS/Manipur
3335.	Himanshu Gupta	IPS/Tripura
3336.	Anurag	IPS/Tripura
3337.	Susanta Kumar Nath	IPS/Orissa
3338.	Yeshwant K. Jethwa	IPS/Orissa
3339.	Ram Singh	IPS/Punjab
3340.	Anita Punj (Ms)	IPS/Punjab
3341.	Praveen Kumar Sinha	IPS/Punjab

3342.	Amardeep Rai	IPS/Punjab
3343.	Rajendra Namdeo Dhoke	IPS/Punjab
3344.	Shashi Prabha Dwivedi	IPS/Punjab
3345.	Ashok Rathore	IPS/Rajasthan
3346.	Govind Gupta	IPS/Rjasthan
3347.	Anil Paliwal	IPS/Rajasthan
3348.	Sunil Dutt	IPS/Rajasthan
3349.	Rajesh Kumar Arya	IPS/Rajasthan
3350.	Sanjay Nag	IPS/TN
3351.	Sidharth Zutshi	IPS/TN
3352.	Vinit Dev Wankhede	IPS/TN
3353.	G. Venkataraman	IPS/TN
3354.	Mahesh Kumar Aggarwal	IPS/TN
3355.	L.V. Antony Dev Kumar	IPS/UP
3356.	Pratap Kumar K.S.	IPS/UP
3357.	Binod Kumar Singh	IPS/UP
3358.	Jai Narayan Singh	IPS/UP
3359.	Raja Srivastava	IPS/UP
3360.	Dhruva Kant Thakur	IPS/UP
3361.	Sujeet Pandey	IPS/UP
3362.	Akhil Kumar	IPS/UP
3363.	Asim Kumar Arun	IPS/UP
3364.	Niraj Kumar Singh	IPS/WB
3365.	Peeyush Pandey	IPS/WB
3366.	Ajoy Kumar	IPS/WB
3367.	Garima Bhatnagar (Ms)	IPS/WB

Training Year: 1995-97; Batch: 1995 -IPS-RR-48

3368.	Khirwar Sandeep	IPS/AGMUT
3369.	Tiwari Madhup Kumar	IPS/AGMUT
3370.	Singh Atul	IPS/AP
3371.	R.S. Praveen Kumar	IPS/AP

3372.	Tewari Anand Kumar	IPS/A&M
3373.	Nongpluh Heimonlang	IPS/A&M
3374.	Tankha Anurag	IPS/A&M
3375.	Venkata Krishna Arige Yag	IPS/A&M
3376.	Gupta Munna Prasad	IPS/A&M
3377.	Mir Ab. Gani	IPS/Bihar
3378.	Saxena Paresh	IPS/Bihar
3379.	Meena Sampat	IPS/Bihar
3380.	Singh Ajay Kumar	IPS/Bihar
3381.	Lathkar Sanjay A.	IPS/Bihar
3382.	S. Raveendran	IPS/Bihar
3383.	R. Malar Vizhi (Ms)	IPS/Bihar
3384.	Jag Mohan	IPS/Bihar
3385.	Saxena Anupam (Ms)	IPS/Bihar
3386.	Swati Lakra (Ms)	IPS/Bihar
3387.	Sasidhar Manoj	IPS/Gujarat
3388.	Bhargava Raju	IPS/Gujarat
3389.	Bali Charu (Ms)	IPS/Haryana
3390.	Chakkirala Sambasiva Rao	IPS/Haryana
3391.	Singh Satinder Pal	IPS/HP
3392.	N. Venu Gopal	IPS/HP
3393.	Goel Shikha (Ms)	IPS/J&K
3394.	Sajimohan	IPS/J&K
3395.	Darad Pankaj Kumar	IPS/J&K
3396.	Singh Shiv Darshan	IPS/J&K
3397.	Kumar Rajesh	IPS/J&K
3398.	Khandare Satish Shriramaj	IPS/J&K
3399.	Namgyal Kalon Tsewang	IPS/J&K
3400.	Dayananda B.	IPS/Karnataka
3401.	Chakravarthy Arun Jeji	IPS/Karnataka
3402.	Paul Amrit	IPS/Karnataka

3403.	S. Suresh	IPS/Kerala
3404.	A. Sai Manohar	IPS/MP
3405.	Jain Mayank	IPS/MP
3406.	Prasad Jaideep	IPS/MP
3407.	Chawla Meenakshi (Ms)	IPS/MP
3408.	Dumbare Ashutosh Karbhari	IPS/Maharashtra
3409.	Salunke Pravin S.	IPS/Maharashtra
3410.	Srivastva Devesh Chandra	IPS/M&T
3411.	Rastogi Puneet	IPS/M&T
3412.	Panda Sanjeeb	IPS/Orissa
3413.	Sharma Radha Kishan	IPS/Orissa
3414.	Ranpise Padmakar Santu	IPS/Orissa
3415.	Priyadarsi Saumyendra Kum	IPS/Orissa
3416.	Thakur Ritu (Ms)	IPS/Orissa
3417.	Bala Santosh (Ms)	IPS/Orissa
3418.	Srivastava Sudhanshu Shek	IPS/Punjab
3419.	B. Chandra Sekhar	IPS/Punjab
3420.	Neeraja Voruvuru (Ms)	IPS/Punjab
3421.	Farooqui Mohd Faiyaz	IPS/Punjab
3422.	Ban Pramod	IPS/Punjab
3423.	Cheema Gautam	IPS/Punjab
3424.	Kumar Naresh	IPS/Punjab
3425.	Prasad Amit	IPS/Punjab
3426.	Srivastava Malini (Ms)	IPS/Rajasthan
3427.	Joseph K. Biju George	IPS/Rajasthan
3428.	Biswas Sushmit	IPS/Rajasthan
3429.	Khare Smita (Ms)	IPS/Rajasthan
3430.	Shrivastava Anand Kumar	IPS/Rajasthan
3431.	N. Sridhar Rao	IPS/Sikkim
3432.	Vinayak Vineet	IPS/Sikkim
3433.	Mittal Sandeep	IPS/TN

3434.	S. Davidson Devasirvatham	IPS/TN
3435.	B. Bala Naga Devi (Ms)	IPS/TN
3436.	Prakash, D.	IPS/UP
3437.	Seth Deepam	IPS/UP
3438.	Singh Alok	IPS/UP
3439.	Bhatia Vijay	IPS/UP
3440.	Mutha Ashok Jain	IPS/UP
3441.	Sengar Amrendra Kumar	IPS/UP
3442.	Lokku Ravi Kumar	IPS/UP
3443.	Kuril Rajkumar Ramnarayan	IPS/UP
3444.	Prasad Paloli Venkata Kri	IPS/UP
3445.	Goyal Vineet Kumar	IPS/WB
3446.	Man Singh	IPS/WB
3447.	Ranade Ajey Mukund	IPS/WB
3448.	Shamin Jawed	IPS/WB

Training Year: 1996-98; Batch -1996-IPS-RR-49

3449.	Anil Shukla	IPS/AGMUT
3450.	Manish Kumar Agarwal	IPS/AGMUT
3451.	Alok Kumar	IPS/AGMUT
3452.	Ajay Chaudhary	IPS/AGMUT
3453.	Ravindra Singh Yadav	IPS/AGMUT
3454.	David Lalrinsanga	IPS/AGMUT
3455.	Charu Sinha (Ms)	IPS/AP
3456.	V. Channappa Sajjanar	IPS/AP
3457.	Anil Kumar	IPS/AP
3458.	V. Srinivasarao Veerisett	IPS/AP
3459.	Rajeev Kumar Meena	IPS/AP
3460.	Vineet Sharma (Ms)	IPS/A&M
3461.	Hiren Chandra Nath	IPS/A&M
3462.	Nelli Kumar Subramanyan	IPS/A&M
3463.	Sudhanshu Kumar	IPS/Bihar

3464.	Vinay Hande	IPS/Bihar
3465.	Nayyar Hasnain Khan	IPS/Bihar
3466.	Sunil Kumar	IPS/Bihar
3467.	Paras Nath	IPS/Bihar
3468.	Anil Kishor Yadav	IPS/Bihar
3469.	Baljit Singh	IPS/Bihar
3470.	Bacchu Singh Meena	IPS/Bihar
3471.	Kamal Kishore Singh	IPS/Bihar
3472.	Sushil Mansing Khopde	IPS/Bihar
3473.	Narasimha N. Komar	IPS/Gujarat
3474.	S. Pandia Raja Kumar	IPS/Gujarat
3475.	Mamta Singh (Ms)	IPS/Haryana
3476.	Satwant Atwal	IPS/HP
3477.	Mukesh Singh	IPS/J&K
3478.	Manish Kishore Sinha	IPS/J&K
3479.	Ritu Mishra (Ms)	IPS/J&K
3480.	Nilkanth S. Avhad	IPS/J&K
3481.	Sunil Kumar	IPS/J&K
3482.	Danesh Rana	IPS/J&K
3483.	Seemant Kumar Singh	IPS/Karnataka
3484.	Bijay Kumar Singh	IPS/Karnataka
3485.	R. Hithendra	IPS/Karnataka
3486.	Umesh Kumar	IPS/Karnataka
3487.	S. Sreejith	IPS/Kerala
3488.	Ajith Kumar M.R.	IPS/Kerala
3489.	Yogesh Choudhary	IPS/MP
3490.	Neeraj Bulchandani	IPS/MP
3491.	Mohd. Shahid Absar	IPS/MP
3492.	Balbir Singh	IPS/MP
3493.	Pradeep Gupta	IPS/MP
3494.	Chanchal Shekhar	IPS/MP

3495.	K.P. Venkateshwar Rao	IPS/MP
3496.	Yogesh Deshmukh	IPS/MP
3497.	Nikhil Jaiprakash Gupta	IPS/Maharashtra
3498.	Chiranjeev Prasad	IPS/Maharashtra
3499.	Ravinder Kumar Singhal	IPS/Maharashtra
3500.	Vinoy Kumar Choubey	IPS/Maharashtra
3501.	Amitesh Kumar	IPS/Maharashtra
3502.	M. Rajamurugan	IPS/M&T
3503.	Mahesh M. Bhagwat	IPS/M&T
3504.	Amitabh Yash	IPS/Nagaland
3505.	Suresh Kumar Palsania	IPS/Orissa
3506.	Sanajay Kumar Singh	IPS/Orissa
3507.	Sunita Kakran (Ms)	IPS/Orissa
3508.	Vibhu Raj (Ms)	IPS/Punjab
3509.	Lakshmee Kant Yadav	IPS/Punjab
3510.	Rajiv Ahir	IPS/Punjab
3511.	Utpal Joshi	IPS/Punjab
3512.	Kapil Dev	IPS/Punjab
3513.	Gollapalli Nageswara Rao	IPS/Punjab
3514.	Sachin Mittal	IPS/Rajasthan
3515.	Binita Yadav (Ms)	IPS/Rajasthan
3516.	Sanjib Kumar Narzary	IPS/Rajasthan
3517.	Prashakha Mathur (Ms)	IPS/Rajasthan
3518.	Dinesh M.N.	IPS/Rajasthan
3519.	Avichal	IPS/Sikkim
3520.	Shalini Singh (Ms)	IPS/TN
3521.	Bhavna Saxena (Ms)	IPS/TN
3522.	K. Shankar	IPS/TN
3523.	A. Amalraj	IPS/TN
3524.	Vikram Thakur	IPS/UP
3525.	A. Satish Ganesh	IPS/UP

3526.	Abhishek Trivedi	IPS/UP
3527.	Jyoti Narayan	IPS/UP
3528.	Navneet Yadav	IPS/UP
3529.	Vijay Prakash	IPS/UP
3530.	Ashok Kumar Singh	IPS/UP
3531.	Ram Kumar	IPS/UP
3532.	Damayanti Sen (Ms)	IPS/WB
3533.	Rashmi Sinha (Ms)	IPS/WB
3534.	Rajeev Mishra	IPS/WB
3535.	Ajay Kumar Nand	IPS/WB
3536.	Mahender Singh Poonia	IPS/WB
3537.	Niket Kaushik	IPS/WB
3538.	R. Sivakumar	IPS/WB
3539.	Anil Kumar -I	IPS/WB

Training Year: 1997-99; Batch: 1997 - IPS - RR - 50 (Golden Jubilee Batch)

3540.	Jaspal Singh	IPS/AGMUT
3541.	Sagar Preet	IPS/AGMUT
3542.	Hargobinder Singh	IPS/AGMUT
3543.	Sharad Agarwal	IPS/AGMUT
3544.	Sumer Singh Gurjar	IPS/AGMUT
3545.	Atul Katiyar	IPS/AGMUT
3546.	Lingala Vijaya Prasad	IPS/AGMUT
3547.	Shankha Brata Bagchi	IPS/AP
3548.	Nidigattu Sanjay	IPS/AP
3549.	N. Madhusudhana Reddy	IPS/AP
3550.	Yaram Nagi Reddy	IPS/AP
3551.	Devendra Singh Chauhan	IPS/AP
3552.	Vijay Kumar- I	IPS/A.P
3553.	Sanjay Kumar Jain	IPS/AP
3554.	Deepak Ratan	IPS/AP

3555.	Manish Kumar Singhal	IPS/A&M
3556.	Binod Kumar	IPS/A&M
3557.	Surender Singh Yadav	IPS/A&M
3558.	Jalli Ajay Kumar	IPS/A&M
3559.	Navin Kumar Singh	IPS/Bihar
3560.	Amit Kumar Jain	IPS/Bihar
3561.	Ajitabh Kumar	IPS/Bihar
3562.	Sanjay Singh	IPS/Bihar
3563.	Ashish Batra	IPS/Bihar
3564.	Suman Gupta (Ms)	IPS/Bihar
3565.	T. Kandasamy	IPS/Bihar
3566.	Omendra Nath Bhaskar	IPS/Bihar
3567.	K.C. Surendra Babu	IPS/Bihar
3568.	Himanshu Bhatt	IPS/Gujarat
3569.	Prafulla Kumar Roushan	IPS/Gujarat
3570.	Anupam Singh Gahlaut	IPS/Gujarat
3571.	Hanif Qureshi	IPS/Haryana
3572.	Matta Ravi Kiran	IPS/Haryana
3573.	Sanjay Kumar - I	IPS/Haryana
3574.	Amitabh Singh Dhillon	IPS/Haryana
3575.	Ajay Kumar Yadav	IPS/HP
3576.	Anand Pratap Singh	IPS/HP
3577.	Peram Lakshmipathi	IPS/HP
3578.	Jaideep Singh	IPS/J&K
3579.	Viplav Kumar	IPS/J&K
3580.	Vijay Kumar - II	IPS/J&K
3581.	Garib Dass	IPS/J&K
3582.	Alok Kumar	IPS/J&K
3583.	P. Hari Sekaran	IPS/Karnataka
3584.	Punit Arora	IPS/Karnataka
3585.	Randhir Prakash	IPS/Karnataka

3586.	S. Murugan	IPS/Karnataka
3587.	K.V. Sharath Chandra	IPS/Karnataka
3588.	M. Nanjundaswami	IPS/Karnataka
3589.	Rajan Singh	IPS/Kerala
3590.	Vijay Shivshankar Sakhare	IPS/Kerala
3591.	Khursheed Ahmed	IPS/Kerala
3592.	Balram Kumar Upadhyay	IPS/Kerala
3593.	Mahipal Yadav	IPS/Kerala
3594.	Gugulothu Lakshman	IPS/Kerala
3595.	Vivekanand	IPS/MP
3596.	Dipanshu V. Kabra	IPS/MP
3597.	Makrand Deouskar	IPS/MP
3598.	Datla Sreenivasa Varma	IPS/MP
3599.	Umesh Joga	IPS/MP
3600.	Solomon Yash Kumar Minz	IPS/MP
3601.	Madhukar Pandey	IPS/Maharashtra
3602.	Brijesh Bahadur Singh	IPS/Maharashtra
3603.	Milind R. Bharambe	IPS/Maharashtra
3604.	Rajvardhan	IPS/Maharashtra
3605.	Md. Quaiser Khalid	IPS/Maharashtra
3606.	Abdur Rahman	IPS/Maharashtra
3607.	Mekala Suresh Kumar	IPS/Maharashtra
3608.	Clay Khongsai	IPS/M&T
3609.	Saurabh Tripathi	IPS/M&T
3610.	Janardan Singh	IPS/Nagaland
3611.	Karuna Kesharwani (Ms)	IPS/Nagaland
3612.	Arun Bothra	IPS/Orissa
3613.	Santosh Dattatraya Vaidya	IPS/Orissa
3614.	Asheet Kumar Panigrahi	IPS/Orissa
3615.	Diptesh Kumar Pattnayak	IPS/Orissa
3616.	Sanjay Kumar - II	IPS/Orissa

3617.	Kutey Dhirendra Sambhaji	IPS/Orissa
3618.	Rekha Khare (Ms)	IPS/Orissa
3619.	Vijay Kumar Singh	IPS/Rajasthan
3620.	Vishal Bansal	IPS/Rajasthan
3621.	S. Sengathir	IPS/Rajasthan
3622.	Hawa Singh Ghumaria	IPS/Rajasthan
3623.	H.M. Jayaram	IPS/TN
3624.	Ayush Mani Tiwari	IPS/TN
3625.	Maheshwar Dayal	IPS/TN
3626.	Sumit Sharan	IPS/TN
3627.	Modak Abhin Dinesh	IPS/TN
3628.	Sanjay Kumar - III	IPS/TN
3629.	Abhinav Kumar	IPS/UP
3630.	Bhanu Bhaskar	IPS/UP
3631.	Namala Ravinder	IPS/UP
3632.	Ram Krishna Swarnkar	IPS/UP
3633.	Vijay Singh Meena	IPS/UP
3634.	Neelesh Kumar	IPS/UP
3635.	Mohit Agarwal	IPS/UP
3636.	Naveen Arora	IPS/UP
3637.	Amit Kumar Sinha	IPS/UP
3638.	Gajendra Kumar Goswamy	IPS/UP
3639.	V. Murugesan	IPS/UP
3640.	Raghubir Lal	IPS/UP
3641.	Sanjay Kumar Gunjyal	IPS/UP
3642.	Bhajani Ram Meena	IPS/UP
3643.	Rahul Srivastava	IPS/WB
3644.	Supratim Sarkar	IPS/WB
3645.	Rajesh Kumar Singh	IPS/WB
3646.	R. Rajasekaran	IPS/WB
3647.	K. Jayaraman	IPS/WB

3648.	Ganji Anil Srinivas	IPS/WB
3649.	Rajesh Subarno	IPS/WB
3650.	Naunihal Singh	IPS/Punjab
3651.	Pavan Kumar Rai	IPS/Punjab
3652.	Rajesh Kumar Jaiswal	IPS/Punjab
3653.	Arun Pal Singh	IPS/Punjab
3654.	Pallakonda Ramesh	R.P.F.
3655.	Pradeep Kumar Gupta	R.P.F.
3656.	Rama Shankar Prasad Singh	R.P.F.
3657.	Ramesh Chandra	R.P.F.
3658.	Saurabh Trivedi	R.P.F.
3659.	Sumati Shandilya	R.P.F.
3660.	Yugal Kishore Joshi	R.P.F.
3661.	Alok Kumar	R.P.F.
3662.	B. Venkateshwar Rao	R.P.F.
3663.	Bohra Alok Sunderlal	R.P.F.
3664.	Md. Nurul Hoda	R.P.F.
3665.	Mohd. Saquib	R.P.F.
3666.	Jehad Ahmed Al-Jurani	P.S.F/Palestine(Foreign)
3667.	Mahmoud O. Abu-Al-Rub	P.S.F/Palestine(Foreign)
3668.	Nedal M.H. Elshaqaqi	P.S.F/Palestine(Foreign)
3669.	Omar F.A. Badawi	P.S.F/Palestine(Foreign)
3670.	Tareq M.A. Dawabshih	P.S.F/Palestine(Foreign)

Bibliography

1. Selections from the Records of Government (Papers relating to the Reform of the Police of India, 1861).

2. *Crime and Police in India*, upto 1861, by Dr. Anand Swarup Gupta - IP (Retd.), UP.

3. *The Police in British India: 1861-1947*, by Dr. Anand Swarup Gupta - IP (Retd.), UP.

4. The Regulations and Orders for the Police of NWP and Oudh.

5. *The Indian Police*, by J C Curry.

6. The Indian Police Committee (Court Committee) Report, 1860.

7. The Indian Police Act (Act V of 1861).

8. The Report of the Police Committee (UP) 1980, KAYE Committee.

9. Police Commission Report 1902.

10. The Civil Police Committee Report, 1919 (About UP Police).

11. The Civil Police Decentralization Committee Report, 1923 (about UP Police).

12. The Report on Re-organisation of the United Provinces Police Force, 1945 (Pearce Committee Report).

13. The Report on Re-organisation Committee Report (U P), 1947 (Sir Sita Ram Committee).

14. The UP Police Commission Report 1960-61 (Ajit Prasad Jain Commission).

15. The National Police Commission (1977-81) Reports.

16. *Constitutional Law of India*, by H M Seervai.

17. History of Police in India: A Chronological Account - A A Ali - National Police Academy Magazine, vol. XXIV, November 1974.

18. *Civil Service Administration in India*, by Dr. R.K. Sapru, Deptt. of Public Administration, Punjab University, Chandigarh.

19. *The Superior Civil Services in India* (A study in Administrative Development, 1947-1957), by V M Sinha, The Institute for Research and Advanced Studies, Jaipur, 1985.

20. *The Police in History*, by A. Kumar IP, DIG, Punjab.

21. *Training of IPS*, by Kaneej Zehra.

22. *Women in Indian Police*, by Shamim Aleem.

23. *Women in Law Enforcement*, by Peter Worne.

24. Several Publications of the SVPNPA, Hyderabad.

25. Indian Police Service - Civil Lists, published by Ministry of Home Affairs, Government of India, for several years.

26. The Indian Police Service (UP Cadre), Gradation Lists from 1955 onwards.

27. *Raj to Swaraj: Changing Contours of Police*, by Sudhir Kumar Jha, IPS, Bihar.

28. *All India Services Manual*, by RN Mishra, SPO (Retd.), Advocate High Court, Allahabad.

29. *Defenders of the Establishment*, K S Dhillon, IPS (Retd.)

30. *Indian Police Journal* (January - June, 1998), BPR&D, Indian Police after 50 years of independence.

31. *The Men Who Ruled India* - Philip Mason.

Index

Notes

Notes

Hon'ble Mr.L.M.Kaye, CIE IP
(23.2.1919 to 30.9.1923)

First IP Officer as IGP of UP

(Chapter 2)

B.N.Lahari, IP
(27.10.1947 to 12.1.1953)
(First Indian I.G. of UP)

T.P.Bhalla, IP
(13.1.53 to 31.3.54)

M.S.Mathur, IP
(1.4.54 to 16.2.61)

Shanti Prasad, IP
(17.2.61 to 9.4.67)
(Honorary ADC to the President of India)

Indian 'IP' Officers as UP Police Chiefs(IG/DG)

(Chapter 3)

Jia Ram, IP
(10.4.67 to 19.2.70)

Islam Ahmad, IP
(18.5.71 to 4.11.71)

N.S.Saksena, IP
(20.2.1970 to 17.5.71)

Amarjit Kumar Dass, IP
(5.11.71 to 30.11.73)

Shrawan Tandon
IGP-UP(27.3.76 to 4.7.77)
& DG, BSF

Lal Singh Varma
(5.7.77 to11.3.80)

Mahendra Singh
(12.3.80 to 23.2.81)

Naresh Kumar
IGP-UP 24.2.81 to 4.3.82
DGP-UP 5.3.82 to 24.4.82

First Batch -IPS-RR-1948
(UP Police Chiefs)

Central Police Training College, Mount Abu

(Chapter 8)

Prime Minister Pt.Jawaharlal Nehru inspecting the "Passing Out Parade"1958

Group Photograph of 1960 Batch with President S.Radhakrishnan on the eve of Passing Out Parade

Probationers of 1963 Batch - Passing Out in 1964 .

Probationers Rowing in Nakki Lake Mount Abu

National Police Academy, Hyderabad

P.L.Mehta, IP
Commandant
(15.9.48 to 31.1.54)

S.Waryam Singh, IP
Commandant
(11.2.54 to 5.11.56)

A.R.Jayawant, IP
Commandant
(8.3.57 to 16.5.58)

G.K.Handoo, IP
Commandant
(17.5.58 to 31.10.60)

← B.B.Banerji, IP
Commandant/Director
(14.3.61 to 28.2.62)

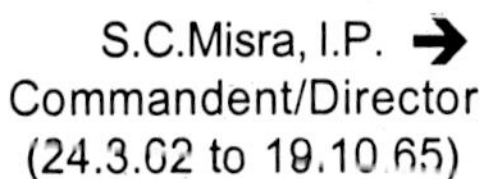

S.C.Misra, I.P. →
Commandent/Director
(24.3.62 to 19.10.65)

Heads of Police Academy

A.K.Ghosh, IP
Director
(1.2.70 to 10.7.71)

S.G.Gokhale, IPS
Director
(1.2.72 to 31.7.74)

←S.M.Diaz, IPS
Director
(11.9.74 to 28.2.77)

R.D.Singh, IPS→
Director
(7.11.77 to 4.2.79)

←P.A.Rosha, IPS
Director
(5.2.79 to 18.9.79)

B.K.Roy, IPS→
Director
(11.11.79 to 31.1.82)

←G.C.Singhvi, IPS
Director
(18.2.83 to 30.11.85)

A.A.Ali, IPS →
Director
(2.12.85 to 31.3.90)

←P.D.Malaviya, IPS
Director
(12.9.90 to 31.12.91)

Sankar Sen, IPS→
Director
(2.4.92 to 31.5.94)

A.P.Durai, IPS
Director
(1.7.94 to 28.9.96)

Trinath Mishra, IPS
Director
(12.11.96 to 6.12.97)

P.V.Rajgopal, IPS
Director
29.6.98 to date

Trainee Probationers Board of Honour
at SVP National Police Academy, Hyderabad

Various Out-door Activities at Hyderabad

Equitation ↑

↓ Target Shooting

Rock Climbing

National Police Academy Colours

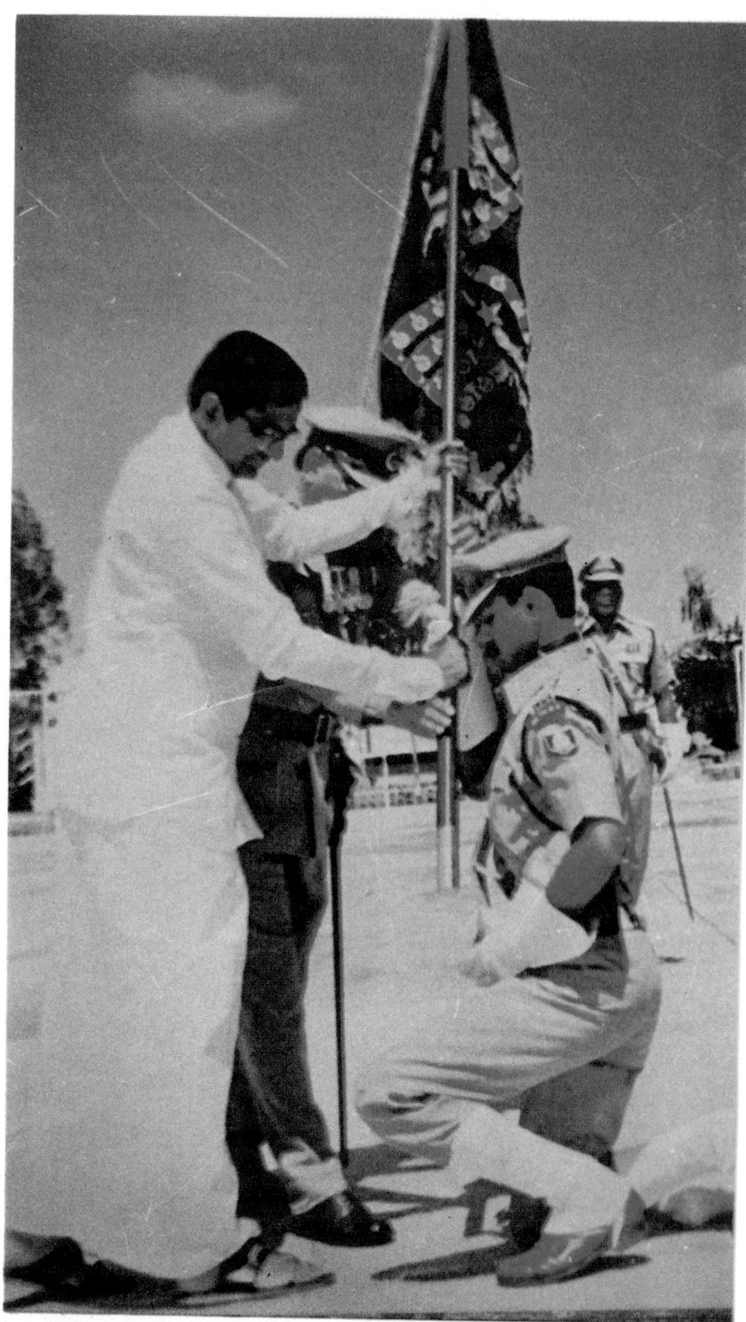

P.Chidambaram, Minister of State for Home, presenting the Colours

Supreme Sacrifice

G.S.Arya

Panch Pagesan

Sewa

Satish Sahney and V.A.Ravi(1963) presenting the memento to A.A.Ali, Director

Officers in Bushirt-working Uniform

(Chapter 9)

Officers in Winter Working Uniform

Officers in Summer Working Uniform

Arun Kumar, SSP Lucknow, Commanding Annual Ceremonial Police Parade in Lucknow, January 1998

Officers in Review Order

Senior Police Officers in Review Order being introduced by S.R.Arun, DGP UP to UP Governor Romesh Bhandari, on Annual Police Parade, **January** 1998 -- Police Lines Lucknow.

S.C.Misra,IP -- Commandant CPTC Abu in Mess Jacket

IPS Officers in Mess Kit Jacket

Mess Night, UP Police Week -- January 1998

Officers in Mess Kit
J.S.Pandey, IPS -- 1976 (Left)
P.K.Tewari, IPS -- 1986 (Right)

Mr.Dodd IGP UP (1925-31)
in two Stars with Crown

Visible Crest on Tie of
Mr.Phillips IGP UP (1937)

IP-- Cap Badge of Mr.Inglis,
IGP UP (1940-45)

Badges of Ranks before 1947

S.K.Rizvi, IGP
IPS-RR-1973
➔

R.N.Gupta, DGP UP
IPS-RR-1954

Subhash Joshi
IPS-RR-UP-1976

Rizwan Ahmad, Selection Grade SP
IPS-RR-1978

Badges of Ranks from 1969

Late Ms. Vandana Malik
IPS-1987-Manipur and Tripura Cadre
who laid down her life while fighting insurgents in 1989

(Chapter 10)

Kiran Bedi, IPS(1972 Batch)

(Courtesy : Ajay Goyal)

Father | Son | Grand Son

Alakh Kumar Sinha
IP, The first IGP of
Bihar in 1939

M.K. Sinha, IP 1928
IGP of Bihar

Jyoti Niwas Kumar
Sinha, IPS - Bihar, 1967

Fathers and Sons

M. S. Mathur
IP-UP, 1931
Former IGP-UP
(Then Police Chief)

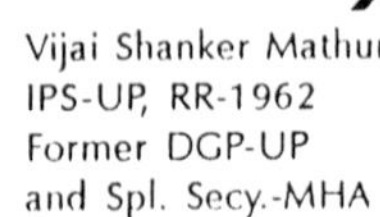

Vijai Shanker Mathur
IPS-UP, RR-1962
Former DGP-UP
and Spl. Secy.-MHA

K.P. Srivastava
SPS/IPS-UP-1951
Former IGP, Arunachal Pradesh

Vikram Srivastava
IPS-UP-RR-1973

(Chapter 11) Family Combinations in IPS

Prakash Singh
IPS-UP-RR-1959
Former DGP, UP
and B.S.F.

Pankaj Kumar Singh
IPS-Rajasthan-RR-1988

Ram Lal
SPS/IPS-UP

(1) Rajiv M. Singh
IPS-Assam-RR-1984

(2) Sujan Vir Singh
IPS-UP-RR-1986

S.R.Arun
IPS-UP-1963(RR)

Asim Arun
IPS-UP-1994(RR)
Son

Sanjeev Shami
IPS-MP-1993(RR)
Son-in-Law

A.K. Sharan
IPS-UP-RR-1965

Sumit Sharan
IPS-Tamilnadu-RR-1997
Golden Jubilee Batch

Brothers

C.K. Mallick
IPS-UP-RR-1963
DG, Vigilance, UP.

A.K. Mallick
IPS-Assam (UP), RR-1979

Fathers and Daughters

Anupam Saxena
IPS-Bihar-RR-1995

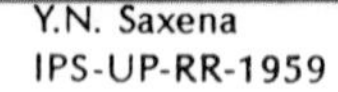

Y.N. Saxena
IPS-UP-RR-1959

Bhagwat Narain Sharma
IPS(PPS-1954)-UP-1968

Vineeta Sharma
IPS-Assam & Meghalaya
RR-1996

Father and Daughter

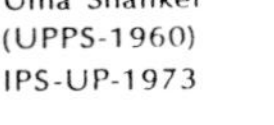

Uma Shanker
(UPPS-1960)
IPS-UP-1973

Karuna Kesherwani
IPS-Nagaland-RR-1997

Sisters

Tadasha Mishra
IPS-Bihar-1994-RR-47

Soumya Mishra
IPS- AP-1994-RR-47

IPS COUPLES

Ashish Gupta
IPS-UP-RR-1989

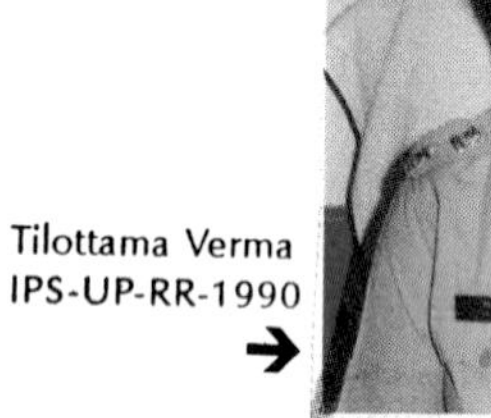

Tilottama Verma
IPS-UP-RR-1990

Inder Singh Mehra (Expired)
IPS-UP-RR-1974

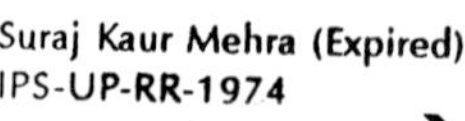

Suraj Kaur Mehra (Expired)
IPS-UP-RR-1974

IPS COUPLES

Shafi Ahsan Rizvi
IPS-UP-RR-1989

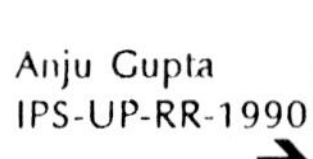

Anju Gupta
IPS-UP-RR-1990 →

Aditya Misra
IPS-UP-RR-1989 ←

S.Renuka Shastry
IPS-UP-RR-1990

Ajai Singh
IPS-Bihar-RR-1993

Anupam Saxena
IPS-Bihar-RR-1995

Fathers-in-Law and Sons-in-Law

H.K. Kerr
SPS/IPS-UP-1941
(Retired as DGP,UP)

(1) Ashish Kumar Mitra
IPS-UP-RR-1970

J.N. Chaturvedi
IPS-UP-RR-1951
(Retired as DGP,UP)

Ranjan Dwivedi
IPS-UP-RR-1979
➔

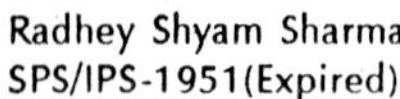

Radhey Shyam Sharma
SPS/IPS-1951(Expired)

M.C. Dewedy
IPS-UP-RR-1963